AF540717

Factional Politics in Rural India

Factional Politics in Rural India

Padma Charan Mishra

&

K. S. Padhy

Dept. of Political Science
Berhampur University
Berhampur
(Orissa)

DISCOVERY PUBLISHING HOUSE

NEW DELHI—110 002

First Published 2000

Reprinted 2026

ISBN: 978-81-7141-566-3

Factional Politics in Rural India

Published by:

DISCOVERY PUBLISHING HOUSE

4383/4B, Ansari Road, Darya Ganj

New Delhi-110 002 (India)

Phone: +91-11-23279245; 23253475; 43596065

Mobile: +91 9811179893 / +91 9871656464

E-mail: discoverybooksindia@gmail.com

orderdphbooks@gmail.com

namitwasan9@gmail.com

web: www.discoverypublishinggroup.com

Printed at:

Infinity Imaging Systems

Delhi

Preface

Factional politics constitutes an important area as well as a pervasive theme in contemporary social science. Factionalism, a growing phenomenon in Indian Government and Politics, has infected almost all organizations including political parties, interests groups, pressure groups, trade unions, voluntary associations, etc. It is very sad to note that even village community and its government and politics are also not free from this political evil. It has assumed so much of importance and significance that this has drawn the attention of social scientists, policy-makers and administrators.

As has been rightly said India lives in villages. But, unfortunately, the rural India, which is visualized under the deceptive and surface appearance of calm and harmony, has, in fact, become a centre of conflict and hostility. The old and long-cherished values of rural India have been declining and are on their wane. Village life has lost its virtues like simplicity, love, sympathy, fellow-feeling, kindness, sacrifice, unity, co-operation, etc. The village atmosphere is no more serene as it is polluted and vitiated. Guided by instinct and passion, people and their leaders have become self-centered, narrow-minded and are more interested in their personal development. As a result, the interests of the village have been thoroughly neglected, ignored and relegated to the background.

Conflict and confrontation but not co-operation and co-existence have become the basis of the village life. The rural society has, therefore, been rightly considered as a faction society. Factors like caste, community, language, personal considerations, desire for higher status, lust for power, greed for wealth, etc., foment the passion of the man and give rise to conflict and tension. Socio-economic changes are also responsible for factionalism in rural government and politics.

It is pertinent to note that most of the scholarly works on factional politics relate to state and national level politics, with special emphasis on the government and political parties. Scholarly works on factionalism in village government are limited, as is evident from the survey of literature.

It may be noted with all humility that the present work will go a long way in fulfilling the aspirations of those who are interested in rural factionalism.

Objectives

The present study seeks to study factionalism in Orissa with special reference to an Orissan village, Nuapada, in the district of Ganjam located in the southern part of Orissa, which came into existence in 1936 and is characterized by backwardness and underdevelopment. With eight per cent of its population living in rural areas, have, naturally, a rural and agricultural background. Casteism still dominates rural orissa and the village Nuapada is not an exception to it. Every caste has its own traditions, customs and its own way of life. There are also kinship groups which have developed different factions in the villages based on socio-political and economic considerations. The introduction of adult franchise and panchayats have increased the role of factions in the rural areas of Orissa.

The main focus of the study is the factional politics in Nuapada village which is, with a population of 2,775, predominantly agricultural. People of this village have a traditional orientation and strong belief in the complex system of caste, religion and other social prejudices. However, with the introduction of the panchayat system, as a form of rural government, and because of socio-economic and political modernization, Nuapada has been undergoing changes. The main thrust of this study is to find out the nature and role of factional politics in rural Orissa on the basis of a micro study.

The present work has made a humble attempt to :

- study the socio-economic and political background of factional leaders of Nuapada as it helps in tracing out the type of leaders who lead factions in the village;

- find out whether the panchayat system has sharpened the factional conflict in Nuapada;
- know the cause of factionalism and study how the factions and alliances are formed in Nuapada;
- study whether factional leaders of Nuapada function independently or act at the behest of leaders at different levels-block, district, state and centre; and
- determine the impact of urbanization and modernization in the growth of factional politics in Nuapada.

Hypotheses

The study of relevant literature on factional politics in rural government has thrown up some of the hypotheses which have been sought to be empirically tested in the present study. They are:

- factionalism tends to be caste-based, issue-oriented;
- it centres around culture, language, region, religion, etc.;
- it tends to be the product of the desire for personal power and prestige;
- an economically dominant caste tends to play a more important role in the process of factionalism than an upper caste in social hierarchy;
- factional leaders tend to hail from the upper strata of the society;
- they tend to be affiliated to political parties;
- they tend to have political linkages with state and national level leaders;
- Panchayati Raj system tends to encourage factionalism in rural government and politics; and, therefore,
- it tends to retard the developmental process in the village. In other words, it tends to be dysfunctional;
- faction groups tend to be permanent;
- they tend to be conflict groups;
- they tend to be primarily non-political;

- they tend to be primarily kinship grouping;
- they tend to be dysfunctional.

Methodology

The success of a research project depends largely on systematic collection and sophisticated analysis of data. This is possible only when all the sources—primary and secondary—are tapped and necessary techniques adopted and made use of. The present work has done its best to go through the available relevant literature to collect data.

It may be noted that the principal tool of investigation is a standardized interview schedule containing both open-ended and multiple choice questions administered to the respondents. In addition, informal discussions and in-depth interviewing furnished considerable revealing evidence. The respondents include 70 factional leaders, both formal and informal of different factions with different socio-economic and political background. The study covers the respondents since independence of the country. In addition, sincere attempt has been made to interview some village leaders without any factional background. 118 villagers selected or chosen on the basis of random sampling were also interviewed. The respondents were questioned in a face-to-face interview by the researcher personally, which was very useful in collecting detailed information form them. The interview schedule is a comprehensive one covering important dimensions of factional politics in rural area.

Empirical data collected through the interview schedule have been processed and tabulated scientifically, so as to make an in-depth analysis of various dimensions of the subject. Various hypotheses have been tested as to reach at right conclusions.

Since the researcher belongs to the nearby village, he has observed factional politics in the village Nuapada from a close quarter. Such observation has been the key element in imparting an insight into and in making a realistic appraisal of factional politics in the village in the modern times.

Review of Literature

Review of literature on a particular subject not only throws much light on its various aspects and dimensions but also helps a scholar to move ahead in the arena of research with a hope and confidence. It gives him new ideas and hardly allows him to grope in darkness. It makes him conscious of his problems that he may or is likely to confront while his work is in progress. It helps him in choosing new areas in the same subject, shedding more light on them and overcoming all those difficulties which his predecessor(s) faced. It also highlights the importance of the subject, exposes its flaws and deficiencies and enables one to assess its relevance and significance. Hence, the importance of the review of literature.

Needless to say, because of its importance, factionalism as a growing phenomenon has drawn the attention of quite a few scholars and critics. Evincing a keen interest in the area, they have thrown much light on its various aspects and dimensions. H.D. Lasswell (1931), R. Firth (1957), D. Pocock (1957), V.W. Turner (1957), Oscar Lewis (1958), A.C. Mayer (1961), R. Nicholas (1963, 1968), Paul R. Brass (1964, 1965), Moshi Shokeid (1968), J.S. Yadav (1968), S.M. Zaidi (1970), Aminul Islam (1974), R.W. Jones (1974), J. Bujra (1975), P.N. Rastogi (1975), G. Murdock (1977), K.C. Panda (1981), J.K. Mohapatra (1985), S.S. Sharma (1985), J. Biossevain (1985), M.S. Mashreque (1992), M. Fukunaga (1993) have made significant contributions to the study of factional politics.

As said earlier, not much work has been done in such a vital area so far as Orissa is concerned, hence the importance of the present study.

Chapterization

The present work spreads over eight chapters. The first chapter has made an attempt to study various aspects of factionalism i.e., definition, meaning, approaches, dimensions, functions, causes, etc. In other words, it is the conceptual framework of the subject for study.

An indepth knowledge about the setting or the environment in which a phenomenon works is quite essential as it helps the researcher to explore the latter in proper perspectives. The second-chapter covers the setting of the village.

It is a fact that economy influences to a large extent the politics of a village, a community or a society. Therefore, an attempt has been made in the third chapter to study the economic conditions of the villagers i.e., how much landed property they have ? What is their profession ? What kind of business activities they are engaged in ? etc.

Factional politics of a village is to be studied in the context of the social structure as the latter throws much light on the working of the former. Therefore, the fourth chapter is devoted to this aspect of the study.

Leaders who are actively involved in factionalism belong to different socio-economic and political background. This has a tremendous bearing upon their role in factional politics. The fifth chapter deals with their profile.

Leaders and villagers have different perceptions on the subject of factionalism. Study of their perceptions reflects their attitudes to the problem. The sixth chapter has, therefore, made an attempt to discuss their perceptions.

Factional politics works at different levels or in different spheres in the village. It is quite interesting to know how it works, how it operates, what is its impact, what are its consequences ? The seventh chapter throws much light on working of factionalism in Nuapada.

The eighth chapter is devoted to conclusion and highlights the findings of the study.

Authors

Contents

1
FACTIONALISM : A Conceptual Framework

Introduction

The term "faction" refers to groups or sections of a society in relation of opposition to one another, interested in promoting their objects rather than those of the society as a whole and often turbulent in their operations.[1] It is a collection of individuals within an organization or institution which operates together in politics long enough or with sufficient regularity to become recognised as a discreet group.[2] It is a group with an articulate set of goals, operating within a larger organization, but not created by or with approval of the parent body.[3] Factions are conflict groups that run along the caste lines and are primarily adnate kinship units.[4] It is a group of households within a caste or sub-caste which rally together for rites, rituals, ceremonies, community activities and which stayed together in a relation of social conflict, co-operation and neutrality.[5] Factions, thus, are sub-groups within groups.

Factionalism is the 'overt conflict in a group which leads to increasing abandonment of co-operative activities'.[6] Factions refers to a number of citizens, whether amounting to a majority or a minority of the whole, who are united and actuated by some common impulse of passion, or of interest, adverse to the rights of other citizens, or to the permanent and aggregate interests of the community.[7] It is considered as a kind of political process.

A faction represents a particular or parochial interest. It may be based on caste, kinship and other social relations. Sometimes, there may be factions comprising different castes. It is relatively unstable, temporary and loose alignments of individuals within a group.[8] Factionalism is different from other units of the structure in that membership is to some extent voluntary unlike caste and lineage.[9]

It may be noted that factionalism has emerged as a tactful strategy to get some position, status and prestige in the society. It is a direct product of the conflicts for power or recognition. Factions also signify a state of polarization with respect to an anterior group in which they have their being. Factionalism has its locus within the orbit of intra-group dissension.[10] Product of the predecessors of modern political parties, they are status groups which typically include individuals of different classes. Among equally privileged individuals, interaction promotes an inclusive corporate identification. But among differently privileged individuals, it spurs conflict and leads to the formation of two or more antagonistic groups.[11] Such groups are amenable to both harmony and disharmony, association and disassociation. Conflicts within such groups are not totally disruptive. In a group it is a normal phenomenon which occurs due to intra-familial, intra-class, inter-clan or inter-ethnic reasons.[12]

Factionalism develops within a political party for the sake of power and prestige. Power, no doubt, is the most important motivating factor for the growth of groupism in a political party. Important political leaders, in their pursuit of power for garnering perceived benefits, seek to dominate the party by organizing groups consisting of their supporters and tend to use these groups to calm down the rival groups within their party, and to bring the party under their complete control. The party would then be used as an instrument of self-aggrandizement by these power-seeking factional leaders. In addition to power, prestige also plays an important role in the formation of factions.[13] A political leader may not have any obsession for power. But he may value maintaining his social prestige more than capturing power. For example, an ex-ruler or an ex-zamindar may not enjoy dabbling in politics. But he would like to keep the inflow of social esteem towards him undisturbed. He would prevent any step which is likely to endanger his social prestige. For example, Raja of Mankapur rebelled against the Congress of Gonda district, because it gave Assembly ticket to his old rival.

Factions emerge through struggle or competition for power resulting in control over official and unofficial positions.[14] As such, they have atleast three aspects : requirements, activity and duration. These three criteria can be utilized in analyzing factionalism at different levels of Indian society. The role of socio-cultural factors like religion, caste and language is very important at different levels.

The emergence of factionalism in a group signifies a basic change in group relationships. If it is deemed as a system output, then the question of input into the system arises. Obviously, the input can come from only two directions: (1) the external environment and (2) the internal elements i.e.,—individuals. The external and internal inputs may act concomitantly owing to the interaction of the system (i.e., groups) across its boundaries with the environment. This would imply a system-state in which the emergence of factionalism is associated with the periods of major changes in the group's environment.[15]

The relationship of factionalism with environmental change is amply borne out by situations ranging from primitive and tribal groups to peasant villages and modern political organizations. Factionalism in tribal communities reflects the pressures of acculturation and assimilation. It may, however, develop along different lines. Turner noted the emergence of two factions among the Ndembu during crises situations. Their composition changed and transcended the lines of kinship.[16] Factional disputes at Chan Kom were largely due to rapid socio-cultural change. They ended when the villages' adjustment to the urban impact was stabilized.[17]

Studies on the topic conducted in different parts of the country show that the transition from an exploitative feudal system to the modern democratic system has invariably give rise to factionalism. It has been found that with the introduction of the panchayat system, the lower caste people have become conscious of their role in the power structure of the village.[18] Rtezlaff shows in his study of a village in Uttar Pradesh that the panchayat elections have brought changes in the power structure of different casts. Patnaik and Lakshmi Narayan have also mentioned that periodical elections to various democratic institutions in India may also be a reason for factionalism in rural areas.[19] Rastogi has observed that factionalism comes to the fore at the time of panchayat elections and that co-operation is at the low ebb on such occasions.[20]

Besides the election to democratic institutions, the actual

working of these institutions also gives rise to creation of factions in the village. The watch-word of democracy is equally in economic, social and cultural spheres. Its aim is to usher in an egalitarian society, free from exploitation. But in actual practice, the fruits of democratic planning are not enjoyed equally by all due to various reasons. Economic and other forms of exploitation continue to plague the society. This creates a situation where there is an unhealthy competition amongst the people; each trying to become a prominent recipient of the economic gains of democracy. Clash of economic interests might give rise to inter-caste or intra-caste factions.[21] Patnaik and Lakshmi Narayan while appreciating this point have observed that new economic opportunities give rise to competitions and are followed by factions because everyone wants to exploit the limited resources of the village.[22] Thus, there is a competition among the people for exploiting the resources of power for their benefit or acquiring a dominance, economic or political, over others. It has been observed that quarrels over the ancestral land, loyalty to particular type of kin, childhood friendship and also gossip group have direct impact on the factional politics.[23]

Factions have five attributes: conflict groups, political groups, non-corporate groups, their members are recruited by a leader and recruitment takes place on diverse principles.[24] These features are mainly found in rural society. Nicholas' study of factions[25] in West Bengal villages shows that factions are formed on the basis of caste, economic dependence, kinship and territory. Political party affiliations, as Nicholas discovers are determined by the nature of factional association.

Issues

Masaki Fukunaga in his study on society, caste and factional politics has delineated four important issues to understand the factional politics in Indian villages. They are : (i) Permanence, (ii) Composition of membership, (iii) Openness of membership and (iv) Political role of factions.[26]

Lewis observed that factions "are relatively inflexible in membership."[27] While the scholars like Mayer (1960), Yadav (1968) and others questioned the permanence of factions, Pocock says that "factions are not permanent but are expedient groupings temporarily created through a confidence or conflict of interest, the resolution of which automatically terminates the faction's *raison* and therefore its existence."[28]

Some of the conflicts which are institutionalized can be solved easily but some other make a permanent cleavage because of their uncompromising nature. These conflicts lead to the formation of permanent groups which are termed as factions. "Factionalism arises out of dissatisfaction of members of a group having dominating character for the creation of a new group to challenge the former after establishing an independent group of separate ideological identity." In every social structure there are occasions for conflict since individuals and sub-groups make claims to scarce resources, prestige or power position.[29]

It is also to be noted that sometimes factions are not found to be permanent. Factions are not permanent groups, but are relative to particular circumstances[30] and sometimes a faction breaks up and its members join other factions in the village. Factions, generally speaking, do not endure unchangingly for a long time. Though a faction group may ally itself with on political party or another from time to time, this need not have any impact on its nature and internal composition. Weiner observes that a faction may support the Congress in one election and the opposition party in the next. It has happened that the same party does not get the votes of members of a faction in a subsequent election through the faction survives during this period.

The membership composition or the alliance of a faction is an important feature which constantly changes depending on various issues in a rural society. Contrary to this, composition stables the core element in the faction. The core element or the nucleus of the factions remains relatively steady.[31] The faction is usually made of a few core families, rich and powerful enough to generate a field of influence and withstand challenges from other families. It is important that the core element does not have to be always constituted by the wealthy men, instead it is only large, influential and well-to-do families which make up the core.[32]

Factions are necessarily "small cohesive groups within castes" or "primarily kinship groupings."[33] But other researchers like Hitchcock,[34] Beals,[35] Berreman,[36] noted that village people provided political support with in the intra-group of kinship or 'jati' as a natural tendency.

As for the openness of membership, factions cut across kinship and caste lines and also tend to provide a common platform of action to the members of different 'jatis' (castes) and kinship to bring them together. Lewis mentions "instance of members of one joint family joining up with opposite factions."[37] Several other scholars also indicated the same situation. Epstein has observed in a south Indian village that only one man of the dominant caste has associated himself with a faction other than that of his lineage.[38] Pocock[39] too reported that even brothers were potential members of opposed factions. Berreman[40] also noted a case where brothers belonged to different cliques. Thus, it is clear that extension of factional membership is not identical with kinship and caste groupings.

The political role of factions is the issue which makes the difference between Lewis's conception and the findings of subsequent researchers. However, the latter emphasized that factional behaviour is one of the most significant indications of the political process existing int he village. As political activity is organized resulting in conflict over power and prestige, factional behaviour becomes political. Even in the case of a conflict, the beginning may involve a purely economic quarrel between two individuals with hardly any political implications but it does not remain so far long. The conflict will involve factional interests very soon, and the original issue becomes a test of strength, prestige and resources between the opposing factions.[41] M. S. Mashreque and M. Rahul Amin have observed that "struggle for power and control over scarce resources appears to be the continuing function of the factional group. Hence, factionalism pre-supposes the existence of hostile relationship of one group with another. Hostility towards other groups is the clearest indication of factionalism."[42]

Factions are non-political groupings or temporary alliances of individuals to fight court cases, although some of them take up political functions and become involved in power politics. Rather they are primarily kinship groupings which carry on important social, economic and ceremonial functions in addition to their factional struggles against one another.[43]

A faction may be either political or non-political in nature. There can not be any faction without any political interest. It must be said that politics does not mean state politics alone, the aim of which is to control the apparatus of the state administration. It may be village politics in its different ramifications. In the beginning, factional politics in rural Orissa seems to be non-political but later on it assumes political colour.[44] It may, therefore, be argued that the root cause of all the factional behaviour is nothing but political interest. The functioning and operation of factions indicates that they feed themselves, keep alive and moving. The only important goal is "bringing down" of the opposing faction.[45] It has been pointed out "where there has been a failure to seize political power ideology helps to build up an opposition to the party in power". What has been missed here, however, is importance of numerical viability.[46]

Motivational Factors

Faction has a direct link with individual's self-interest rather than group or community interest. In the modern society it means something by which one can get some sort of prestige and status in society by adopting some strategy tactfully. It arises in struggle for power or recognition of leadership. It represents a division on details of application and not on principles. Perception of self-interest is the main objective of individuals in joining a faction. The term 'self-interest' may designate, in the words of Rastogi, the struggle of individuals for ideals, beliefs and ideology as well as their bids for power, status and resources.[47] Another primary motive may be personal animosity. Talking about a major factional dispute in Namhalli, Beals observed that "..... the goals of each faction appeared to be based upon the personal motivation of the individuals involved.[48] Cohn in his study on "the Chamar of Senapur" observes that 'personal animosity' and the 'wish for personal gain and power' are reported to be the main driving forces for factions in Senapur."[49] The complex of individual motivations may variously comprise the preservation of self-identity, ego-expansion and material rewards. Membership of a factional group may then represent the individual's response to dynamic social situations in the context of their motivational requirements.[50] The associational character of individuals is the dominant factor in the formation of factions.

However, due to the process of modernization and democratization, a group of rural elites has emerged in village level. These elites try to gain the political support by patronizing their cause. Accordingly, when factions occur at the village level, the leader becomes more cautious to keep his followers under him and support the cause even at the cost of irregularities lest they should align with another faction and thus jeopardize his position.[51] This is the way in which a political leader acts as a link between the factions at the village level and the political activity at the higher level. Periodical elections to various democratic institutions in India may also be a reason for factionalism in rural politics. As a result, new factions based on divergent membership have emerged on the rural scene reflecting the dynamics of the people as well as the forces of change, especially after the introduction of schemes of rural development and Panchayati Raj institutions in place of traditional micro-structure.[52] No doubt, these factions some time forget their differences and jointly work for village upliftment. But their loyalty to their faction still remains. Patnaik and Lakshi Narayan have rightly said that "they (factional interest) may be latent, nevertheless they run as under-current in sustaining a faction.[53] Besides the elections to democratic institution, the actual working of the democratic institutions also gives rise to emergence of factions in the village. No doubt, democracy believes in an egalitarian, social and economic order, but in actual practice the fruits of democratic planning are not enjoyed equally by all. This creates a situation which leads to unhealthy competition among the people trying to grab the major economic gains. Such competitions give rise to factions in different terms. Factionalism in Indian villages has been intensified due to adoption of measures like Zamindari abolition. This has led to a sharp decline in the prestige and powers of Zamindars (landlords) on the one hand, besides affecting the interests of traditional caste leaders. It was they who acted as arbitrators in most cases of disputes within a village. Now, it is no longer so as the situation has undergone a radical change and the tension escalates. Factions developed among rural Israeli immigrants as a consequence of the pressure of adaptation to the new environment consisting of unfamiliar institutions like village co-operatives.[54] They also emerge with a change in the social structure and democratization of the society. For example, in Madras, the backward caste movement led Harijans and other backward castes to form a rival group and challenge the supermacy of Brahmins.

By the 1980s, factionalism had transformed the shape and background of the village activity and at the same time strengthened the activational force in the daily life of the villagers in North India, specially the members of the lower caste, who were the subjects of discrimination, played a positive role in political activity. Besides the improvement in the economic status had shaken the structure of political control by the dominant caste in the villages. It is considered that after Independence the faction itself has been responsible for encouraging intensification of enemity and disputes and alsó the widening of cracks within the society.[55] Factions also emerge due to population explosion, economic mobility, mass education, adult franchise, break down of joint families.[56]

Factions: Functional and Dysfunctional

There is a general tendency to treat a faction as dysfunctional. But it is both functional and dysfunctional, it has both integrative and disintegrative functions. Factional politics, as a part of disintegrative role, accepts neither the doctrine of majority rule nor institutional mechanism to resolve the conflicts with other factions. Defeated faction leaders tend to describe an unfavourable vote as a corrupted vote, a misguided vote or a vote of betrayal in a conflict where arbitrators are no longer available. A real danger exists when the activities of faction may lead to a split in the party. Sometimes faction leaders may run against the official candidate or sabotage election campaign from within the organization. A disaffected faction leader does not mind participating in the defeat of the entire local congress organization, if this is the only way to defeat his faction rivals. This is the observation made by Brass in his study on Uttar Pradesh factional politics.[57] Secondly, factional politics in traditional societies is based on personality, status and power. Conflict between faction leaders for the sake of status leads to intense factional disputes which are often in their very nature insoluble. When prestige or honour becomes of primary importance in politics, the possibilities of resolving conflicts are reduced, for honour can not be shared. The disintegrative impact of factional politics may lead to a decline in the electoral strength of a political party. The Congress in Uttar Pradesh polled only 35 per cent of votes in the state Assembly elections held in 1962, making the Congress Party in Uttar Pradesh the weakest state congress party in India.[58]

But, factions also make positive contributions by its integrative role in the society. Bhargava and Torgal have observed that factionalism weakens the traditional authority. To them, till 1978 traditional leaders were at the helm of panchayat affairs. In 1978 elections, factions came to the fore by effectively challenging and ousting leadership based on traditional authority. As a result, there emerged new leaders in the political scene. In this respect, it acts as a ladder for the advancement of leaders.[59] Secondly, it encourages wider or greater participation by groups and individuals because they are necessary to defeat traditional authority.

Thirdly, factions serve as a new source of communication between people from different kinship groups and villages of the area. Factional politics mobilises individuals and groups of different back-grounds.[60] It also acts as a source of check and balance in the panchayat administration. It exposes the misdeeds and loopholes in policy and actions of opponent groups. In this sense it acts as an agency of making others responsible. It also helps in putting checks on corruption and monopoly of bureaucrats by bringing their activities to lime light. Factional leaders to enhance their prestige and position in their area invite ministers and officers of higher influence to their locality. Before such people visit the area, many local problems get solved. This makes the community highly beneficial.

It may be noted that integrative functions though less prominent are more important int he long run. The disintegrative role of factionalism is more manifest but ultimately less important. It means a faction has properties of fission as well as fusion, i.e., a single faction or components of more than one faction may come together and form a new faction. The inter-play between fission and fusion comes into being through re-alignment of interest in terms of redefining factional loyalties.

Thus, we find factions have both functional and dysfunctional roles to play in every society. It, often, becomes inevitable. Where factions do not exist, despotism may crop up. Factionalism is gradually becoming more vivid day by day especially with the emergence of participatory democracy and working of Panchayati Raj system in India. The desire for more power, position and higher status has made the factional politics more active and dynamic.

It is true and must be expected that there will always be factions in society. "The diversity in the faculties of men, from which the rights of property originate, is......an inseparable obstacle to a uniformity of interests." Despotism will end factions, but the cure is no better than the disease. Liberty is to faction what air is to fire, an element without which it instantly expires.[61]

Thus, factionalism can not be avoided in our society as it has become the mania of the 20th century mankind.

Approaches

There are different approaches to the study of the faction and Nicholas has mentioned about two of them. While one of them focuses on the analysis of political conflict the other one lays emphasis on the study of political organization.[62] It means the study of political organization and analysis of political conflict must go side by side, otherwise it will be infructuous.

Structural approach regards factions as groups occupying mutually opposing positions in their struggle for political power with a view to further the interest of their respective members. The other variation of the structural view is the social structure model suggested by Lasswell. To him, factions are mutually opposed not only in their struggle for political power but also in several non-political spheres as well. These groups may stand in a relationship of the total opposition to each other. They do not confine their activity to the political sphere but extend it to various other spheres such as ritual, economic, commensal etc.[63]

Mayer talks about the particular nature of the disputes and considers them as the pivotal criteria of faction formation. He regards factions as specific variety of action sets.[64] This approach has been called as conflict approach since its primary aim is to emphasize the nature of conflict between different groups and individuals.

Dimensions

Studies on factions can be classified under two categories: first, they centre around village communities, their social organization, stratification and class and power relations and such kind of studies have been undertaken by social anthropologists; second, studies made by political scientists high-lighting inter-party factions and intra-party factional alignments and focusing on mechanisms of sharing political power at local, regional and national levels.

Factionalism may be understood either as a tool of structural analysis or as an ideology. In the first instance, there are several studies of factions in which kinship divisions are considered as factions. This model of analysis of factions, however, denies the role of leadership and factions are viewed as spontaneous divisions in a given society; they are intrinsic to social structure where in class or lineage heads become leaders of these factions (clans) by virtue of their hereditary positions.

The other view i.e. factionalism is an ideology refers to the role of leaders in dividing people into their respective followings. They assume the role of patrons in different political parties and within the parties. Factional leaders try to channelize developmental resources in favour of the region and community to which they belong and from which their following is largely derived. Present day power politics, developmental scheme and allocation of resources can be examined from this perspective which regards factionalism as an ideology. But these two views can be blended together and synthesized because factions by their nature are comprised of structural as well as ideological elements. In structural terms a faction is a kind of group and in ideological terms, it is an alliance of structurally divergent elements. A group of people who come to share the same goals either by force or by circumstances of otherwise, tend to form a faction in opposition to other groups and people. The structural similarity of these groups and people contributes to the formation of factions.[65]

An analysis of both kinds of studies on factions reveals that several criteria have been used in arriving at a single classification of factions. Two of them used generally are recruitment as the basis of faction formation and the permanent or temporary character of factions. Micro-structural studies of factions, however, are based on the criteria of caste, kinship and lineage etc. and consider factions as enduring phenomena. The macro-structural studies consider factors as issue or problem-oriented, hence imply that factions are emphemeral and interest-based and cut across caste and kinship lines.

There are a number of studies in which the faction is considered as a group comprising of members drawn from different castes. Factional alignments are formed whenever there is a controversial issue. In such a situation different factions take various stands in order to safeguard their respective interests. Since factions are formed on the basis of certain issues they tend to be short-lived, that is either they dissolve themselves or their membership changes as soon as the issue in question gets settled.

A faction may operate at a different level of state and local administration to have control over the administration. At the village level factional activities seem to be non-political at the beginning. But subsequently when such groups gain momentum, they become political in nature. There is a basic difference between the factions operating at the state politics and those which get involved in village politics. At the state level factions may emerge due to conflict and difference of opinion with the party high command to get important portfolios and position in the ministry, to become the chairman of the party, etc. Such groups may break the party or the ministry depending upon the situation. But according to Lewis, faction int he village occurs "...... as a result of (i) quarrel over the inheritance of land, (ii) quarrel over the adoption of sons, (iii) quarrel over house site and irrigation rights, (iv) quarrel over sexual offences, (v) murders, (vi) quarrel between castes......".[66]

Brass maintains that factions and factional conflict in India are a part and parcel of the indigenous social and political order.[67] Factional politics develops in a given society under certain conditions and is a manifestation of the leader-follower relationship in the countryside. A factional leader must ensure the continued loyalty of their followers. Moreover, they would try to increase the number of their followers by recruiting new members who are not yet members of any faction or by enticing some members of rival faction to defeat and join their groups. While supporting his factional leaders, a follower expects some patronage. So long as he receives such patronage, he would support his leader. Otherwise he would desert him and join the rival faction if he is offered tempting terms by the latter. The factional leader distributes benefits among his supporters for getting their loyalty and support in his fight against the leader of the opposing faction. Thus, the relationship between the leader of a faction and his supporters is reciprocal; both need each other and neither can thrive at the expense of the other. People tend to affiliate with others in order to better achieve their goals. The affiliation lasts while it remains profitable to both parties. Fukunaga in his study observes that political power is not the privilege of the "village elite." It is shared by every member of the community who participates actively or passively, positively or negatively—in the overall affairs of village.[68]

Sisson has correctly observed, "Factional coalitions are contracts of mutual benefit and can be broken by either supporter or supported when benefit appears more attractive through an alternative alignment, although these coalitions have usually existed over a fairly long period of time with marginal adjustment."[69] Therefore, it is said that factions are the predecessors of modern political parties. Cohn notes that in Senapur factionalism, rivalry, jealousy and friction between groups had always existed and often found expression in open fights, killings and house burnings.[70] The uncompromisable nature of conflict leads to the formation of a permanent group which, in political term may be called faction. Some conflicts are resolved and some are not. Where the conflict is resolved, it is not factional. But as pointed out by Miller, most of the conflicts are periodically or temporarily resolved.[71] Yet the conflict continues, perhaps on different issues, along different dimensions and involving different persons. So, whatever it may be, conflict occurs from time to time in human societies and factionalism is a characteristic form of conflict.[72]

Studies of factions, those dealing with conflict, form one of the central themes in the studies of village life. Siegel and Beals[73] in a study of factionalism, have distinguished two kinds of conflicts. According to them there may be conflict between cohesive subgroups within the larger groups. They have called it schismatic factionalism. The second type may involve the groups, the composition of which changes rapidly and radically. It has been termed as pervasive factionalism.

As village politics is at the bottom of the state politics and is the pre-training ground of most of the politicians, most of the factions emerging and developing at the village level are also apt to the political in nature. Of course, there is a lot of difference in the formation of such groups in the state and village level. Factionalism runs vertically either way. It may run from the top to the bottom or from the bottom to the top. If there is conflict in a political party at the state level, it would percolate to its lower units like district units, block units and village units. The factional leaders at the state level would tend to mobilize resources and support not only at the state level, but also at the lower levels. This they would do by exploiting primordial loyalties like caste, religion, language and region. They would also seek to win over party members by distributing or even promising different kinds of benefits. Factionalism may also run in the reverse gear. If a village unit of a party, for example, suffers from factionalism, the leaders of rival groups would tend to win the support of the leaders placed at the higher level of the party. Rarely, would the party at a higher rung of the ladder be split due to the split at a lower point of the ladder. But if there is already a division in the party at the higher level, the lower level split of the party would mesh in with the higher-levels split. In other words, it would be easier for the leaders of village factions to gain the alliance of higher-level leaders who are already placed in charge of rival factions. Therefore, it is apparent that factionalism would tend to run faster from the top to the bottom than the bottom to the top.

The formation of factional groupings differ from that of the state to the village level. At the state level such groups may form: (i) due to conflicting opinion with the party boss; (ii) to acquire the chair of party's important position; (iii) to have enormous control over the ministry; (iv) when power or portfolio of a minister is taken away by the leaders; (v) when a party's district or any comparatively important leader's word or interest is ignored; and (vi) when other political parties declare prizes to topple the ministry etc. Such groups sometimes split the monolith the party or ministry as the case may be. They may also paralyze the state administration. But at the village level the reasons for formation of such groups and their functions are otherwise. In micro-politics, the aim is limited. The aim of the village leaders is neither to acquire power in the state administration nor to change a ministry, nor even to establish a position in state politics. Being limited in their aim, their universe is limited and ultimately their goal is also limited to this small universe.[74]

Bailey discovered various factions all of which were rooted in caste division.[75] He also found that factions of different castes which approved of each other in their day-to-day functioning bridged their differences and acted as a unit whenever there was a common threat or problem faced by the village community.

Factions being inseparable part of social system are created in the village and members from different castes align with different factions and in the process, multi-caste alliances come into existence. These alliances are generally the foci of power rather than the caste as a whole.[76] These alliances are clearly visible during panchayat elections. The candidature of the contestants is sponsored by the multi-caste alliances and they are sure to gain political power, if their candidate is elected. Since candidates of the same caste contest against each other, the caste as a factor is losing importance and political factions and personal ambitions cut across caste loyalties.

In Indian village, and elsewhere in under-developed societies, the influences of modernization and democratic norms of political participation created a situation where traditional rules of social segmentation began to change. This led to further status ambiguity in a changing socio-economic situation by providing free access to new power positions irrespective of traditional norms of social hierarchy. The competition for power, status and economic opportunities under such anomie conditions led to the development of interest-oriented grouping of non-traditional bases. These groupings or factions then became social devices to enable individuals to achieve their aims in situations where they lack their customary groups and effective norms.[77] These studies reveal that power structure in the villages is changing and loyalties cut-across the caste boundaries; because of numerical superiority, the lower castes are also gaining power; because of voting rights new alignments are taking place and traditionally powerful men are losing ground; factionalism has, thus, become a part of the village politics. On the basis of these studies it can be said that in different spheres—whether in exercise power and dominance in elections, in decision-making, developmental activities or articulation of leadership, the intra-caste unity is questioned.[78] Scholars generally agree that the castes are split into various power-wielding groups, known as factions. These factions in the form of multi-caste alliances are most active, operational and effective. Even within the faction the role of influential individuals is more pronounced.

Factional Leadership

Leadership, an integral part of inter-personal behaviour, plays an important role in shaping the socio-economic and political life of the rural communities[79] and has been considered as an activity which influences the group behaviour in order to effect co-operation towards some desirable goals. The status as well as the role of the leader mobilize the group to achieve the desired goal and thus, ultimately, effecting structural changes. In a changing social structure, from the traditional to the modern one, leadership is also prone to change. The introduction of community projects, land reforms, decentralized local administration and adult franchise, which at the reconstruction of rural society, have brought forth the importance of leadership.[80] It is believed that the success or failure of development plans and indeed of more general ideological aspirations as embodied in our constitution, may well depend upon the type of leadership available at village, town and the district levels.

Every society more or less witnesses predominance of a leader who makes the group activity a happy and satisfying experience for group members. Leadership is an inter-personal influence exercised in a situation and directed through communication process towards the attainment of a specified goal or goals.[81] Accordingly, a factional group also operates under the influence of a leader. There can be only one leader in a faction. Where there is more than one leader, there exists more than one faction or a coalition of factions. The ideal Indian faction leader has seniority, education, integrity; he has an understanding of people's personal problem and struggles; he is personally conciliatory in temperament and is able to solve the disputes, he is politically adept; he has "tact" and he knows the art of political manipulation. Most important, he is selfless and generous and provides money and job to his followers.[82] Faction leaders are ordinary competitors and mostly well-to-do and have great control over resources. Where resources are dispersed, there the chances are more for emerging factions. In such a situation, the leaders of the several factions tie with one another to beg resources, support etc., from their counterparts. The loss of one is the gain of others.[83]

According to Bogardus, leadership may be classified on the basis of personality types and social roles; mode of exercise of their leadership; relationship between the leaders and the led; origin of leadership and some other multiple criteria.[84] However, in case of factional leaders, loyalty to their respective followers is the main quality of a leader. According to Bailey, this loyalty is the moral commitment on the part of the party workers and voters to the political party. The absence of such a commitment in Orissa reflects the failure of party to achieve legitimacy in the society.[85]

A leader must be a man of wealth, highly educated, intelligent, magnanimous etc., in nature. He must look after the interest of the followers and should be prepared to sacrifice some of his interest, otherwise his leadership may not last long. The factional leaders while making their own advancement must also see the advancement of his followers.

To be successful in factional politics, one has to work behind the scene, to go behind the back, not only of one's enemies but also of those who appeared to be one's friends and to set a high value on secrecy and conspiracy.[86] These secret, clandestine and behind-the-scene activities are very much necessary to keep him on the alert for making pre-emptive strikes on his opponent groups when required.

Though national politics centres around urban and semi-urban areas, the village faction can not be said to be completely different. At the village level also faction leaders try to keep contact with urban leaders and sometimes act as their agents. They do this with the hope of getting some rewards from the urban leaders. Accordingly, such faction leaders support the cause of their followers in the village. For external relations with others, faction leaders are often motivated more by considerations of prestige than by the desire for power only.[87] According to Bhargava at any level of panchayati raj a leader should have a support base inside the council for his continuation in power. At the same time, he should establish links with higher level leaders who could serve as "political umbrella" of him.[88]

K. S. Dhillon, discusses rural leadership so as to recognise its protean forms and its unreliability as a mechanism for extension work. According to him, rural leaders have brought to light the varied roles of kin and caste oriented factions in the decision-making process in rural India.[89]

Irving Krikerbocker has, however, defined the term leader as the individual who is selected, elected or voluntarily accepted by a group because of his possession or control over the means which the group desires to utilize to attain its objectives.[90]

Roy's study provides some features about the types of personal emerging as leaders in Indian villages and the modes of their operation. He derives a generalization from his study that people with higher educational standard, better income and higher standard of living, having large family members, participate in new organizations and become leaders. According to him, caste and age never determine who would be the leader.[91]

Articulate leadership is an important determinant for the successful functioning of a faction. Leaders of both the major and minor factions draw strength and help from different sources and different people in the village. Nicholas, in his study of Govindapur village, observed that the people in the village helped their leaders because they were "kinsmen", some were "economically dependent on their leaders", some backed their neighbourhood head men", others helped on the ground of caste relations whereas still another group of people helped their leader, "in hopes of defeating their enemy".[92]

After analysing all these concepts it can be said that in rural area, faction leaders' sole aim is to achieve power and prestige and in that process to annul the attempts of others who are opposed to them. These leaders are very selfish and ambitious and their politics is politics of *status quo*. They utilize local bodies or co-operatives or any such decentralized organisations, since they serve as strategic power points, the control on which will help them to ascend to higher level power.[93] As Myron Weiner has pointed out that "whenever there is power, there must be politics—a law as fundamental in Political Science as supply and demand in Economics.[94]

References

1. Raymond Firth, "*Introduction to Factions in Indian and Overseas Indian Societies.*" The British Journal of Sociology, Vol. 8, No. 4, 1957, p. 292.
2. Rodney W. Jones, *Urban Politics in India: Area, Power and Policy in a Penetrated System*, Berkeley: University of California Press, 1974, p. 71.
3. Myron Weiner, *Party Politics in India: The Development of a Multi-party System* Princeton: University Press, 1957, p. 237.
4. H.S. Dhillon, et al, *Leadership and Groups in a South Indian Village* New Delhi: Planning Commission, Government of India press, 1955.
5. Baljit Singh, *Next Step in Village India* Bombay: Asia Publishing House, 1961, p.4.
6. A. R. Beals and B. J. Seigel "*Pervasive Factionalism*", American Anthropologist, Vol. 62, 1960, p. 399.
7. Federalist, (New York: Modern Library) pp. 53–62, In Reinhard Bendix and Seymour Martin Lipset (ed.) *Class, Status and Power: Social Stratification in Comparative Perspective*, London: 1974, p. 2.
8. P.N. Rastogi, *The Nature and Dynamics of Factional Conflict*, New Delhi: The Macmillon Company of India Ltd., 1975, p. 32.
9. M. N. Srinivas, *The Remembered Village*, New Delhi: Oxford University Press, 1979, p. 221.
10. N. Patnaik and H. D. Lakshmi Narayan "*Factional Politics in Village India*", Man in India, Vol. 49, 1969, p. 162.
11. Hechter Michael, "*Group Formation and the Cultural Division of Labour*", American Journal of Sociology, Vol. 84, NO. 2, September 1978, pp. 297–98.
12. N. K. Behura, "*Conflict, Politics and Harmony*", Man and Life, 1978, p. 35.
13. J. K. Mahapatra, *Factional Politics in India*, Allahabad : Chugh Publication, 1985, p. 4.
14. B. K. Nagla, *Factionalism, Politics and Social Structure*, Jaipur: Rawat Publications, 1984, p. 5.
15. Beals & Siegel, *op. cit.*

16. Quoted in Rastogi, *op. cit.* p.30.
17. *Ibid.*
18. Quoted in P. K. Choudhury, *Caste and Power Structure : A study of a Haryana Village*, Unpublished Ph.D. Dissertation, 1984, p. 12.
19. Patnaik and Lakshmi Narayan, *Op. cit.*
20. Quoted in Choudhury, *Op. cit.*, p. 12.
21. C. Parvathamma, "*Elections and Traditional Leadership in a Mysore Village*", The Economic Weekly, Vol. xvii, No. 10, 7 March 1964, p. 470.
22. Patnaik and Lakshmi Narayan, *Op. cit.*, p. 185.
23. D. K. Samanta, "*Determinants of Political Factions in a Deccan Village*," Journal of Indian Anthropological Society, Vol. 17, 1982, p. 222.
24. Ralph W. Nicholas, "*Factions: A Comparative Analysis*" in Nicholas (ed.) Political System and Distribution of Power, ASA, Monographs, London : Tavistock Publication, 1963, pp. 21–61.
25. ________________, "Village Factions and Political Parties", Journal of Common Wealth Studies Vol. 2, 1963 pp. 17–32.
26. Masaki Fukunaga, *Society, Caste and Factional Politics, Conflict and Continuity in Rural India*, New Delhi: Mahohar, 1993.
27. Oscar Lewis, *Group Dynamics in a North Indian Village*, New Delhi: Planning Commission, Government of India, 1954, p. 14.
28. D. F. Pocock, "*The Bases of Factions in Gujarat*", British Journal of Sociology, Vol. 8 No. 4, 1957, p. 296, 300.
29. Quoted in Patnaik and Lakshmi Narayan, *Op. cit.*
30. Pocock, *Op. cit.*, p. 296.
31. F. G. Bailey, "*The Study of Politics in Village India*", a paper presented at the 16th Annual Meeting of the Association for Asian Studies, Washington D.C., March 1964, (Memeo), p.2.
32. G.D. Berreman, *Hindus of the Himalayas*, Berkeley : University of California Press, 1963, p. 266.
33. Lewis, *Op. cit.*, p. 14.
34. John T. Hitchock, *The Rajputs of Kohlapur: A Study of Kinship, Social Stratification and Politics*. Unpublished Ph.D. Dissertation,

Cornell University, 1956, pp. 258–59.

35. A. R. Beals, "*Cleavage and Internal Conflict: An Example from India*," Journal of Conflict Resolution, 1961, Vol. 5., No. 1, p. 34.

36. Berreman, *Op. cit.*, p. 267.

37. Oscar Lewis, *Village Life in Northern India*, Urbana: University of Illinois Press, 1958, p. 148.

38. T. S. Epstein, Economic Development and Social Change in South India, Manchester: Manchester University Press, 1962, p. 130.

39. Pocock, op. cit.

40. Berreman, op. cit.

41. Fukunaga, op. cit., p. 9.

42. M. S. Mashreque and M.R. Amin, "*Politics ofFactionalism in Rural Bangladesh*," IASSI Quarterly, Vol. II, No. 2, 1992, pp. 145–46.

43. Oscar Lewis, Quoted in Anthony Carter, *Elite Politics in Rural India*, p. 102.

44. K.C. Panda, *Factional Politics in Rural Orissa*, Unpublished Ph.D. Dissertation, Sambalpur University, 1981, p. 9.

45. Fukunaga, op. cit., p. 9.

46. Patnaik and Lakshmi Narayan, op. cit., p. 171.

47. Rastogi, op. cit., p. 32.

48. A.R. Beals, *Culture, Change and Social Conflict in a South Indian Village*, (Berkeley: University of California, 1954), p. 206.

49. Fukunaga, op. cit., p.24.

50. Rastogi, op. cit., p. 32.

51. Patnaik and Lakshmi Narayan, op. cit., p. 165.

52. Nagla, op. cit., p. 36.

53. Patnaik and Lakshmi Narayan, op. cit.

54. Shokeid Moshe, "*Immigration and Factionalism: An Analysis of Factions in Rural Israeli Communities of Immigrants*," Quoted by Rastogi, op. cit., p. 30.

55. Fukunaga, op. cit., p.4.

56. Panda, op. cit., p. 20.
57. Paul R. Brass, *Factional Politics in an Indian State: The Congress Party in Uttar Pradesh*, Berkeley: University of California Press, 1965, p. 145.
58. *Ibid.*
59. B.S. Bhargava and V.N. Torgal, "*Factionalism: A Study of Panchayat in Karnataka*", Quarterly Journal of the Local Self Government Institute, Vol. 51–52, Bombay 1980–82, p. 247.
60. *Ibid.*
61. Jannet Bujra, "*The Dynamics of Political Action: A New Look at Factinalism*", Anthropologist, 1975, p. 75.
62. Ralph W. Nicholas, "*Factions: A Comparative Analysis*" in Michael Banton (ed.), Political Systems and the Distribution of Power, Quoted in Bhargava and Torgal, op. cit., p. 242.
63. Nagla, op. cit., p. 6.
64. Adrian C. Mayer, *Peasent in the Pacific: A Study of Fiji, Indian Rural Society*, London: Routledge and Kegan Paul, 1961, p. 122.
65. Nagla, op. cit., p. 4.
66. Lewis, op. cit., p. 503.
67. Brass, op. cit., p. 234.
68. Fukunaga, op. cit., p. 35.
69. Richard Sisson, *The Congress Party in Rajsthan: Political Integration and Institution Building in an Indian State*, Delhi: University of California Press, 1972, p. 314.
70. Quoted in Fukunaga, op. cit., p. 13.
71. D. F. Miller, "*Faction in Indian Village Politics*", Pacific Affairs, Vol. 38, No. 1965, p. 18.
72. J. S. Yadav, "*Factionalism in a Harayana Village*", American Anthropologist, Vol. 70 1968, p. 898.
73. Beals and Siegel, op. cit., pp. 394–97.
74. Panda, op. cit., p. 10.
75. F. G. Bailey, *Caste and Economic Frontier*, Manchester: Manchester University Press, 1957, pp. 186--98.

76. Choudhury, op. cit., p.11.
77. Rastogi, op. cit., p. 32.
78. Choudhury, op. cit., p. 12.
79. Satinderjit Kaur, et. al., "Role of Village Leaders in Rural Upliftment" Kurukshetra, Sept. 1993, p. 11.
80. Ibid.
81. Tennenbaum, et. al., op. cit.
82. Paul R. Brass, "*Factionalism and Congress Party in Uttar Pradesh*", Asian Survey, Vol. 4. (1964), p. 1042.
83. Pattnaik and Lakshmi Narayana, op. cit., pp. 163–64.
84. E.S. Bogardus, in P.C. Dev and B.K. Agarwal, "Rural Leadership in Green Revolution, Delhi: Researcheo Publications, 1974, p.2.
85. F.G. Bailey, "*Politics and Society in Orissa*", Advancement of Science, May 1962, p. 27.
86. __________, "*The Definition of Factionalism*" (Unpublished), 1977, p. 8.
87. Brass, *Factional Politics in an Indian State*....., op. cit., 237.
88. B.S. Bhargava, *Political Administrative Dynamics in Panchayati Raj System*, Delhi: Ashish Publishing House, p.3.
89. Dhillion, op. cit.
90. Irving Kikerbocker in Browne, Cohn and Danville (eds.), *The Study of Leadership,* The Inter-State Printers and Publishers: 1958, pp. 10–11.
91. Pradeepta Roy, "*The Characteristics of Emergent Leaders*", in L.P. Vidyarthy (ed.), Leadership in India New Delhi: Asia Publishing House, 1967.
92. Nicholas, op. cit., p. 46,
93. K. Sesadri, "*Indian Politics: Then & Now*", Patterns of Leadership in India, p. 111.
94. Quoted in Bhargava, op. cit., p.3.

2
THE SETTING

(A) Orissa : A Profile

One of the twenty five states (Federal units) of the Indian Union, situated in the north eastern zone of the Indian peninsula, located between 17^0–50' and 22^0–34' of north latitude and between 81^0–27' and 87^0–99' east of Greenwich, bounded in the North by Bihar, in the West by Madhya Pradesh, in the North-East by West Bengal and in the South by Andhra Pradesh and with a land area of 1,55,707 Sq. Kilometers, the State of Orissa is divided into thirty[1] district for administrative purposes. It has four well defined physical regions: the hilly region (Plateau) of the North and North West, the Eastern Ghats, the central plateau and the coastal plains. The dominant physical features of the state are: the Bay of Bengal on the East, the alluvial coastal plains, the plateau to the North and Western part of the state and the mountainous southern Orissa, which forms part of the long chain of the hills known as Eastern Ghats. Geographically Orissa is broadly divided into western uplands and the coastal plains.

The coastal plains cover the district of Balasore, Cuttack, Puri and Ganjam and constitute 25 per cent of the total area of the State. The hill regions in the North and North-West constitute the mineral belt of the State. The State frequently suffers from flood and cyclone as well as drought both in the plateau areas as well as the hilly portions.[2]

Orissa's Population, as per the 1991 census, is 31,512,070. Of them, 27,279,615 live in villages and the rest 4,232,455 live in urban areas. India has the second largest population in the world, while the State of Orissa occupies the eleventh position among all the States in the country.[3] While India has 2.42 per cent of total geographical area of the world, it accounts for about 16 per cent of the world population. Spreading over 4.74 per cent of total geographical area of the country Orissa accounts for 3.73 per cent of India's population.[4] India has a density of population of 267 per sq. km. while it is 202 in case of Orissa. The districts which have a higher density than the state average are undivided Cuttack, Balasore, Puri and Ganjam. The reasons for it can be ascribed to the fertile soil having irrigation facilities, increased industrial activities, growth of urbanization, good communication facilities, etc. The literacy in Orissa stands at 48.55 per cent as against the national average of 52.11 per cent.[5] It shows that in the field of literacy, Orissa trials behind the national average. Literacy promotion drives are to be taken to eradicate the problem of illiteracy. Of course, attempts are being taken by the government in this regard. As a result, Ganjam and Gajapati districts are declared as cent per cent literate districts of Orissa. The literacy rate in the coastal division is much higher than that of the highland division. A unique feature of Orissa is the very high percentage of scheduled castes and scheduled tribes constituting 38 per cent of the total population of which 22 per cent are tribals and 16 per cent scheduled castes.

Orissa is predominantly rural state where 86.57 per cent of its people live in its 50,872 villages. It is, therefore, one of the least urbanized and industrialised States in the Country. The Urban population of the state constitutes only 13.43 per cent of the total population of the State, as per the 1991 census. The percentage of Urban population of India and Orissa may be seen from the Table 2.1.

Table 2.1

Census Year	*Percentage of Urban Population*	
	India	*Orissa*
1941	13.86	3.00
1951	17.29	4.06
1961	17.97	6.32
1971	19.91	8.41
1981	23.34	11.79
1991	25.72	13.43

Though the percentage of urban population is gradually increasing, Orissa has a low level of urbanization compared to that of the national figure as is evident from the above table.

Agriculture is the basis of its economy. Nearly 74 per cent of its population are engaged in agriculture. The following statement gives us an idea about the involvement of the people of Orissa in agriculture as well as of those at the National level.

[Table 2.2] Percentage Distribution of Main Workers by Cultivators and Agricultural Labourers, in India and Orissa by Residence and Sex during 1981–1991.

Sl. No.		Total/ Rural/ Urban	Persons Males Females	Percentage of the Total Main Workers			
				Cultivators		Agrl. Labourers	
				1981	1991	1981	1991
1.	India	Total	Persons	41.58	38.75	24.94	26.15
			Males	43.70	40.01	19.56	20.90
			Females	33.20	34.55	46.18	43.56
		Rural	Persons	51.10	48.47	29.88	31.77
			Males	55.16	51.79	24.00	26.11
			Females	37.07	38.98	50.20	47.94
		Urban	Persons	5.13	4.99	6.05	6.66
			Males	5.20	4.90	4.66	5.35
			Females	4.66	5.54	16.57	14.89
2.	Orissa	Total	Persons	46.94	44.21	27.76	28.85
			Males	51.27	48.35	22.65	22.96
			Females	24.50	26.03	54.24	54.73
		Rural	Persons	51.78	49.30	30.14	31.64
			Males	56.91	54.52	24.70	25.37
			Females	26.26	27.77	57.21	57.50
		Urban	Persons	7.08	6.44	8.20	8.19
			Males	7.49	6.75	6.70	6.70
			Females	4.02	4.03	19.45	19.72

Thus the people of Orissa mainly depend on agriculture for their livelihood. More than 2/3rd of the working population are cultivators and agricultural labourers and the remaining are engaged in the cottage industries or doing other work. The cultivators constitute 44.21 per cent of the main workers of the State as against the national average of 38.75 per cent. Similarly, at the national level agricultural labourers constitute 26.15 per cent while at the State level it comes to 28.85 per cent which is more than the national average. Hence, the percentage of cultivators and agricultural labourer in Orissa have slowly been increasing during the last decade.

Land reforms[6] and land ceiling measures have not been effective and they have hardly helped in changing the agrarian structure of the State. Because Orissa is still gripped by semi-feudalism and small tenants and agricultural labourers, by and large, are still attached to their old "land lords"[7]. Because of this continued traditional loyalty, they are not able to identify themselves with an economic class of identical interests. As a result, a conscious agrarian class has failed to emerge in the State.

Orissa is rich in resources but poor in economic development.[8] In other words, the State is rich but its people are poor. Its economy is agriculture dominated and the process of industrialization has been slow. Inspite of the vast forest, mines and other natural resources, it still remains one of the most industrially backward states. A "Sad symbol of man's ingratitude to Nature", she presents a paradox in plenty. The vast industrial potentials of the State have been mainly concentrated in the hill regions. She is a large producer of high grade iron and manganese ores. The Rourkela Steel plant and Tata Iron and Steel Co., depend mainly upon Orissa's Iron ores. Twenty five percent of the total manganese in India is produced in Orissa and it contributes to enrich the foreign exchange position of India.

Orissa has very inadequate means of transport in relation to agriculture and industrial potential as also mineral wealth and forest resources. Transport and communication constitute the nerves of economy. Unfortunately, it also lags behind most other States in India in transport and communication.

Geographically, Orissa is regarded as a State of Eastern India, but culturally it is as much a part of North India as that of the South. This has influenced its history to a great extent. While the coastal districts have their affinity with North India, South Orissa comes closes to the South India because of their homogeneity.

Orissa is, thus, a confluence of two streams of Indian culture. Its language, culture, art and architecture bear indelible marks of *Aryavarta* (Northern) and Dakshinatya (Southern) civilizations.

Orissa has a very rich and glorious history. The people of Kalinga (as they were known 2000 years ago) were seafaring, making it a prosperous maritime state. Till the early part of the 19th century, the Oriya seamen kept the maritime flag of this country flying in the waters of South East Asia but the Portuguese pirates and enterprising British dealt a death-blow to its prosperous maritime trade. It may be mentioned here that ancient Orissa had an overseas empire with colonies in Burma and the oceanic islands. Oriya merchants and missionaries carried their art and culture even to the far off flung lands of Peru and Mexico and helped to build the old Maya civilization in central America.[9] Even they had voyaged to distant lands of Sumatra, Java, Bali which are now parts of Indonesia and other South East Asian countries and one comes across buildings and temples in the Orissa school of Architecture which bear testimony to the effective functioning of the people from Orissa as messengers of culture and good will through the medium of personal contact and commercial intercourse.

From time to time migrants from different parts of India, speaking different languages and worshiping in different shrines visited Orissa. Many of them settled down here and different cultures were blended into an organic whole. Thus, developed a catholicity of outlook. The Tantra culture of Kamroop, the Dravidian culture of Gondwara and the Aryan culture of the North have all gone to evolve the cult of Jagannath, the cult of love and tolerance. Oriyas have great faith in their secular Lord Jagannath who is conceived as cosmopolitan deity; where all the sectarian religions of India have been merged and assimilated. Thus, the cosmopolitan deity, Jagannath, has inspired the cosmopolitan outlook, manners and the way of life among the people of Orissa. All religious, social customs and the cultural activities in Orissa veer round Lord Jagannath. In short, Orissa's culture means Jagannath and Jagannath means oriya culture.

The temple of Lord Jagannath[10] at Puri, Lingaraj[11] temple at Bhubaneswar and the Sun temple[12] at Konark are known throughout the length and breadth of the country. For centuries,

Orissa's history was one of peace and progress. Temples and monuments and well-knit village communities still bear testimony to the glorious days of spiritual greatness and material prosperity. It seems that the geographical situation of the State, its physical features, political strength, inner creativity of the people, its economic condition and social circumstances have contributed to the building up of its cultural edifice. But unfortunately, the cultural edifice of Orissa was shakened because of British rule over it in 1803.[13] During this period the natural Orissa was dismembered and Oriya-speaking tracts lay scattered in the neighbouring administrative units-Bengal, Madras and Central province. Oriya culture and language were in danger of disappearing F.G. Bailey, a keen British scholar on Orissa, says :

"Oriya culture was despised. Bengalis even attempted to prove that oriya was a mere dialect of Bengali, where as Oriyas pointed out that, Bengali with equal justification could be considered a corrupted form of Oriya. Many Oriyas lost their lands to Bengalis. Estates were sold to meet arrears of tax and the sale took place in Calcutta, often without the knowledge of the Oriya owner".[14] All this happened in the heart of Orissa in which Oriyas were in a clear majority. Worse happened in those tracts where they were minority.

The history of Orissa is remarkable for its political greatness, economic prosperity, social upliftments, architectural and artistic attainments and religious movements through all its ages[15]. It is well known that Orissa was a prosperous country under its own independent kings. This is evident from the writings of both early travellers and later historians. Orissa was subjected to successive foreign dominations for a long time. The Marathas ruled the land from 1751 to 1803.[16] They divided the territory into two political divisions, namely Mughalbandi and Garjats. Mughalbandi division consist of the coastal plains was under their direct rule while Garjat division comprised the hilly regions of the North and North Western parts of Orissa. The two areas were, no doubt, connected both culturally and economically, for they had same language, religion and cultural values. But there are many other aspects responsible for fundamental diversities between the hill and the coastal division. For about a century and half these two divisions had experienced two different types of government. The

Mughalbandi areas of Cuttack, Puri and Balasore were conquered by the British from the Marathas in 1803 and were ruled by them. The Garjat areas which lay in the hilly regions in the North-Western part of Orissa were ruled by the local chieftains during the Maratha period. The British did not interfere in their internal administration and they were left almost undisturbed in the hands of the rulers on payment of fixed annual tributes, which partly contributed to overall backwardness of the region.

The Mughalbandi areas had land-settlement in the days of Akbar,[17] while the Garjat area was the traditional home of feudal lords and the rulers of the feudatory states.[18]

On account of historical accident, Orissa remained dismembered and the Oriya-speaking tracts scattered broadly within three British administrative units, viz., Bengal, the Central Provinces and Madras. Till 1936; it continued without any substantial change except that there was a slight alteration in the year 1905 when the district of Sambalpur, which had then been included within the Central Provinces was transferred to Orissa division.[19] Although the status of Orissa was markedly improved by the creation of the province of Bihar and Orissa, yet it, by no means, satisfied the aspirations of the Oriyas. It was because of their continuous demand for a separate state. Montagu-Chelmsford report[20] suggested for an early consideration of the question of formation of provinces on the basis of language. Subsequently, the Legislative Councils of Bihar and Orissa passed resolution, recommending the amalgamation of Oriya-speaking tracts. It afforded a striking example of they unity of opinion among the representatives of Orissa in that Council.[21] Afterwards, the Government of India appointed the Philip-Duff Committee to make a detailed enquiry on the spot in order to ascertain the attitude of Oriya-speaking people of the Madras Presidency on the question of their amalgamation with Orissa. The committee recommended that there was a genuine, long-standing and deep-seated desire on the part of the educated Oriya classes of the oriya-speaking tracts for amalgamation of these tracts with Orissa under one administration.[22]

The formation of the separate state of Orissa in 1936 was the result of a protracted Oriya nationalist agitation since 1903. The formation of "Utkal Samilani" (Utkal Union Conference) provided a forum for carrying out the movement for the integration of the Oriya-speaking tracts under one administration. Madhusudan Das realized that the political development of the Oriyas would not be possible if different Oriya-speaking areas remained scattered as appendages to other provinces. Thus, the movement led by Madhusudan Das, 'the grand old man of Orissa', was perhaps the earliest demand in India, for a homogeneous linguistic state.

The historic meeting held on 30th and 31st December, 1903 at Cuttack was truly a National Assembly, where the first resolution moved by the Ruling Chief of Keonjhar, emphasized the administrative union of the Oriya tracts. The resolution was a sequel to Lord Curzon's proposal.[23] The Conference symbolized the awakening of the Oriyas[24] and gave an impetus to the struggle for amalgamation of Oriya tracts. Madhusudan das was its chief architect. As such, he inspired a new awakening among the people of Orissa and symbolized the new sunrise at the end of a century of darkness.[25]

Das went to England in 1907 and organized the movement there too. During his short stay in London, he was very much exercised with the Orissa question. He addressed several meetings interviewed some important members of parliament and circulated a pamphlet entitled "Unrest in India", which he had printed in England.[26] He could enlist the sympathy of the British people in support of the 11 million Oriyas. Even a large number of journalists of the day reviewed the matter favourably and gave importance to the cause of Orissa. Various British newspapers of that time highlighted Orissa and the Oriya movement.[27]

Convinced of the legitimacy of the demand, the Simon Commission,[28] recommended a separate province for Orissa. The question came up before the Round-Table Conference in London in 1931 and Orissa was given a separate provincial status under the Government of India Act, 1935. In January 1936, an order-in-Council was promulgated by His Majesty, creating the separate Province of Orissa.

On 1st April, 1936, the province of Orissa was inaugurated and it consisted of six districts, namely Cuttack, Puri, Balasore, Sambalpur, Ganjam and Koraput.[29] It comprised an area of 32,695 square miles with a population of 80,43,681.[30]

On the eve of the inauguration, the British King in his "Message of Greetings" stated that the province of Orissa was the first outcome of the Government of India Act of 1935 and wished that the new province would draw inspiration from the past and prove worthy of the historic tradition of the "Holy land of Orissa".[31]

On 1st April, 1936, The statesman, Published from Calcutta, stated that the creation of Sind and Orissa led to an end of long agitation and praised those who served for the cause of these lands and greeted them as they proved their case to the satisfaction of the British Government by demonstrating unflagging zeal.

A meeting, organized on 1st April, 1936 at Cuttack to observe the oath-taking ceremony of Sir John Austin Huback, the first Governor of Orissa,[32] was attended by various sections of the people from the urban and rural areas. The leaders who had identified themselves with the cause of Orissa from the inception of Utkal Union Conference since 1903, expressed great happiness, as they could see their attempts translated into reality. But the exclusion of the essential outlying Oriya tracts like Saraikala, Singhbhum, etc. kept the aspirations of the people unfulfilled. The process of unification of all Oriya-speaking tracts could be complete only during 1948-49. After India's Independence, the princely states (Garjats) attached to Orissa claimed sovereignty. The Prajamandal Movement and diplomatic moves by the Government of Orissa under H.K. Mahatab's astute leadership virtually forced the princely states to merge with Orissa. By 1949, twenty-four of the princely states had merged with Orissa except Saraikala and Kharswan which remained the bone of contention between Orissa and Bihar until the States Reorganization Commission, 1956 recommended their inclusion in Bihar. After the merger of princely states, Orissa consisted of 13 districts.[33] It is important to note that the process of princely state's integration in India began in Orissa. But for administrative convenience, the number of districts in Orissa has been raised to 30 by the Biju Patnaik government in 1993.

Orissa is a traditional caste-ridden Hindu society and the talents for the political, economic, social academic leadership in the state are provided mainly by the caste Hindus. High caste Hindus, mainly *Brahmins* and *Karans* monopolize elite positions in the state. Since independence *Kshartriyas* hailing from the families of ex-rulers and *Khandayats* constitute the largest caste group in the state emerging politically influential.

Political Culture of Orissa

The term 'Political culture' refers to the pattern of individual attitudes and orientations towards politics among members of a political system.[34] It is the product of the collective history of a political system and the life histories of the individuals who currently make-up the system.[35] Political culture refers to specifically political orientations towards the political system and its various parts and attitudes towards the role of the self in the system.[36] It includes not only the attitudes towards politics, political values, ideologies, national character and cultural ethos, but also the style, manner and substantive form of politics.[37] It is the manifestation, in aggregate, of the psychological and subjective dimension of politics.

The present Orissa acquired its politics identity after being carved out as a separate state only in 1936. However, politics in Orissa prior to that as discussed earlier, veered round the agitation for a separate state from 1903 to 1936.[38]

Elections under the 1935 Act were first held in Orissa, and it was being freely said in those days that this was deliberately done by the Government of India because they thought that the cultural clash and the influence of the Zamindars would give a jolt to the congress party and thus would give lead and set an example to the rest of India.[39] But in 1937 the Congress in Orissa secured 36 seats in the newly formed 60-member Legislative Assembly. In the Assembly Elections of 1946 the Congress was able to repeat its success by winning a majority of seats. The electoral success of the Congress in 1946 (Congress got 45 seats out of 60) was made possible due to two factors. By that time it was the only important political party in the State. Other political parties had practically no popular base in the State. But later on the Congress politics in the province had developed certain unfortunate tendencies on the issues of caste, class and region, whose impact was bitterly felt in later years.[40]

The congress party in Orissa in the pre-independence period was faction-ridden. This factionalism was largely on the lines of the development at the national level. There were three groups in the State unit of the organisation viz.–(i) The Swaraj group (ii) The orthodox Congressmen known as "Gandhians" and (iii) The communists and the Socialists. Each one of these groups had a distinct role in the struggle for independence. The Swarajists and the Gandhians fought between themselves to capture the State Congress. The intra-Congress conflict was also based on age, caste and region. The Swarajists, in fact, were old congress people, Brahmin by caste and belonged to Puri district. Important among them were Nilakantha Dash, Godavarish Mishra, Lingaraj Mishra, Krupasindhu Mishra and Harihara Dash, all of them were close colleagues of Gopabandhu who established an ideal school at Satyabadi near Puri. The other group included Harekrishna Mehatab, Nabakrushna Choudhry, Nityananda Kanungo and Raja Krishna Bose who belonged to Balasore and Cuttack districts. They were younger in age and most of them were non-Brahmins. Though this group accepted Gopabandhu Das as its leader, yet it shifted its loyalty later towards a rival group known as Alaka Ashram Group with its head quarter at Jagatsinghpur.

At the time of the formation of the first Congress Government in Orissa in 1937,[41] the factional rivalry between the two groups in the organisation came to a stage of open hostility. The leadership of Nilakantha Das and Godabarish Mishra was not accepted though the credit for returning a Congress majority was squarely attributed to the organizing ability of Dash. Biswanath Das of Ganjam formed the cabinet with Nityananda Kanungo of the Alaka Ashram Group and Bodhram Dube of Sambalpur as its other two members. However, the Das-Mishra group made their last bid to capture the Pradesh Congress Committee in 1939. This time Godabarish Mishra contested for the Presidentship, but was defeated by a candidate of the Alaka Ashram group, Radha Krishna Biswasray from Koraput backed by Mahatab. From 1939 onward the Pradesh Congress Committee was practically under Mahatab's control. The Das-Mishra group steadily lost ground and fell from the grace of the High Command due to Mahatab's efforts. Through political contacts with central leaders, Mahatab became the member of the All India Congress Working Committee.[42]

The Congress Ministry in Orissa resigned in 1939 on the issue of the Second World War and Orissa for the first time came directly under the Governors' rule. Nilakantha Dash and Godabarish Mishra made a bid for an alternative ministry but Mahatab's tactical moves foiled their attempt. Being disgusted, they resigned from the Congress alongwith seven other members and joined hands with the opposition. By taking advantage of the situation, they eventually succeeded in forming a government in 1941. It was the second minority government headed by Krishna Chandra Gajapati Narayan Dev, Maharaja of Paralakhemundi, with Godabarish Mishra and Sobhan Khan as ministers. The Ministry had to resign in 1944 due to personal incapability among the members of the cabinet. Thus for the second time, the Governors' rule was promulgated and it continued till 1946.

Factional conflicts in Orissa Congress forged fresh alliance in the nineteen forties. An important outcome of this conflict was the emergence of Mahatab as the undisputed leader of the Congress party. By the time of the 1946 elections the younger generation led by H.K. Mahatab had firmly established themselves as leaders by replacing the Satyabadi group.

However, during the British period, politics and society, so to say, were bifurcated from each other. Except a very privileged few, the vast mass of India did not have any share in the political process of the country. Only a few kinds, Zamindars and other supporters of the British enjoyed some political power, to the extent, allowed to them by the alien ruler. But the situation began to change rapidly in the aftermath of India's Independence. With the introduction of adult franchise in 1952 and the establishment of the Panchyatiraj in later part of 1950's in different states. Democracy could reach the common man. Both the rich and the poor, the urban and rural people, and the feudal lords and the commoners were given equal legal rights to compete for power and make policies for their betterment.

The villages, of late, politically came to the limelight. But, ironically enough, some parochial and infrastructural forces like casteism, communalism, ethnicism and regionalism have gained ascendancy. In this restricted sense, as Morris Jones has pertinently pointed out, in the wake of Independence, politics and society came to meet.[43]

The electoral history of Orissa can be divided into four distinct phases. From 1951–52 to 1961 it was an era of uncertain mandate. The second phase from 1961 to 1967 marked the Congress being voted to power and maintaining political stability. The third phase (1967–76) witnessed an era of political coalitions with no party commanding an absolute majority in the State Legislative Assembly and the last one since 1977 onwards has been the phase of positive electoral choice.[44]

The verdict of the people of Orissa was uncertain till 1961 mid-term poll, as no single party could manage to win an absolute majority in the State Legislative Assembly so as to form the government. In 1961 the Indian National Congress in Orissa led by Biju Patnaik, for the first time got an absolute majority. The verdict was not clear in the elections held between 1967–1977. Since 1977, the electoral verdict gave altogether a different picture, where people voted a particular party so as to secure an absolute majority. A study of electoral politics in Orissa suggests that though a large number of political parties (like Ganatantra Parisad, Socialists, Swatantra, Praja Socialist Party, Jharkhanda etc.) have entered the political arena a very few could get positive response from the people. The Congress is the only party which consistently entered the electoral arena from the beginning (except 1977 and 1990) and has emerged as a party with reasonably good support base. It is also found that Orissa has practically become a citadel of political instability and no government has completed a full term of five years till 1980. Though Naba Krishna Choudhry remained in office for a period of six years i.e., from May 1950 to October 1956, it may be divided into two periods : The first period was from May 1950 to December 1951, and the second was from March 1952 to October 1956. The politics in Orissa was characterized by politics of coalition[45] and defection.[46] The game of defection had been so flippant that ministry after ministry has collapsed like a house of cards. For long years the State of Orissa has become famous for the political drama staged mainly by coalition actors. Groupism in the Congress and infighting among the coalition partners have been the principal causes of the down fall of the different ministeries.[47] The mandate of the Orissa voters has always been uncertain till 1977. Therefore, it gave birth to coalition experiments for a great length of time.

The post–1980 political scenario, however, represents an era of stability. The Congress (I) party led by J.B. Patnaik swept the polls in the May 1980 Assembly elections. He earned the credit of leading a stable government in the State and enjoyed political proximity with the central party leadership.[48] No doubt, the Congress Party government, experienced factional rivalries. But it completed its full term of five years. The Congress Party swept the December 1984 and May 1996 elections to the Lok Sabha from Orissa and repeated its performance in the 1985 and 1995 Assembly Elections.

Factionalism has influenced the politics of Orissa before and after independence. It has resulted in politics of defection causing in the collapse of different governments, giving rise to coalition politics and politics of instability. There were many regional parties which appeared on the political scenes, shared power and after some time disappeared from the political scene as a result of factionalism. Dissidentism or factionalism is not a Peculiar development inside the party in power. It has also its ramifications in the parties in opposition. Factionalism in the state level bears a reflection of the factional politics of the respective parties at the national level. Factional politics acquires a predominant position when a political party is voted to power with a slender majority in the legislature and finds it difficult to maintain the political balance.

In Orissa, the issue of political corruption was raised frequently. Most of the politicians of the state have been accused of indulging in favoritism and political corruption. But, so far no politician in Orissa against whom charges of corruption were made and even adverse findings were made by inquiry commission, was punished in the courts of law. Political corruption has become a party in the game of politics and politicians indulge in it with impunity. Since its formation as a separate state in 1936, the political atmosphere in Orissa has been vitiated by political corruption.[49]

In Orissa, the power structure is dominated by elite castes. Orissa's political culture indicates that it has a very small group of middle-class elite. High caste politicians dominate the leadership structure of all parties and factions in Orissa.[50] They include *Brahmins, Karans, Kshatriyas,* and *Khandayats.* The Table 2.2 throws light about the sharing of power at different levels by different castes.

[Table 2.3] The Successive List of Prime Ministers/ Chief Ministers of Orissa alongwith Castes (1937–1996)

Prime Minister/ Chief Minister	*Caste*	*Duration*	
		From	To
Prime Minister			
Maharaja Krishna Chandra Gajapati Narayan Deo	Kshatriya	01-04-1937	19-07-1937
Biswanath Das	Brahmin	19-07-1937	06-11-1939
Maharaja Krishna Chandra Gajapati Narayan Deo	Kshatriya	24-11-1941	30-06-1944
Hare Krishna Mahatab	Kshatriya	23-02-1946	12-05-1950
Chief Minister			
Naba Krishna Choudhury	Karan	12-05-1950	06-04-1957
Hare Krishna Mahatab	Kshatriya	06-04-1957	25-02-1961
Biju Patnaik	Karan	23-06-1961	02-10-1963
Biren Mitra	Karan	02-10-1963	21-02-1965
Sadasiva Tripathy	Brahmin	21-02-1965	08-03-1967
R.N. Singh Deo	Kshatriya	08-03-1967	09-01-1971
Biswanath Das	Brahmin	03-04-1971	14-06-1972
Nandini Satapathy	Brahmin	14-06-1972	03-03-1973
Binayak Acharya	Brahmin	29-12-1976	30-04-1977
Nilamani RoutRay	Khandayat	29-06-1977	09-06-1980
J.B. Patnaik	Karan	09-06-1980	09-03-1985
J.B. Patnaik	Karan	10-03-1985	06-12-1989
Hemananda Biswal	S.T.	07-12-1989	04-03-1990
Biju Patnaik	Karan	05-03-1990	14-03-1995
J.B. Patnaik	Karan	15-03-1995	Continuing

(B) DISTRICT OF GANJAM—A PROFILE

Ganjam, one of the southern districts of Orissa lies between 18°46'N and 20°17'N latitudes and between 83°48'E and 85°11'E longitudes. It is bounded on the north by Boudh-Khondamals and Puri district, on the South by Srikakulam district of Andhra Pradesh, in the West by Boudh-Khondamals and Koraput districts and in the East by Puri districts and Bay of Bengal.

The name Ganjam owes its origin to the Persian word "Ganj-i-am", which means the grainary/greenery of the world.[51] The district justifies this name as it contains some of the most fertile lands of the State of Orissa.[52]

The district divides itself easily into two broad divisions, the coastal plain areas in the east and the table-land in the West. The eastern and northern frontiers of the coastal plains consist of thick forests with well-grown sal trees. Towards the centre and the south it is hilly with beautiful well-watered valleys running towards the sea. The south-eastern portion is fertile and contains extensive multi-cropped areas, well served by many irrigation projects, both major and minor. The extreme south-east is occupied by a portion of the Chilka lake, its immediate vicinity being good for fishery and salt manufacture though not so good for cultivation. The table-land of the Western sector of the district is a continuation of the great line of the Easter Ghats, and is chiefly formed by two plateaus conspicuously featured by some of the highest mountains of Orissa. The highest hills in the district are Singaraju Parbat (4,973 ft), Mahendragiri (4,923 ft.) and Devagiri (4,534 ft.).[53]

The district has alluvial soil in its eastern part and laterite soil in the west, with small patches of black cotton soil at the centre and in the north-east close to Chilka lake. Forest covers a total area of 6,882 square kilometers in 1989–90 of being 54.9% to the total geographical area of the district.

The earliest historical relics in this district are the Rock Edicts of Ashoka inscribed on a hill (then known as Khapingala Parbat) at Jaugada on the bank of river Rushikulya.[54] The Ganjam area was a part of ancient Kalinga which was occupied by Ashok after a fierce battle in 261 B.C. close to the hill containing the Edicts was located the township of Samapa,[55] which was the second capital of Kalinga under Asoka and was the seat of administration of an Executive Officer called Rajavachanika. This area continued to be in the Maurya empire probably till the last Maurya king.[56] In the first century B.C. Kharavela made Kalinga powerful and prosperous and led his invincible army in all directions of India. The Ganjam area came under the rule of the Satavahans in the 2nd century A.D. The port of Palura, which was probably the same as Dantapura developed during the early Christian centuries into an important emporium of trade, carried on commercial relations with different parts of Roman empire.[57]

In the middle of the 4th century A.D., Kalinga region was invaded by Samudragupta, the king of Magadha. By that time this region comprised of several petty principalities, viz., Kottura ruled by Swamidatta, Pistapura ruled by Mahendragiri, Erandapalla ruled by Damana and Devarastra by Kuver.[58] Out of these, Kottura of Swamidatta was, without doubt, in the territory comprising the present Ganjam district. During the post-Samudragupta period a new dynasty called Mathara came to power in Kalinga with their capital first at Sripura (Batia Sripura near Parlakhemundi) and then at Simhapura (Modern Singupura). Under the rule of this dynasty the Ganjam region became very prosperous. The Matharas ruled up to 550[59] A.D., when Eastern Gangas came to power and ruled over the territory comprising district of Andhra Pradesh. About 570 A.D., Kings of Vigraha family became powerful in North Ganjam. But by the 7th century A.D., the Sailobhava dynasty founded a new state called Kongoda-mandala comprising north of Ganjam district and southern part of Puri district. The Eastern Ganga and Sailodbhavas ruled as contemporary powers for some time over southern and northern parts of Ganjam respectively.

In the 8th century A.D., the Bhauma-Karas rose to power in Utkal with Viraja (modern Jajpur) as their capital.[60] Kongoda then comprising the north Ganjam area became a feudatory state under the Bhauma-Karas. A new Ganga family founded a territory called Swetaka with Swetakapura (modern Chikiti) as head quarters and ruled as feudatory of the Bhauma-Karas.[61] In the 9th century A.D., the Bhanjas of Baudh region were driven out by the Somavamsis and founded a kingdom comprising north-western part of Ganjam and Western part of Puri district. They were also the feudatory of the Bhauma-Karas and ruled from their headquarters Vanjulvaka which is not properly identified. About the 10th century A.D., a new Bhanja house came to power in Russelkunda region with Kolada-Kataka as headquarters and this family continued to rule till 1835 when they were ousted by the British.[62]

The Bhauma-Karas were supplanted by the Somavamsis in the 10th century A.D., and under them the Eastern Gangas of south Ganjam and Bhanjas of north Ganjam continued to rule as feudatories. In 1022 A.D. Rajendra Chola took possession of the major part of modern Ganjam district. The Eastern Ganga king Vajrahasta V. became independent after the death of Rajendra Chola in 1040 A.D. His son Rajaraja became master of an extensive territory and defeated Karna Deva, the Sanavamsi king of Utkal. The Gangas were, however, driven away by the army of the Pala king of Gauda. Rajaraja was succeeded by his son Chodaganga dev who occupied Utkal in 1100 A.D. and organised an extensive empire from the Ganges to Godavari. The present district of Ganjam remained as part of the empire of the later Gangas and after its fall in 1435 as part of the empire of the Suryavamsi Gajapati kings. During the rule of the Suryavamsis a number of feudal states were created in Ganjam region and many of these states continued till the British period. The major part of Ganjam was, however, organised as an administrative unit which continued till the British period. The major part of Ganjam was, however, organised as an administrative unit which continued to be so till the rule of the Moghuls. During the rule of the last Suryavamsi king Prataparudra Deva, Ganjam became a strategic area at the time of war between Orissa and Vijayanagar led a successful campaign up to Simhanchalam near Vizagapatnam and Prataprudra had to cede part of his territory to the south of the Godavari to the victor. After the death of Prataprudra Deva (1540) Quli Qutb Shah of Golkunda extended his territory quite close to the present district of Ganjam. Orissa was occupied by the Muslims in 1568 when Mukunda Hari Chandan, the last independent king was killed in the battle. In 1571, Ibrahim Qutb Shah taking advantage of the chaotic condition of Orissa organized his authority over Chicacole Sircar which included the district of Ganjam South of the Rishikulya River.[63] In 1687, the emperor Aurangzeb annexed the Qutb Shahi kingdom to Moghul empire. But soon after his death, the affairs of the Deccan became chaotic and the Mahattas extended their power over Ganjam about the year 1740. By that time the English and the

French entered into struggle for getting privileges in South India and the French with the help of Nawab Salabatjang got supremacy over the Northern sircars including the Chicacole Sircar. In 1757, the French commander Bussy personally marched into Ganjam and realised the arrears of tribute from the feudal chiefs. The English, however, were ultimately successful in defeating the French in the Deccan and the latter had to abandon Ganjam in 1759.[64]

The district of Ganjam was under the formal possession of the British in 1765 by a "Farman" of the Mughal Emperor. The British were to enjoy the Northern circars as 'Inams' or free gift.[65] The English took the possession of Ganjam in 1766.

Under the orders of the Madras government, Cotsford proceeded to Ganjam in early 1767 A.D. and found the prevailing conditions disturbing.[67] In 1787, the Circuit Committee investigated the revenue resources of the Ganjam district and submitted a report on 25 April, 1788, which was based on the permanent settlement effected in the district by Pater Cherry in 1804. The office of the Collector, Ganjam was established in 1794. Early in the 19th century Ganjam became a hot bed of political troubles as most of the Zamindars revolted against, Mohiri and Parlakhemundi had become very serious since 1817. Orders were restored with great difficulty after military operation for a long period which ended in 1836.

In 1839, the hill areas of Ganjam and Vizagapatnam districts were excluded from the jurisdiction of the Civil court and placed under the Agent to the Governor. In 1845, a special Commissioner was appointed for suppression of Meriah sacrifices among the Khonds. In 1856, disturbances broke out among the sabaras in Parlakhemundi headed by Radhakrishna Dandasena of Gaiba. The rebellion was put down in Parlakhemundi, but it extended towards Kalahandi and Phulbani through a veteran leader Chakrabisoi, who could not be suppressed by the British. During the second half of the 19th century the British rule was consolidated and Ganjam breathed an atmosphere of peace and order.

In 1857 A.D., there was a country wide demonstration against the British Administration. Even though, the British called it the Sepoy Mutiny, actually it was the First War of Independence. During that time, there was unrest in the district of Ganjam.[68]

The Oriyas outside Orissa suffered from various disabilities and difficulties. Padmanabha Narayan Deo of Parlakhemundi founded an organisation known as Utkal Hitainshini Samaj to fight against the injustice done to the Oriyas of Ganjam.[69] The exclusion of Oriya as the court language of Sambalpur, created a great sensation throughout Orissa.[70] Towards the end of the 19th century, the feeling for administrative union of Ganjam with Orissa became very intense. For their unification, the Oriyas agitated for one administration. This was recognized by Cooke, I.C.S., the then Commissioner of Orissa, in the Annual General Administrative Report in 1894-95.[71] He proposed to extend the boundaries of Orissa by the addition of Sambalpur and Ganjam districts.[72]

In September 1897, Madhu Sudan Das, on behalf of Utkal Sabha, as mentioned earlier, visited London and met Lord George Hamilton, the Secretary of State for India and presented him the recommendation of the commissioner Cooke, for the union of Oriya tracts.[73] On the advice of Hamilton, Das presented his demand for Orissa before Viceroy Lord Curzon.[74] During the later part of 1902, Curzon paid a visit to Orissa. He was the first Viceroy to visit Orissa. The people of Ganjam submitted a "Monster Memorial to Curzon."[75]

The memorialists stated that they were unnaturally dissociated from the Oriya brothers of Orissa and they prayed the Government of India to bring together the scattered divisions inhabited by oriya-speaking people.

At the beginning of the 20th century, struggle for amalgamation of the oriya tracts was keenly organized in Ganjam. Oriya had been recognized as official language in the district in the year 1896 and a definite move for amalgamation of Oriya-speaking tracts started in the year 1907.

In the meantime, the Indian National Congress had the session in Madras where the Telugus got a resolution passed opposing the separation of Ganjam from Madras province.[76] This thoughtless action of the National Congress in disregarding the claims of smaller nationalities in the interest of larger ones was unfortunate. However, the Congress later on realized the merit of constituting provinces on the basis of regional dialect.

In Orissa, the collectors of the districts invited the opinions of the public regarding the question of the proposed union. The public regarding the question of the proposed union. The public opinion was in favour of a separate province, constituted of all the Oriya-speaking tracts under a chief commissionership. In Madras too, the opinion was invited on the proposal of the Government. Sir Murray Hammick, Chief Secretary to the Government of Madras under Lord Ampthill, strongly opposed the suggested amalgamation of Ganjam and Vizagapatnam Agency with Orissa.[77]

Sir Andrew Fraser, the Lieutenant Governor of Bengal, pointed out that geographically and ethnically, the Ganjam district and the agency tract should belong to Orissa.[78] To the misfortune of the people of Orissa, Lord Curzon went on leave to England and Lord Ampthill officiated. When the question was referred to him for decision, he put a seal on the fate of Oriyas, by a resolution of the Government of India, which gave up the transfer of Ganjam and Vizagapatnam Agency to Orissa, though the proposed transfer of Sambalpur to Orissa was approved.[79]

The Oriyas of Ganjam in a Memorial to the Viceroy protested against the grounds advanced in the resolution to abandon the proposed amalgamation and suggested for the appointment of a non-official commission to enquire into the details of the subject, for which they were prepared to incur the expenses. These people continued their agitation for amalgamation with unabated energy.

The Oriyas of Ganjam were repeatedly sending memorials to the Government of India, as well as, the Madras Government with appeals for the administrative union of Orissa. The Government introduced many palliative half-measures to reduce the evils of the condition of dismemberment. In fact, it was the people of Ganjam who had kept the hope and dreamt of separate Orissa province despite the disheartening and hopeless conditions, they were subjected to.[80]

During the British period, Ganjam was divided into several Zamindaris, Sub-Zamindaris and other tenures. This intermediary system had been created by the British for strengthening their hold over the people. With the help of these intermediaries, who were the favoured few. After independence these intermediatory interests were, however, abolished.[81]

The Phillip-Duff Committee report (1922) categorically stressed the need for transferring the Oriya Zamindaris to Orissa as they had century-long connection with it.[82] The leading Oriyas of the districts of Vizagpatnam and Ganjam including the Rajas and Zamindars of Jeypore, Mandasa, Tekali, Jalantara, expressed their views emphatically supporting amalgamation of Oriya tracts.[83] Krishna Chandra Gajapati of Parlakhemundi suggested for the formation of a separate province for the Oriyas on linguistic basis, based on principles of formation of linguistic provinces, recommended in the Montague-Chelmsford Report.[84]

The Phillip-Duff committee in its report said: "Our enquiry has shown that there is a genuine long-standing and deep-seated desire on the part of the educated Oriya classes of the Oriya-speaking tracts of Madras for the amalgamation of these tracts with Orissa under one administration."[85] As far as possible, it seems that this was the first enquiry at the government level for the creation of provinces on linguistic basis.[86] After a detailed enquiry, the Committee came to the conclusion that Oriya-speaking areas of Madras including Ganjam Agency and Vizagpatnam Agency should be amalgamated with Orissa. Being guided by the views and wishes of Maharaja of Parlakhemundi, the Phillip-Duff Commission in 1922 and O'Donnel Commission in 1932 recommended amalgamation of major portion of the then Ganjam district with Orissa.

The recommendation of the Phillip-Duff Committee was duly considered by the Simon Commission in which Krishna Chandra Gajapati took a leading part. The Commission said: "An urgent case for consideration and treatment is that of the Oriya-speaking people. They were so much impressed with Orissa's claim that they appointed a special sub-committee presided over by major Atlee to look into the question.[87]

The Sub-Committee was of the view that the grievance was well-founded and the demand was substantially supported by the people.[88]

The report of the Sub-Committee provided much inspiration to the people of Orissa to pursue the matter at the highest level.[89] However, it was Krushna Chandra Gajapati who could raise the question on Orissa in the 1st Round Table Conference, although the matter did not find place in the agenda. His demand for the creation of Orissa on linguistic basis evoked general support from the members of 1st session of the Round Table Conference.

In 1931, earlier to the appointment of O'Donnell Committee, the census operation was conducted in Madras Presidency and as a result, the Oriyas of Ganjam and Vizagapatnam districts became cautious to protect their own interests, "as from the past records they found that their number in presidency was artificially reduced on account of manipulation by some Andhra Enumerators.[90] The aim of Andhras was not to allow a single inch of land from Ganjam or Vizagapatnam to Orissa as demanded by the Oriyas.[91] The members of Utkal Hitainshani Samaj of Parlakhemundi took timely and proper steps, despite the stiff oppositions and threatenings that they received from two powerful English officials, namely, Dixon, the Collector of Ganjam and Yeats, the Census Superintendent of Madras.

The Boundary committee received evidence and memoranda from the main contesting parties, namely, the Oriyas and Telugus at Gopalpur and Ganjam. Yeats (the Census Superintendent), on behalf of Madras Government, deposed before the Committee "counter plotting" against the Oriya demands.[92]

The Ganjam Land-holders Association presented a memorandum to the Chairman and members of the Boundary Committee, during their camp at Cuttack. Among other things, it was pointed out that, 'the district of Ganjam is almost all Zamindari and the Zamindaris who have acquired vested interests and got a large stake in the district, have derived their power and estates from the Gajapati kings of Orissa, who granted them their lands on condition of feudal service and of keeping in check the wild aboriginal tribes of the hills'.

The Ganjam Zamindars were very powerful, wielding considerable influence on the local people including the Kondhs and Saoras. There was also a strong feudal attachment which bound the local people to the Zamindars. The Muslim rulers of Hyderabad had to depend on the local Zamindars for the collection of revenue and maintenance of law and order within their respective territories as Ganjam lay about seven hundred miles from Hyderabad.[93] These Zamindars were the hereditary collectors of revenue, who held office theoretically during good behaviour.[94]

The following were the Zamindaries and proprietary estates in the district of Ganjam:

Zamindaries

1) Khallikote and Athagarh.

2) Palur.

3) Birdi

4) Huma

5) Dharakote

6) Badagada

7) Katingia

8) Seragada

9) Sana Khemundi

10) Bada-Khemundi (Digaphandi)

11) Chikiti

12) Surangi

13) Jarada

14) Jalantara

15) Budarsingi

16) Mandasa

17) Tarala

18) Parakhemundi

Proprietary Estates :

19) Aska Estate
Kurla Estate
Devabhumi } Aska Malukdari

20) Barua Estate

21) Urlam

22) Raghunathpur (Tekkali)

23) Puruna Tekkali, and

24) Nandigam.

Besides these, there was the Ghumsur estate which was one of the ancient Zamindaries in the district. Most of the Zamindaries were permanently settled.

Historically speaking, therefore, the district of Ganjam was an integral part of the Orissan Empire for centuries with the hoary civilization until its disruption in 1565. All the chief land-holders of the district have got their kith and kin among the feudatory chiefs and Zamindars of present Orissa and their separation from the same is a mere matter of accident due to several causes, and Ganjam a relic of disrupted Orissa is subjected to several disabilities-social, linguistic, religious, administrative and political.

On 1 April 1936, when the separate province of Orissa was formed, the Present district of Ganjam became a Part of the new province after being transferred from Madras presidency.

Area and Population

The undivided Ganjam district has an area of 12,531 sq. kms. and a population of 31.43 lakhs as per the 1991(p) census. It accounts for 8.06 per cent of the total area of the state and accommodated 9.97 per cent of the state's population.[95] However, the district was reorganised by the Government of Orissa on 2 October, 1992 whereby the Parlakhemundi sub-division has become a new separate district named "Gajapati", leaving the other parts in the district of Ganjam.

Now the district of Ganjam has an area of 8.033 sq. kms., having 26,84,379 population and the Gajapati district has an area of 3,056 sq. kms. with 4,58,741 population.[96]

The density of the population of the undivided Ganjam district is 251 as against 202 persons per sq. kms. of the State in 1991 census. The Table 2.4 shows the growth of population of the district from 1901--1991.

The table indicates that except for the decade 1911–21 in all other census years the population has registered steady increase from that of the previous census year. In 1971, this increase has

[Table 2.4] Decadal Variation in Population and Growth Rate of Population in the District Since 1901

Decade	*Strength of Population*	*Decimal Growth Rate of Population*
1901	11,41,963	------------
1911	12,69,686	(+) 11.18
1921	12,68,465	(–) 03.25
1931	13,91,069	(+) 13.24
1941	15,60,669	(+) 12.19
1951	16,24,829	(+) 04.11
1961	18,72,530	(+) 15.24
1971	22,93,808	(+) 22.50
1981	26,69,899	(+) 16.40
1991 (p)	31,43,120	(+) 17.72

Source : Government of Orissa, District Statistical Hand Book 1990–91, Ganjam, p. 10.

registered the highest percentage being 22.50. The decrease of population in 1921 might be due to the fact that, the census operation was conducted in Madras Presidency and the number was artificially reduced by some Andhra Enumerators.[97]

The district is predominantly rural. Though there is a growing tendency towards urbanization during the last two decades in the district; the percentage of rural population to the total population of the district is 85.0398 (1991 census). The Table 2.5 indicates the urban and rural agglomerations of the district :

It may be noted that the sex ratio of the district is 1012 females per 1000 males. In rural area, it is 1024 : 1000, while in urban area it is 947:1000; While the sex ratio at the state level is not favourable to women, Ganjam district has certainly given them a solace as is evident from the Table 2.5.

The undivided Ganjam district had 4 sub-divisions, 14 Tahsils, 33 Police stations, 29 Community Development Blocks, 466 Gram Panchayats, 2 Municipalities, 18 Notified Area Councils, 16 Sub-Registrar Offices and 4 Agricultural districts. The head-quarter of the district is Chatrapur which is 20 kms. away from Berhampur, the most populous town of the district.

[Table 2.5] Population of Urban/Rural Agglomerations in the District as per 1991 (p) census

State/District Urban Agglomerations		Population			Growth Rate		Sex ratio 1991 (Females per 1000 males)
		Person	Male	Female	1971–81	1981–91	
Orissa	Total	3,15,12,070	1,59,79,904	1,55,32,166	20.17	19.50	972
	Rural	2,72,79,615	1,37,12,156	1,35,67,459	15.73	17.28	989
	Urban	42,32,455	22,67,748	19,64,707	68.54	36.08	866
Ganjam	Total	31,43,120	15,62,128	15,80,992	16.40	17.72	1,012
	Rural	26,72,718	13,20,501	13,52,217	12.56	16.74	1,024
	Urban	04,70,402	02,41,627	02,28,775	46.38	23.66	947

Source : Government of Orissa, District Statistical Hand Book 1990–91, Ganjam.

River System

The Rushikulya, the Bodonadi, the Mahendratanaya, the Bansadhara, the Bahuda, the Harobhangi, the Dhanei, the Ghodahada and the Baghua are the important rivers of the district. Rushikulya, the longest river stretching a distance of 160 kms. and covering major areas of the district, constitutes the prime source for irrigation of the districts. Besides this, there are also some other irrigation projects on other rivers which facilitate for the growth of agriculture in the district.

Agriculture

Agriculture is the most important activity of the people of the district. Paddy is their principal crop. Ganjam used to export the finest variety of rice to Madras, while it was under Madras presidency.[99] The plains area of the district contains most fertile lands in the state. The adequate rainfall facilitates for paddy cultivation. The cultivation in the agency area of the district is comparatively small. The principal crops of the district in order of importance are paddy, ragi, green-gram, sugarcane, groundnuts, til, and gingilly etc. It is because of large scale agricultural production in the state labourers engaged in it usually get employment for six months in a year.

Socio-Cultural Aspect of the District

For the purpose of making an analysis of the social and cultural habits of the people, the district may be divided into two regions: the agency tracts and the plains. The former is inhabited by Kondhs and Saoras who continue to live with their age old traditions and superstitions. Living in agency area their life is hazardous. However, with the efforts of Christian Missionaries, Voluntary organizations and governmental agencies etc., the tribals are slowly initiated into the main stream of development. Therefore, a quite significant change in outlook has taken place in recent years. Yet in interior areas, the tribal people are yet to change their traditional way of life.

The plains are inhabited by different ethnic groups. The value pattern of these people is changing day by day. The literacy is on the increase and there is a growing desire for advancement in social life. An overwhelming majority of people speak Oriya language.

However, a section of them speak Telugu language because of their long association with Madras Presidency. Historically, in Ganjam there are two Aryan and two aboriginal races forming the bulk of the population. The two Aryan races are the Oriyas and the Telugus and the two aboriginal, the Kondhs and the Saoras, who are confined to the mountaneous tracts of the district. The Oriya language resembles Hindustani.

The Telugus of the Madras Presidency are mainly Saivaites while the majority of Oriyas are Vaishnavites. The Oriyas follow the Vaishnavism of Chaitanya, the great Hindu reformer of the Northern India. The rituals and different ceremonial observations attached to this system of Vaishnavism are entirely different from those of rituals and ceremonies of Ramanuja of South India. A Telugu Vaishnava creed preached by Ramanuja is kept insulated from the Dravidian Brahmins. Inter-marriage and inter-dining among them were strictly prohibited. The Vaishnavism as advocated by Chaitanya recognised no such distinctions.

In the district of Ganjam there are many sites and monuments of archeological importance. Archeological relics are found at the places like Jaugarh, Budha Khol, Athagargh, Khallikote, Aska, Palur, Surangi and other places. Under the influence of the Jagannath cult temples were built at places like Athagarh, Chikiti, Surangi, Parlakhemundi, Khallikote, Digapahandi and Berhampur. Ganjam has a fair contribution in the field of literature. It had contributed significantly in the making rich tradition of culture and literacy heritage of Orissa. It is revealed from the medieval Oriya literature that majority of the poets of medieval time hailed from Ganjam. The long association of Ganjam with Madras presidency had, in no way resulted in losing the cultural identity of the people.

Political Culture

As mentioned earlier, political culture not only refers to the pattern of individual attitudes and orientation towards politics, but also the style, manner and substantive form of politics. Undoubtedly, political culture gets reflected in political behaviour of the people, which includes and covers political participation and the electoral behaviour of the people. Needless to say, political participation constitutes a significant variable of political development in a democratic polity. Political parties, which seek the mandate of the people in fixed intervals of time, achieve legitimacy for their political authority if they are supported by the majority of the electorate in their battle for power. The electorate exercises control over the executive through the elected representatives and this constitutes the very basis of responsive democratic government. An election may be said to be a procedure recognised by the rulers of an organisation, be it a state, a club, a voluntary organization, where all or some of the members choose a small number of persons to hold an office or officers of authority within that organization.[100] It is a means through which voters exercise their right to franchise to choose their representatives. It is also an important instrument which helps a society to organize itself and make formal decisions. Where elections are free and fair and when right to vote is exercised without any restraint, a political system secures political obedience without any difficulty. Since people participate in a common act of electing representatives, elections "lend authority and legitimacy to the acts of those who wield power in the name of the people".[101]

Elections may be understood to reflect changing opinions and social conception about citizenship and equality.[102] All persons are equal before the ballot box, even if they are not so in other respects. Elections enhance political consciousness and motivate the people to channel their energies collectively towards the attainment of basic goals of development and give a new meaning and reality to their sense of citizenship.[103] It is the key mechanism of consensus and at the same time an important means of institutionalizing conflict among different groups.[104]

The elections were held in January 1937 to the Orissa Legislative Assembly under the Government of India Act, 1935. Thirteen members represented the Ganjam district from various constituencies including nominated ones. After the delimitation of the constituencies, now the Ganjam district covers 15 Assembly constituencies[105] out of which two seats are reserved for the Scheduled Castes and one for the Scheduled Tribes and Two Lok Sabha constituencies.[106]

The district was in political limelight of the State from 1936 to 1944. Its leaders took the leadership of Orissa province and played a dominant role in state-politics. Prominent politicians from Ganjam like Maharaja Krushna Chandra Gajapati Narayan Deo of

Parlakhemundi, Biswanath Das, Dibakar Patnaik, Rama Chandra Mardraj Deo, the Raja of Khallikote and Mandhata Gorachand Patnaik dominated the politics of the state.

In the later period, however, the politicians from other costal districts like Cuttack, Puri and Balasore occupied predominant positions in the party and the Government at the state level. There has been a steady decline in the quality of political leadership in Ganjam district, as a result of which their bargaining power vis-a-vis the party leaders belonging to other coastal districts of Orissa has diminished. This has adversely affected the economic development of the district.

(C) THE VILLAGE : NUAPADA

The Village Nuapada, one of the most populous and developed villages in Orissa comes under Chikiti Block in the district of Ganjam in Orissa. It is located at latitude of 19.10'N and 84°.30 longitude and at a distance of 18 kms. from Digapahandi, the Tahasil head-quarter and 45 kms. away form Berhampur, Sub-divisional headquarter. During the first General Election of India in 1952, Nuapada was under Parlakhemundi Assembly Constituency and Bhanjanagar (Scheduled Caste) Parliamentary and Assembly Constituencies order, 1961 and the Gazette of 1965, it was transferred to Ramagiri (Scheduled Tribe) Assembly and Koraput (S.T.) Parliamentary constituencies in the fourth general election.[107] In 1974, it was transferred to Chikiti Assembly Constituency and in 1977 it was brought under the Berhampur Lok Sabha Constituency.[108] Till 1966, Nuapada was the headquarter of the Panchayat which consisted of thirty-two villages. At that time it enjoyed much political significance which, of course, gradually started eroding after the creation of new Panchayat headquarters in the neighbouring village called Lalamenta, and Chandapur in the year 1966 and 1983 respectively. Similarly because of the delimitation of the Panchayat Samiti, the village was transferred from Digapahandi to Chikiti Panchayat Samiti in 1962. Its geography, people, history, economy and politics have an unique style in comparison to other villages in the district of Ganjam.

Location and the People

Surrounded by the forests, mountains, agricultural lands and the river Bahuda the climatic condition of Nuapada, which spreads over an area of 141.24 acres of land, is moderate. Its population, according to 1991 Census, was 2,374 which, by the end of January 1994, went upto 2775. Since the whole population profess the same religion i.e. Hinduism, there have been no communal disturbance.

The Table 2.6 indicates the caste-wise population of the village.

[Table 2.6] Caste-wise Population

Sl. No.	*Caste*	*Nature of the Caste*	*No. of House-holds*	*Population*	*% Proportion to Population*
1.	Barber (Bhandari)	Other Back-ward Caste	22	123	4.43
2.	Barika	Schedule Tribe	06	34	1.23
3.	Bauri	Schedule Caste	07	23	0.83
4.	Brahmin including Kamma Brahmin	Upper Caste	56	256	9.23
5.	Carpenter	O.B.C.	04	20	0.72
6.	Dandasi	S.C.	40	179	6.45
7.	Dera (Weavers)	O.B.C.	04	20	0.72
8.	Dhobi (Washerman)	S.C.	42	218	7.86
9.	Goldsmith	O.B.C.	10	62	2.23
10.	Gudia	O.B.C.	12	79	2.85
11.	Hadi	S.C.	13	58	2.09
12.	Jangum	O.B.C.	03	18	0.65
13.	Kampa	O.B.C.	37	168	6.05
14.	Karan	U.C.	11	40	1.44
15.	Keuta (Fisher Man)	S.C.	34	182	6.56
16.	Khadura	O.B.C.	28	163	5.87
17.	Khandayat (Oriya)	O.B.C.	14	98	3.52
18.	Komti	U.C.	70	356	12.83
19.	Mali (Archaka)	O.B.C.	03	22	0.79
20.	Parcelia	O.B.C.	05	29	1.05
21.	Redika	O.B.C.	12	89	3.21
22.	Sundhi	O.B.C.	04	27	0.97
23.	Teli	O.B.C.	09	41	1.48
24.	Other Backward Castes including Scheduled Tribes	———	16	68	2.45
		Total	**537**	**2775**	**100.00**

No doubt, Nuapada is represented by the people of different castes, but the Dera, Komti, Brahmin, Dhobi, Keuta, Dandasi, Kampa, Khadura, Barber are the predominant castes in the village. However, a detailed analysis of the castes has been made in another chapter on Social structure of the village. The male and female ratio of the village is 1381:1394.

House Pattern

Like other villages in the region, Nuapada has mainly four types of houses namely pucca building houses, houses of stone walls and tiled roofs, brick walls with thatched roofs and mud-wall houses with thatched roofs. For a long time, the village had some houses with stone walls and tiled roofs. All the houses (except three) of this category were owned by the Komti caste. Two houses belonged to the Brahmins and another one to a Dera. Because of modernization all such houses have been remodelled and now a very few houses of this type exist. Earlier, rich people only preferred such type of house. The wooden threshold and doors of these houses are very heavy.

Now all such rich and well-to-do families have constructed pucca buildings. The walls are made of local stone and bricks available at very cheap rates; the doors and their frames are fashioned by local carpenter and are often decorated on the outside with carvings of geometrical designs. Now-a-days the people prefer folded doors with ventilation chamber on it. Due to urban contacts and influence the houses show certain marks of sophistication: two storeyed, marble floors, septic tanks, attached bathrooms, big rooms (four to six in number) with free ventilation facilities, etc. These houses are also so well-furnished that one may not believe whether gadgets life has become more sophisticated and comfortable. Household utensils are well arranged in the dining rooms. Generally, steel, aluminium and brass utensils are found in the rich families. Silver utensils are found in privileged few.

The middle class people build two-room thatched or tiled houses. The walls are made of local bricks with mud clay, are plastered by cement. Floors are made of cement. Economically better-off people go for houses with tiled roofs. But poor people are forced to construct houses with thatched roofs which are to be repaired or replaced with straws, before monsoon. The one-sided, undecorated and simple doors and frames are made by local carpenters at a very low cost. Some of the houses have pit-latrines in the back-yards and some have septic latrines. But unfortunately, sixty percent of the houses belonging to such category do not have latrines. They generally go out into the fields or the sands of the river for answering the call of nature even after fifty years of independence of the country.

The poor people build one-room or two-room thatched houses. The walls are made of mud and some have wattled walls. The roof is always thatched. A selective few of these houses have least furnitures. The few metal utensils which the family possesses are among the most treasured parts of the household property. The household utensils are generally made by the local potter. It is very interesting to note that some of these houses have cattlesheds close to the living-rooms. Since there is no electricity in these houses, people collect some fuel as well as small quantities of edible and marketable minor forest produce from the local scrub jungle.

History of the Village

The history of Nuapada is the history of few generations and of modern origin. Available sources reveal that it came into existence after the settlement of a few families of Deras and Komtis. The Komtis, who were appointed as Mustadars in Zamindaris were impressed by the fact that settlement in this place would give them a better scope to undertake their trade and commerce extending upto Turubudi and Chelligada. It is also said that once there was a heavy drought in some Telugu-speaking area under the Madras presidency. Starvation and death forced some members or families of that area to leave for some other place which could provide them food and security. They landed at Chariapada, the earlier name of Nuapada as there was transaction of trade and commerce between Chariapada and their native place. They made Chariapada their new-found home land. They set up a colony near Chariapada and in due course of time; Chariapada along with the new colony came to be known as Nuapada (new habitation). It is significant to note that after this new habitation trade and commerce expanded gradually.

Though Nuapada Village took its shape from the village Chariapada, it started with a new type of settlement having strict caste orientation. New settlements have been made in different parts of the village on the basis of caste. Castes in Nuapada like Komti, Dera, Brahmin and Hadis occupy houses in compact blocks on contiguous patches of lands, but in close proximity. The houses of people belonging to other communities are also found.

Economy

Nuapada is not economically a poor village. Farming, weaving, handicrafts and business are their main occupational source of income. The functional basis of the Indian caste system is generally well understood, but integration of different castes into the economic pattern of the rural community organization of India is not so well known. The occupations and functions of different castes are not wholly exclusive, but the economic system of rural India is founded mainly on their functional specialization and interdependence.[109] For example, agriculture is the main occupation of the Kamps. But other castes-both high and low-can also cultivate land, if they have any besides following their traditional occupation. Similarly, trade and commerce was originally considered to be the monopoly of the Komti caste, but now other caste have also jumped into the fray. However, even now a large number of crafts and occupations in rural India may be said to be the monopoly of different castes.[110] Nuapada is no exception to it. Tradition has given to each group a definite position in the structure of the community and with that position also goes a definite economic function which is the major source of livelihood for that group. As agriculture is the mainstay of the rural economy of India, the crafts and occupations of the country-side are generally integrated with it.[111] In a traditional agricultural village in India, those who control land also control the people.[112] The landlord-tenant relationship is probably the most important patronage relationship in traditional Indian village life.[113]

In village politics, the dominant caste must have an excess of land to manipulate. That is, if they are to remain dominant, members of dominant caste must have more land than they can cultivate themselves, so that they can have dependent tenants. Through manipulation of land-tenure relationships the Komtis of Nuapada have been able to retain their economic dominance in the village, inspite of land reform legislation. They still own approximately 50 per cent of the total wet land of the village and in nearby villages also they have lands.

The economic condition of all the castes is not the same. As the Komtis are being traders, money-lenders and land-holders, their financial condition is better than other castes. Deras are labourers engaged in traditional weaving, Brahmins are the priests and do not have sound economy, Kampas are marginal farmers or agricultural labourers, Khanduras are traders engaged in their trade outside the locality and others engaged in their professional occupation or are labourers. So in the list, the Komtis top the list where as the Redikas and other communities list the last. The economic jealousies among the caste members within and across the kinship group have, however, resulted in the development of factions in this village. However, a detailed analysis of the economic structure of the village has been made in the next chapter of the present study.

Education and Culture

Prior to independence, Nuapada like other Indian villages was economically, culturally and educationally poor, backward and lagged behind. Previously the percentage of literacy in Nuapada was very negligible. It was due to lack of any facilities for education in the area. However, gradually, the public consciousness for education grew among the noted personalities of that period. They were Epari Lingaraju, Narasingha Panigrahi, Sunkuru Ram Das, Tumulu Eghnesu, Essety Lingaraju, Ravi Laxmaji and Tumulu Krishna Murty who took leadership in bringing an alround development to the village. A village "Chatasali" (School) was started by Narasingha Panigrahi, one of the then literates of Nuapada. Gradually it was converted to an M.E. School and was also in receipt of government grants. In the year 1922–23, the King, Krupamaya Dev, of Badakhemundi Zamindari paid a visist to Behrampur taluk, which was under his jurisdiction. On the way to Behrampur the king camped under a mango groove, now situated near the play ground of the Government High School of Nuapada. A severe storm lashed at the king's camp site, destroying everything including the temporary shelter constructed for the king's stay. In a make-shift arrangement, the king was housed in the house of Raghunath Tripathy, which was lying vacant in the Chariapada village. And in front of the house, where the Revenue Inspector's Office is still there, the king started his own office. Availing this opportunity the enthusiastic mass approached him for help and support in opening a high school at Nuapada. The king as a token of love and encouragement gave five hundred rupees to them. Since the among was too meagre, it was decided to rotate it so that it would grow up with accumulated interest. It was placed under the custody of the Komti Pentho which charged one rupee as interest per month per one hundred rupees. With compound interest the principal amount of Rs. 500/- got multiplied by ten times in the early 1940s.

There was a widow woman among Komti community named Tumulu Patita, who died without any legal heir. She left some property (in cash) with T. Krishna Murty who donated a part of it to the opening of a high school. Dibakar Patnaik, the President of the District Board of Ganjam held a detailed discussion with Murty for the spread of education in Nuapada area. Following this, on a memorable day a High School was established at Nuapada in July 1941. At that time there were only seven High schools in the district of Ganjam.[114] They were established in important towns like Berhampur, Chatrapur, Purusotampur, Aska, Bhanjanagar, Sorada and Parlakhemundi. So the eighth high school of the district was started in a remote and under developed area of Nuapada under Badakhemundi Zamindari. Inspite of lack of communication facilities, people from different parts of the district came to Nuapada for education. The villagers donated lands and money for the growth of the high school. The Dera community constructed one or two thatched rooms. Sunkuru Ram Das Ratna Subudhi, the richest persons of the village, spared his choultry, which is close to the High school, for hostel purpose. The M.E. school was also merged with the high school having class VI to XI. It was under the control of the District Board from 1945–57. Subsequently, it became a grant-in-aid school in 1958 and a government institution on 1 June, 1964.

Though the High School was established, the dream of T. Krishna Murty was not fulfilled as he was eager to spread the women education too. He dreamt for the establishment of a college also. A cultural centre known as "Taruna Rangalaya" was established in which the village women were imparted education in music and training in handicraft. To enrich the educational and cultural atmosphere of the villagé, dramatic clubs and libraries have been established. In 1947, a public library named as "Jayanti Pathagar" with a good reading room, was set up. Newspapers and magazines were subscribed. Now it is having more than 8000 books and various types of magazines and journals. It also extends its cultural and educational facilities through the Non-formal-education project since 1 April, 1989 to the non-school-going children and drop-outs of this area. Being a voluntary organization it also par takes to remove the illiteracy of this area. Besides, several training and orientation camps are also undertaken in Adivasi and Harijan villages of this area. In the year 1980, after persistent efforts, a college was set up. But, unfortunately, these centres of learning have become the centres of factional feud because of conflict among different sections of the people in the village. A detailed analysis, however, has been made in subsequent chapter. But on the otherhand, it is an axiomatic truth that these educational institutions have made 90 per cent of the population of the village literate.

Medical Facilities

Health is wealth. If wealth is lost nothing is lost and if health is lost everything is lost. Thus, goes the adage. Therefore, efforts on the part of the villagers under the leadership of T. Krishna Murty, resulted in setting-up of a dispensary on 7 March, 1947. Spreading over 3.5 acres of land donated by the people, it was later converted to a ten-bedded Hospital. In 1989 it acquired the status of additional public health centre as per the decision of the Government of Orissa. Thus, before India got her Independence in August 1947, the people of Nuapada could avail medical facilities in their own village. People from far away places like Turubudi, Tumba, Surangi, Khariaguda were depending solely on this hospital for their health care.

The people of Nuapada have evinced a keen interest in providing medical facilities not only to themselves but also have done their best to look after their pet and domestic animals by taking their maximum health care. The Intensive Cattle Development Centre functioning at Dabhar village near Nuapada from February, 1973, was shifted to Nuapada on 15 December, 1977. A milk society was formed in 1979. It was installed as a Chilling plant. Of course, it could not function properly due to mismanagement by the members of the society. However, during the Congress

Government led by Janaki Ballav Patnaik the villagers could successfully motivate the local M.L.A. in having a Veterinary Hospital in Nuapada. The same was inaugurated on 26 January, 1981.

Road and Communication

Like any other backward village in India, Nuapada, until 1968, was not well-connected by road. As a result, transport and communication facilities were very poor. It was only after 1968, it was linked with the Tahasil head-quarter at Digapahandi and block head-quarter at Chikiti. There was a single bus which was plying from Berhampur to Chikiti via Digapahandi. The people had to cross the river Bahuda at three points to go to the Domuhani Bus Stand. Now this place Domuhani is known as Kalingadala Dam or Bahuda Dam where a water reservoir is constructed for irrigation purpose. It was Krishna Murty who, realising the importance of transport and communication, strived hard to improve them and succeeded to a large extent in his attempt. Roads were completed. Buses and other vehicles started plying. But because of the river Bahuda these could not reach Nuapada. As a result, they had to stop at Chandanpur, a nearby village and from that village again the people had to walk through the river to reach Nuapada. The river Bahuda was their "sorrow" as far as transport and communication was concerned.

The situation, however, improved in 1984–85 when a bridge was constructed on the Bahuda river following persistent demands by the people. Now the village is well linked with important towns of the district. After the construction of the bridge the roads are also extended to Turubudi, Khariaguda, Surangi, Gada Govindpur and other places. It may be observed that availability of or nearness to modern means of transport and communications modifies the setting and fabric of the village.[115]

Political

The village Nuapada has a great political tradition. During the Pre-Independence era, its people actively participated in the freedom struggle of the country as they were highly conscious of the political environment. T. Krishna Murty, popularly known as 'Gandhi' in the area, was their leader. He was a dedicated and committed worker. He attended not only several meetings of

Mahatma Gandhi, the father of the nation but also was greatly influenced by his ideology. He, therefore, organised the villagers and the local people not only to protest the British regime but also fight against the exploitation of the people by the Zamindars. He came in contact with several political leaders of the district and the state like Biswanath Das, the former Prime Minister as well as the Chief Minister of the State, Niranjan Patnaik, Uma Charan Patnaik, V.V. Giri, former President of India, Dibakar Patnaik, popularly known as the "Iron Man" of Ganjam district and several important leaders.[116]

It is significant to note that Murty had attended almost all the sessions of the Indian National Congress. During Dangi March, people of the village under his leadership broke the salt law of the British Government and were arrested. During this period this village had a political link with the state congress and All India National Congress inspired and motivated them to fight against British imperialism.

During the Pre-Independence days there was a strong political tussle between the leaders of the Indian National Congress and Justice party formed by the kings and Zamindars. In this tussle, political leaders of Nuapada always sided with the former and accordingly had set Murty as a candidate from Congress Party in Digapahandi taluk against the Zamindar (Justice party) for the membership of the District Board in 1936. But because of Justice party's conspiracy against Murty, he was defeated by a narrow margin. But this election made the farmers of this area quite conscious of their rights. And under the leadership of Murty they were organised to fight against the zamindars who used to exploit them. In fact, at that time Mustadars were acting as the middle men between the zamindars and the tenants (farmers) to collect revenue. Since they were collecting the revenue tax from the farmers without giving any receipt, time and again they forced the farmers to pay the same. Murty took the initiative to protest against such oppression and formed a Raiyat (farmers) Association. The people of Nuapada with the help of other prominent leaders like Biswanath Das and Dibakar Patnaik moved from village to village to organize the farmers. They also held a Raiyat Samilani (farmer's conference) at Deokhali which is 8 kms. away from Nuapada and in that meeting the then President of the Congress Pandit Nehru had addressed the people. They brought it to the notice of the district administration and were convinced about the mischief of Mustadars and Zamindars. People were organized not to pay tax without any receipt. After much struggle the Mustadar system was abolished from Badakhemundi Zamindari in 1947. Besides the Raiyat Movement, there was also a social reform movement in the village during the freedom struggle.

Untouchability is perhaps the greatest social evil in India and undoubtedly it is one of the greatest maladies that has afflicted our country. Krishna Murty organised the untouchables and requested the police to bring this social disease to an end. Because of interference of the local police and initiative taken by the freedom fighters, practise of untouchability could be brought to an end.

The people of Nuapada also had organised a movement against alcohol, and were arrested for picketing in front of the liquor shops. They were conscious of the dangers of alcoholism. Because of such socio-political movements the people of Nuapada could create a healthy social and political atmosphere in the village. They are politically conscious and have concentrated on developmental projects like irrigation project over river Bahuda for the benefit of the farmers, establishment of educational institutions, hospitals, etc.

But after Independence the political scenario of the village has changed. Politics has become more self-oriented, caste dominated and faction-ridden. Villagers are now completely divided among themselves and after the introduction of Panchyati Raj village politics in Nuapada has become more and more faction-ridden.

References

1. 1) Angul, 2) Balangir, 3) Balasore, 4) Baragarh, 5) Boudh, 6) Bhadrak, 7) Cuttack, 8) Deogarh, 9) Dhenkanal, 10) Gajapati, 11) Ganjam, 12) Jagatsinghpur, 13) Jajpur, 14) Jharsuguda, 15) Kalahandi, 16) Kendrapada, 17) Keonjhar, 18) Khordha, 19) Koraput, 20) Malkangiri, 21) Mayurbhanj, 22) Nawapara, 23) Nayagarh, 24) Nowrangapur, 25) Phulbani (Kondhamala), 26) Puri, 27) Rayagada, 28) Sambalpur, 29) Sonepur, 30) Sundegarh.

2. Report on Agricultural census of Orissa, 1970–71, Board of Revenue, Orissa, p. 2.

3. Census of India, 1991, Series 19, Orissa (provisional), p. 5.

4. Ibid., p.5.

5. Ibid., p.16.

6. Tiller's right over the land has been protected under various land reform enactments like 'Madras Estates Land (Orissa Amendment) Bill, 1947' 'Orissa Tenancy Protection Act, 1948', and 'Orissa Land Reforms Act, 1975'. For details see: K.M. Patra, Orissa State Legislature and Freedom Struggle, 1912–47.

7. Mahapatra, op. cit., p. 27.

8. B.B. Jena, Orissa: people, culture and polity (Delhi:Kalyani Publishers, 1980), p. 27.

9. Mahapatra, Op. cit., p. 37.

10. The earliest Ganga monument of Orissa, the construction of this huge structure was started by king Anantavarma Chodaganga (1078–1150 A.D.) and completed by Ananga Bhima Dev III (A.D. 1216–1238), one of his successors. With the height of around 216 feet, it is said to be the loftiest, spectacular and magnificent religious edifice of Orissa. The shrine of Jagannath became very famous from the beginning of the Ganga rule in Orissa in the early part of the twelfth century A.D. Built on the charming sea-shore, it is not only one of the holiest pilgrimage centres for the Hindus but also has become one of the most attractive tourist spots. For details see: K.C. Panigrahi, History of Orissa (Hindu period) (Cuttak: Kitab Mahal, 1981), pp. 406–407; 339.

11. The Lingaraj temple, with a height of 180 feet and built by Yayati Kesari who may be identified with Yayati II (1025–1040 A.D.) of the Somavamsi dynasty, provides sufficient evidence to believe that this Saiva shrine was influenced by the Jagannath cult. For details see : Panigrahi, Ibid., p.400, 342.

12. The Sun temple at Konarka, "the grandest achievement of the Eastern School of Architecture", is situated some twenty miles away in north-easterly direction from Puri. King Narasimha (1238–1264 A.D.) built at Konarka, a temple for the Sun to live in with other Gods". Grand in conception and great even in its ruin, the stupendous undertaking stands with its disfigured beauty in a desolate tract of ever-drifting sands. For detail see: Panigrahi, Ibid, pp. 410–415.

13. N. K. Sahu et. al., History of Orissa (Cuttack : Nalanda, 1985), p. 376. Also see: B.C. Ray, Foundations of British Orissa (Cuttack: New Students Store, 1969), pp. 44–45.

14. F.G. Bailey, Politics and Social Change, Orissa in 1959 (Bombay: Oxford, 1961), p. 162.

15. Hare Krishna Mahatab, History of Orissa, Vol. I (Cuttack; Prajatantra Prachar Samiti, 1959), p.1.

16. B.C. Ray, Orissa under Marathas, (1751–1803) (Allahabad: Kitab Mahal, 1960), p. 127.

17. Akbar's proclamation in 1556 as the successor of Humayun marked the real beginning of the Mughal Empire in India. He, however, assumed fully the reigns of government into his own hands in 1562, which continued till 1605.

18. K.V. Rao, "The pattern of Orissa Politics", in Iqbal Narain (ed.), State Politics in India, (Meerut: Meenakshi, 1967), p. 216.

19. Report of the Administrative Enquiry Committee, Government of Orissa, 1958, pp. 10–11.

20. In 1917, the British government deputed E.S., Montague, Secretary of State, with a small committee consisting of Earl of Donoughmore, Sir William Duke, Bhupendra Nath Basu and Charles Roberts, to consult the Indian Government andn politicians on matters relating to the formation of the provinces on the basis of language. Montague, therefore, visisted different parts of India along with the Governor-General, Lord Chelmsford, in order to make an indepth study of the problem. In this regard he also visited Orissa to enquire into the demands for amalgamation of Oriya-speaking tracts.

21. Jena, Op. cit., p. 251.

22. Orissa review, 1 April, 1961, Bhubaneswar, p. 4.

23. Lord Curzon, the Viceroy of India, had prepared a scheme of some territorial adjustment in the country, which was outlined in the famous Risely circular of 3 December, 1903. In that document, the problems of the Oriya-speaking tracts and how they affected the administration of the local governments were fully discussed. Taking all factors into consideration it was decided "to unite the whole of Oriya-speaking peoples, both hill & plain under one administration and to make that administration, of Bengal." (Two Bachelors of Arts., The Oriya Movement Appendix D. Risley Circular, pp. 312.8) (Aska, 1919).

24. Prabhat Mukherjee, Utkal University, History of Orissa Vol. VI, p. 425.

25. Surendra Mohanty, Satavidra Surya (Oriya) (Cuttack: Lark Books, 1970), p. 706.

26. P.S.N. Patra, K.C. Gajapati Narayan Deo, The Maharaja of Parlakhemundi, (Berhampur : Gyan Prakashini, 1981), p. 39.

27. Ibid.

28. The Simon Commission arrived at Patna on 12 December, 1928. The Simon Commission was convinced that it was "an urgent case for consideration and treatment". While surveying the problem it observed as follows: The province of Bihar and Orissa, which was constituted in 1912, is the most artificial unit of all the Indian provinces. It was formed by bringing under a single administration three areas which differ markedly not only in physical features, but in many social, linguistic and cultural characteristics." (Report of the Indian statutory commission. Vol. I (Calcutta: 1930), p. 68.

    (A small number of Oriya leaders accorded a warm reception to the Simon Commission at Patna Railway Station on 12 December, 1928) (The Prajatantra, Oriya Daily, 17.12.1928).

29. Orissa Review, op. cit., p. 10.

30. P. K. Jena, Orissa–A New Province (Calcutta: Punthi Pustak, 1988), p. 53.

31. The Statesman, 2 April, 1936.

32. Satya Samachar, Oriya Weekly, 38th issue, Utkal Sahitya Press, Cuttack, 8th Apri, 1936.

33. Balangir, Balasore, Cuttack, Dhenkanal, Ganjam, Kalahandi, Keonjhar, Koraput, Mayrubhanj, Phulbani, Puri, Sambalpur and Sundargarh.

34. Almond andn Powell, Comparative Politics: A Developmental Approach (New Delhi: Gulab Primilani Amerind Publishing Co. Pvt. Ltd., 1966), p. 50.

35. Fred I Greenstein and Nelson W. Polsby (Eds.), "Handbook of Political Science" Vol. III (Massachusetts: 1973), p. 15.

36. Gabriel, A. Almond and S. Verba, "The civic culture" (Boston: Little Brown, 1965), p. 201.

37. S. P. Varma, Modern Political Theory: A critical survey (New Delhi: Vikas Publishing House Pvt. Ltd., 1975), p. 292.

38. B.B. Jena, "Political Parties in Orissa", in I. Narain (ed.), State Politics in India (Meerut: Meenakshi, 1967), p. 485.

39. K.V. rao, "Politics in Orissa, Social Ecology and Constitutional Compulsions", Indian Journal of Political Science, Vol. 26, 1965, p. 103.

40. S. C. Das, "Government and Politics of Orissa", Indian Journal of Political Science, Vol. 26, 1965, p. 85.

41. After the elections in 1937 in Orissa, the Congress did not form the Government. A minority government was installed on 1 April, 1937 headed by Krishna Chandra Gajapati Narayana Deo, the Maharaja of Parlakhemundi. The other two members of the ministry were Mandhata Gorachand Patnaik and Latifur Rahaman. This Ministry continued for three months. In July 1937 Biswanath Das formed the government.

42. Mahatab came into contact with Janaki Nath Bose, father of Subhash Chandra Bose at Cuttack and came close to Subhash Chandra Bose who become Congress President in 1938 and nominated Mahatab as member from Orissa to the Congress Working Committee.

43. W.H. Morris Jones, The Government and Politics of India, (London: Hutchinson, 1971), p. 15. See also Biplab Dasgupta and W.H. Morris Jones, Patterns and Trends in Indian Politics; An Ecological Analysis of Aggregate Data on Society and Elections, (New Delhi: Allied, 1975), p. 17.

44. Surya Narayana Mishra, "Election and Political Development in Orissa" in A.P. Padhi (ed.) Indian State Politics: A Case Study of Orissa, (Delhi: B.R. Publishing Corporation, 1985), p. 49.

45. For details see Sukadev Nanda, Coalitional Politics in Orissa, (New Delhi: Sterling Publishers Pvt. Ltd., 1979).

46. For details see B.K. Patnaik, The Politics of floor-crossing, (Cuttack: Santosh Publications, 1985).

47. B.C. Das, "The Dynamics of Factional Conflict: A Study of the Dimensions of Electoral Conflict in an Assembly constituency in Orissa", The Indian Political Science Review, Vol. XI, January 1977, No. 1, p. 60.

48. B.C. Choudhary, Social Change, Social Culture and Modernization: A linkage process of political development in an Orissan district, Unpublished Ph.D. Dissertation, Berhampur University, 1991) p.14.

49. For details see Krushna Singh Padhy, Corruption in Politics: A Case Study, (Delhi: B.R. Publishing Corporation, 1986), K.S. Padhy and P.K. Muni, Corruption in Indian Politics: A case study of An Indian State, (Delhi: Discovery Publishing House, 1987) and K.S. Padhy, Politics of Corruption in Orissa, in A.P. Padhi (ed.), Indian State Politics: A Case Study of Orissa, (Delhi: B.R. Publishing Corporation, 1985).

50. B.C. Das. "Government and Politics in Orissa since Independence—A Bird's Eye View", The Indian Political Science Review, Vol. XII, 1977, p. 178.

51. W.W. Hunter, The Imperial Gazetter of India, Vol. V, (London: 1985), p. 1.

52. District Statistical Hand Book, Ganjam, 1965, District Statistical Office Ganjam, Berhampur, p.1.

53. District Statistical Hand Book, Ganjam, 1978 and 1979, pp. 1–2.

54. V.A. Smith, Asoka: The Buddhist Emperor of India, (New Delhi: S. Chand & Co., 1964), p. 25.

55. Cunningham, Inscriptions of Asoka, p. 17.

56. According to V.A. Smith the Magadhan empire of Asoka after the death of his son Kunala was divided into two parts. Dasaratha, the son and successor of Asoka, became the ruler of the eastern part of the kingdom with his capital at Pataliputra. The Western part of the kingdom was under the charge of his brother Samprati, and his capital was Ujjain. The Magadhan empire gradually declined during his reign and Kalinga became an independent kingdom in 223 B.C.

57. Census of India, 1961, Orissa, District Census Hand Book, Ganjam, vol. 1, pp. 1–7.

58. Ibid.

59. Biswarup Das, The Bhauma–Karas–Buddhist Kings of Orissa–and their times, (New Delhi: Oriental Publishers and Distributors, 1978), p.12.

60. Ibid., p. 101.

61. Ibid. p. 105.

62. Census of India, 1961, op. cit.

63. Hunter, op. cit. p. 3.

64. The control of British was recognised by Nizam Salabat Jung under the provisions of the treaty of friendship signed with the British on 14 May, 1759.

65. J.J. Maltby, The Ganjam District Manual, Government of Madras, 1918, p. 85.

66. Patra, op. cit., p. 12.

67. S.C. De (ed.), History of Freedom Movement in Orissa, Vol. I, pp. 43–44.

68. Patra, op. cit., p. 14.

69. Patra, op. cit., p. 17.

70. Ibid.

71. Memorandum on behalf of the people of Orissa, from, Indian Statutory Commission, Vol. XVI, His Majestry's Stationary Office, London, 1930, p. 389.

72. Bimbadhar Patnaik, "The Oriya Problem, Utkal Union Committee", (Patna: University Press, 1931), p.2.

73. Samuel Hoare, Maharaja of Parlakhemundi, (An article), from souvenir, Our Homage to the Father of New Orissa, Maharajas 78th Birth Day Celebration Committee, Cuttack, 1969, English Section, p. 13.

74. Dharitri, An Oriya Daily, Cuttack, 1 April, 1976.

75. Patnaik, op. cit.

76. De (ed.), op. cit., Vol.·II, p. 126.

77. Quoted in Patra, op. cit., p. 21.

78. De (ed.), op. cit., p. 127.

79. Resolution of the Government of India, No. 2491, dated 19th July, 1905, Bengal Archives.

80. Surendra Mohanty, "Kulabrudha" (Oriya), (Cuttack: Lark Books, 1978), p. 65.

81. This was done under the provision of the Orissa Estates Abolition Act, 1952.

82. Patnaik, op. cit., p. 28.

83. S.N. Rajguru, "History of the Gangas", Part II, p. 268.

84. Ibid.

85. Orissa Review, 1 April, 1961, p. 4.

86. Natabar Samanta Ray, "A short History of creation of Orissa as a separate State", Utkal Prasanga, Special issue (Bhubaneswar: 1975), p. 11.

87. Patnaik, op. cit., p.4.

88. Simon Commission Report, Vol. II, p.25.

89. K.M. Patra, "Orissa under the British, A Political Sketch", Side-lights on History and Culture of Orissain M.N. Das (ed.) (Cuttack: Vidyapuri, 1977), p. 170.

90. Rajguru, op. cit., p. 277.

91. Ibid.

92. Ibid.

93. See, Choudhury, Op. Cit., p. 166.

94. Ibid.

95. District Statistical Hand Book, 1990–91, Ganjam, pp. 1–2.

96. "Pragatibadi", An Oriya Daily, special supplement, dated 01–04–93.

97. Rajaguru, Op.cit., p. 277.

98. District Statistical Hand Book 1990–91, op. cit., p.2.

99. Choudhury, Op. cit., p. 177.

100. W.J.M. Mackenzie, "Elections", International Encyclopaedia of Social Science (New York: Collier Macmillan, 1968), p.1.

101. Herbert Emmerich and Richard Garnett, "Electoral Processes" in Encylopaeida Britanica (Macro), Vol. 6 (U.S.A.: The University of Chicago Press, 1977), p. 530.

102. K.S. Padhy and P.P. Tripathy, "Volting behaviour of Tribals in India", (Delhi: Kaniskha Publishers & Distributors, 1994), p.3.

103. Joseph, P. Harris, "Elections" Encyclopaedia of Social Science, Vol. V–VI, (New York : Macmillan, 1962), p. 452.

104. S.M. Lipset, "Political Sociology", in N.J. Smelser (ed.), Sociology: An introduction, (New Delhi: Wiley Eastern, 1970), p. 456.

105. Jagannath Prasad (S.C.), Bhanjanagar, Suruda, Aska, Kavisurya Nagar, Kodala, Khallikote, Chatrapur, Hinjili, Gopalpur (S.C.), Berhampur, Chikiti, Mohana, Ramagiri (S.T.) and Parlakhemundi.

106. Berhampur and Aska Lok Sabha Constituencies.

107. See the Orissa Gazette, Extraordinary No. 1503, Cuttack, 27 June, 1965.

108. See Third Supplement to Hand Book of important Notification Circulars & Order. Home Election Departments, 1978.

109. S.C. Dube, Indian Village, (New Delhi: Allied Publisher, 1967), p. 57.

110. Ibid.

111. Ibid.

112. S.L. Hanchett, Changing Economic, Social and Ritual Relationship in a Modern South India Village, (University Micro Films International, 1970), p. 162.

113. Ibid.

114. B.S. Panda, Gandhi Krushna Murty (Oriya) (Berhampur : Gopinath Press, 1979), p. 22.

115. Dube, Op. Cit., p.6.

116. Panda, Op. cit., p. 30.

3
VILLAGE ECONOMY

The village economy constitutes an important area of the study as it helps one to understand the sub-dynamics of factionalism in the rural government and politics. Although, agriculture continues to be the core sector of India's rural economy,[1] the changed industrial and economic scenario in the Country has left a tremendous impact upon the village economy.[2] It is a fact that development in the field of communication and transport has brought about significant changes in the economic drive of the villages. As a result, the Indian village is undergoing a process of urbanization. Agriculture products are now marketed in urban centres. The village can no longer be strictly called an agricultural community. However, with such economic changes the power equation has not changed. Till today, the rural rich in villages monopolize the economic and political power and obstruct the improvement of the rural poor.

It may be mentioned that the economic structure of Nuapada, the village taken for the present study, has got many facets. It is not strictly an agricultural economy as people have started adopting a number of other sources of income too. It is worthwhile to present the observations on all the determinants of Nuapada's economy. Such determinants are (A) land and agriculture, (B) Patron-Client relationships (C) occupations and services (D) business.

(A) LAND AND AGRICULTURE

The village Nuapada spreads over an area of 268.81 acres of land, out of which habitation accounts for 19.27 acres. It is to be noted that about thirty five acres of land are not fit for cultivation as they yield neither grain nor grass. The Royat area (Cultivated land) for which revenue is charged is, thus, 197.84 acres. This land yields an annual revenue of Rs. 723.80 ps. excluding water tax of Rs. 459.50 ps. and cess fee of Rs. 363.05 ps. There are four tanks covering 16.13 acres of land. Though agricultural land constitutes the main economic resource in the village, not everyone in the village possesses the land of his own. Those who own, own it disproportionately. The pattern of land ownership is reflected in the following Table.

[Table 3.1] Caste-wise Landownership in Village Nuapada in 1994

Sl. No.	*Caste*	*Size of land ownership in Acres*	*% in Proportion to the total cultivable land*	*No. of households*	*% of the total households*
1.	Brahmin	10.40	05.25	40	(08.37)
2.	Komti	52.47	26.52	66	(13.81)
3.	Kampa	31.03	15.68	32	(06.69)
4.	Parcelia (O.B.C.)	07.88	3.98	05	(01.05)
5.	Khandayat (O.B.C.)	07.31	3.69	10	(02.09)
6.	Dera (O.B.C.)	06.57	3.32	78	(16.32)
7.	Temple and Institutions	69.82	37.24		
8.	Kamma	02.28	1.15	03	(00.63)
9.	S.T. (of other villages including Matia	02.42	1.22	--	--
10.	Teli (O.B.C.)	01.57	0.79	09	(01.88)
11.	Goldsmith (O.B.C.)	01.13	0.57	09	(01.88)
12.	Khadura (O.B.C.)	01.14	0.58	28	(05.86)
13.	Keuta (S.C.)	00.64	0.32	34	(07.11)
14.	Karan	00.05	0.03	03	(00.63)
15.	Dhoba (S.C.)	00.04	0.02	41	(08.58)
16.	Barika (S.T.)	Nil	--	06	(01.26)
17.	Dandashi (S.C.)	Nil	--	40	(08.37)
18.	Barber (O.B.C.)	Nil	--	21	(04.39)
19.	Gudia (O.B.C.)	Nil	--	11	(02.30)
20.	Redica (O.B.C.)	Nil	--	12	(02.51)
21.	Hadi (S.C.)	Nil	--	13	(02.72)
21.	Shundhi (O.B.C.)	Nil	--	04	(00.84)
23.	Bouri (S.C.)	Nil	--	07	(01.46)
	Total AC	197.84 Cents	100.00%	472	(100.00%)

The Table 3.1 indicates that the komtis occupy the 1st position in respect of land-holding in the village, followed by other castes like Kampa, Parcelia, Khandayat, Dera and Kamma. The present study reveals that the komtis have lands not only in Nuapada but also in other villages surrounding it. This can be partly attributed to the fact that during the Zamindari system, the komtis were the Mustadars[3] and Sahukars[4] and by virtue of their such positions they were able to exploit the people and acquire more land. They used to lend money to the poor people and charged heavy interest. The borrowers had to mortgage their lands or part of the crops or gold ornaments depending upon the sum of money which they borrowed. When they were not able to repay the loan, they usually surrendered whatever they had mortgaged to the sahukars. Besides this, the komtis also used to purchase the land in nearby villages at throw-away prices. It is because of their dominance in the sphere of economy, they have acquired a status in the Socio-political sphere of the village and act as the main agent of factionalism in Nuapada village.

While agriculture sector continues to dominate the economy of the state (of Orissa) absorbing 80% of the work force and contributing more than 50% of the state domestic product,[5] the village under study accommodates about 35% of the house holds to be the possessors of lands and another 30% engaged in agrarian sector as agricultural labourers.

Thus, the scarcity of means and their alternative uses to satisfy unlimited wants give rise to a series of choice-making phenomena which in the context of the village happen to be woven round the Matrix of agriculture.[6] The agriculture sector even in the 1990s continues to function as the backbone of the Indian economy as the highest contributor to Gross Domestic Product (GDP) and also as provider of large employment.[7]

Land ownership is the most important basis of rural economy in India.[8] Nearly every village resident has a direct or indirect relationship to the land economy. The social and religious life of a rural society centres around the agricultural cycle and is profoundly influenced by fluctuations in climate and crops. Land is also, as in other villages, the most valued item in Nuapada and the present study supports the earlier study made by H.S. Lorraine on a South

Indian village that land is a source of prestige and influence for those who have some control over it.[9] It supports the study of M.N. Srinivas on Mysore village that land is the ultimate basis for most of the relationships that unify the various castes in his Mysore village.[10]

Baljit Singh's study on "Next step in village India" also supports our study on Nuapada village that income, security and prestige in rural society are almost directly proportional to land-holdings.[11]

Ownership of land confers status position, prestige and it makes on powerful in all respects and in every sphere of life-social, economic and political. Greater the ownership of land, higher is one's importance and prominence in the society. Economic power helps a lot or goes a long way in making one politically powerful. Thus, political power and economic dominance are often close companions and go together. The landlord or the Zamindar was practically the master of his village where law way usually equated with his will.[12]

The study also supports K.K. Singh's observations in his article "Rural restlessness" that over the centuries, a pattern of social relationships developed around land and agriculture. The economically dominant rural elites controlled local affairs and also had some influence at the higher centres of power.[13]

In Nuapada, there are, as mentioned earlier, 537 houses. Each house represents a family. From this 41 families of government officials, who are not the permanent residents of the village, can be deleted. 173 families have some land of their own and remaining 323 families are landless. Those who have no land, and those who have little land are left with the alternatives of either working as whole-time agricultural labourers or of cultivating land taken on lease or on share cropping. Since land has a socio-economic and political value, the people feel that "a villager without land is like one without caste: thus the landless are the de-classed of the rural society." It is significant to note that people belonging to some castes like Kampa have a deep sense of attachment to their lands. Therefore, they cannot think in terms of disposing of their land. But sometimes they are forced to sell a part of their land. The day on which it is sold, it happens to be one of the saddest days for them. It is a day to mourn. The women folk may even wail and shed tears of real grief. For several days the family atmosphere remains overcast with gloom. Land is indeed the most precious and coveted possession of the village people.[14] With the exception of women's ornaments and the house itself, land is the only property they can have which gives them a feeling of tremendous security.

Agriculture in Nuapada village is quite progressive. Around 80% of the area is irrigated and some farms are irrigated more than once. Before 1980 there were 3 major tanks utilized for irrigation purposes. But later on, with the initiation of the village people, the then M.L.A. Chintamani Dyana Samantara, had moved the government of Orissa and accordingly some lift irrigation points were installed by the Government. Besides this, there are 3 private lift irrigation points which provide sufficient water for cultivation. But during summer season, as the river "Bahuda", which passes nearly by village, becomes dry, the irrigation points also become dead. By digging the river, the private owners of the lift irrigation points irrigate some of their lands for vegetable product. A canal named "poichandia" is extended up to Nuapada. But people do not get any water from it at the time of need. However, with the exception of 1986–87 (Which was a drought year of the entire Ganjam district), despite irregular mansoon and rainfall, the lands are cultivated and give better or more yields. The main crops are rice, ragi, kulthi, mung, biri, groundnut and vegetables. The cropping intensity in the village is around 170–190 per cent.

The use of modern inputs in agriculture is limited to a few big farmers who have access to irrigation facilities. There are only three tractors which are owned by big farmers of the village. Some farmers cultivate their lands by tractors on hired basis. Most of the agriculturists plough their lands with bullock-drawn wooden ploughts even today. Some farmers have changed their plough only to the extent that a new piece of Iron is tagged on to it at its furrowing end. Despite this, the agriculture in Nuapada is progressive. Though no important agro-processing Industries has come up in the village so far, the farmers use HYV seeds, fertilizers and pesticides on any significant scale to increase the production and productivity of their land.

It is to be noted that the demand for hired labour is generally no so high in Nuapada village as the family members of the backward or low castes make themselves fully engaged in the land, beginning from the transplantation of the seedlings to harvesting of paddy as they have not enough land. The other castes like Komti, Dera, parcelia and Brahmins hire labour during busy seasons for paddy transplanting, harvesting etc. It is quite interesting to note that often they get labour at a cheaper rate since labourers from nearby villages including Brahmin Nuapada are prepared to sell their labour for a low price when they do not have any work in their hands. Thus poverty and unemployment force them to work hard for a meagre income.

It may be pointed out that with the overall increase in the price of different goods and commodities over the years, the price of land has also gone up as is evident from the following Table.

[Table 3.2] Land and Its Value

	Type of Land	*Grades of Land and Price per Acre in Rupee*			*Year 1994*
		A	B	C	
1.	Dryland	27,000/-	24,000/-	20,000/-	
2.	Wetland	60,000/-	50,000/-	40,000/-	,,
3.	Orchard	40,000/-	----	---	,,

It may not be wrong to observe that the value of wet land has gone high because of irrigation facilities. Therefore, even if the area does not get much or sufficient rain the farmers do not feel disappointed as they can yield some crops.

Interaction between Nuapada and other surrounding villages in respect of trade and commerce is quite encouraging. The business men of this village purchase paddy, ragis, mung, Kolthi, etc. from nearby villages and export them to the nearby towns.

In Nuapada village as is the case with other villages, land-holding continues to be the deciding factor in socio-political and economic activities of the village. But since all the land-holders do not cultivate their land, they give the same to the tenants who cultivate and share with the former a part of the crop that was yielded. Such a phenomenon creates a different type of political equation in the village. Accordingly a study has been made in landlord and tenant relationship.

(B) LANDLORD AND TENANT-RELATIONSHIP

Though a number of Socio-economic reform measures have been introduced in the rural society, the forces of tradition continue to resist progress and do come in the way of effective implementation of developmental schemes in Nuapada village. For example, even after the legal abolition of landlordism, there continues to exist on a fairly large scale the land-lord-tenant relationship in one form or another. As mentioned earlier, India is mainly an agricultural economy and land is wealth. So the farmers of Nuapada, as in the case in other villages, do believe that they are economically secure only when they are the owners of some land.[15]

In general, an Indian village consists of peasants office-goers, artisans and untouchable castes. The relation among the castes in the village has been traditionally hierarchical, although the land owning caste is the pivot of the village community irrespective of its ritual status. In fact, the land-owning caste is the patron and the service-holders, artisans and unfree labour castes are its clients. In this study those who cultivate the land of the landlords are considered as the tenants. The relationship between the landlord and tenant is the most important patronage relationship in the traditional village life like Nuapada. Under the old system of diffuse mutual obligation numerous and varied exchanges were made. The most important contribution of the landlord to his tenants is his land. By permitting the tenant to cultivate a crop, he gives him an opportunity to partake in the wealth of the agricultural system. Consequently the tenants are obliged to the landlords. Thus, the introduction of the concept of individual proprietary right over land witnessed integration of the villages into the mainstream of Indian nation, monetization of economy, and the establishment of a network of roads and railways. The social relations of agricultural production have also under gone change. However, it is still argued that "even today in the village diverse castes continue to come together for agricultural production.[16]

The agrarian structure of traditional or pre-British Indian village is different from that of Post-British and free Indian village. The concept of individual right over land was unknown to the people before the British rule. Land was not a marketable commodity. However, some households belonging to one or a few castes had the right to use the land. They were the dominant castes of the village. Thus, in the village under study, the Komtis have vast land in surrounding villages. They are the traders and they usually distribute their land among several tenants to cultivate on share-cropping. This, they do mainly to bring them under their control and increase their political influence. The landlord as patron provided his tenant with other kinds of help as well. In exchange of all this, the client gives his physical service whenever and wherever it is required to the patrons or the landlords. Thus, the relationship between a patron and client is based on an exchange with each giving what the other needs most. Hence the study supports the findings made earlier by Hanchett[17] on a south Indian village wherein a client is also free to beg shamelessly and almost to become angry when he feels neglected.

Thus, the tenants also in their turn feel obliged to the landlord who comes to their assistance in crucial times by extending credit to them. The interest rate is exceedingly high and sometimes even compound interests is charged. In some cases the interest amount is far above the principal and the vile landlord succeeds in taking possession of the land in lieu of the credit amount. This happens in spite of the presence of the rural banking sector. This is because of the strong influence of the old tradition of the tenant looking up to the landlord for assistance for every conceivable purpose. Secondly, the ignorance of the villagers makes them feel that the banks are inaccessible to them and banking is yet to become their habit. The rural poor strongly believe that the banking is for the rich only and it is of no use for them. Also, the fact that the banks insist on some formalities deter the tenant and the rural poor from approaching them. On the other hand, the rural landlord insists on no formalities (except a signed paper, the contents of which are mostly not known to the debtor). This is a tempting factor to approach him for monetary assistance. But unfortunately he does not known what is in store for him in future. Unable to repay the loan which he had borrowed, the tenant has no other choice except to surrender his land or ornaments in his possession to the landlord. It is a very common thing that the landlord always tries to keep the debtor under the permanent obligations by collecting interest only and not insisting on the repayment of principal amount.

Thus, the dominant economic power in the hands of Brahmin and Komti landlords enables them to exercise the greatest influence in the socio-political sector also. Further, the komtis as a community are more cunning than the Brahmins and manage to keep their clients in good humour. Thus, among the predominant communities in the village they play a more dominant role in the village and the surrounding areas. A keen observation of the factional politics in Nuapada village reveals that the komti community leads a very powerful faction inspite of the occasional attempts made by the Brahmins, the Deras, the Kampas, etc. to form another faction and resist the domination of the former who with their greater financial power and extensive landholdings in surrounding villages successfully obstruct the attempt of other communities in their factional power-struggle. Further the educational level of the komti community is far higher than that of the other communities. Many from the younger generation of this community have become engineers, lawyers, lecturers, pharmacists, etc. giving an added advantage to the prestige of the community. Thus, the hold of the factions led by the komtis in the village politics is greater than that of the other factions headed by the Brahmins and others.

The role of castes also is worth examining. It is interesting to note that at least in Madras presidency area, where the Cornwallis' land revenue system was implemented, Brahmins were not appointed as Zamindars. A few inams were given to them during the Muslim rule. By and large, the Zamindaris were looked after by the non-Brahmin communities and it is of interest to note that the British deliberately encouraged the non-Brahmin movement in Madras presidency since the Brahmins were the first to join the national movement.[18]

Caste-wise again, the Brahmins generally not being good agriculturists at least in south, migrated to the urban areas seeking jobs under the government. In most places the agricultural communities were other than the Brahmins. In many places, since a Brahmin could not stand the rigors of rural life after the general political awakening, he ceased to be of importance in the village. Thus, mostly, the rich landlords after the abolition of the Zamindari system are non-Brahmins. Those who sought jobs in the urban areas had slowly to yield their position by selling away their lands since land to the tiller had become an accepted principle in general, though no formal legislation was made.[19]

Land reform measures have been undertaken by the government from time to time to provide socio-economic justice to the people in the society. In spite of the "Orissa Tenancy Protection Act, 1948", "Orissa Tenant Relief Act of 1954", "The Estate Abolition Act" of 1951, the tenants could not be free from the exploitation of the intermediaries.

Undoubtedly these acts went a long way in releasing many of the tenants from the clutches of the intermediaries. But unfortunately the poor and ignorant tenants were not aware of these Acts. As a result and for no fault of theirs, they, in many places of Orissa, continued to be mercilessly exploited by these intermediaries who, in fact, did not possess any land in their name, yet they were the worst oppressors of the tenants. Lack of knowledge or information about these acts also prevented the latter from reporting their oppression by the intermediaries to the Tahasildars who were invested with power to investigate into such kinds of oppression. Enactments notwithstanding, peasants' sufferings could not be prevented. It is very unfortunate to observe that no steps were taken either by the Public Relations department or by the Revenue department in educating the tenants about so many laws made to improve their living conditions. Therefore, the connivance of Zamindars with Revenue officials proved highly detrimental to the interest of the poor tenants.

However, a progressive legislation relating to agrarian reforms and land tenures consequent upon the gradual abolition of intermediary interest, known as "Orissa Land Reforms Act 1960" came into existence. The Chapter 4 of the Act deals with ceiling and disposal of surplus land and it came into force in January 1972.

For the first time in Nuapada, after rigid implementation of Land Reforms Act in 1975, the discontentment of the labourers, specially agrarian ones, was engineered against the landholders of this village and some outer agencies and political parties tried to exploit the prevailing situation to make political capital out of it. As a result, the situation was complicated. The then M.L.A. representing the Chikiti Assembly constituency, also sided with the agitators and turned a deaf ear to the requests of komtis, the major landlords and other village elites of nearby villages. But it is quite disheartening to note that this agrarian revolt, instead of being successful, released some new economic and political forces. Landlords in this village have always exploited the innocence, simplicity, illiteracy and ignorance of the poor tenants. As a result of this revolt, landlords rather made a mischievous plan of driving the villagers by offering lands to the landless to cultivate the land for two years freely without paying anything. It was done under the guise of landlords' benevolency to perpetuate their exploitation of tenants. Because it gave them an opportunity to take away their lands after some time from those tenants. Because it gave them an opportunity to take away their lands after some time from those tenants. In this way inspite of enactment of the Orissa Land Reforms Act, the fact remained that the new Act could not guarantee a better deal for the tenants. Rather some of them were denied an opportunity to cultivate the land. As a result, they were thrown into the abyss of poverty. Thirdly, village life was changed from a 'Community life' to a "divided life", because division was marked even among the landless. Above all, landlords throughout Orissa started supporting the new political party i.e. the Janata Party, which emerged in 1977 as a force to reckon with, following the imposition of "National Emergency" in India in June 1975. Janata Party came to power in many states including Orissa. It is disheartening to observe that after assuming power, the new party kept the Orissa Land Reforms Act in cold storage allowing the traditional exploitation of tenants by Zamindars to continue. Surprisingly the courts in Orissa have also proved to be Pro landlord by and large.[20] Because in this regard nearly 83,589 cases were instituted out of which 79,268 were disposed of, benefiting only 22,405 persons involving 9,559 hectors in the entire State of Orissa.

Thus, the land-lord-tenant relationship is based on 'bourgeois economic model' of exploiter-exploited syndrome. Landlords have utilized the same for their social, economic and political gains.

(C) OCCUPATION AND SERVICES

Together with land, occupation and services do contribute to the exercise of great influence in the Socio-political arena of the village, Nuapada. It is realized that different occupations enjoy a different degree of prestige relative to one another. In a society, which is dynamic in nature, many factors are responsible for its economic and social changes. But with the process of urbanization, one finds that there is a consistent pattern of socio-economic changes in the village Nuapada. Land values, occupation, modes of living and thinking, food habits and dress, the relations between different generations, the inter-caste relationships all these have changed considerably.

Urbanization has had its impact on the occupational structure of the village more than on anything else. Nuapada village as a whole has come under the impact of urbanization with reference to occupation. Previous occupations were mainly agricultural, trading and working on daily wages, etc. But today, occupations of the people include not only these but various types of industrial work such as weaving, spinning, store-keeping, factory labourer etc. Many of them are also engaged in road-building, house-building, brick-laying and some also serve as engineers, doctors, teachers down to the peons etc. in the offices of the various parts of the country. Thus industrialization and Urbanization have influenced occupational mobility and super-imposing new values on the rural people.[21]

Thus, the Table 3.3 indicates that in the village under study, there are twenty-two engineers, two doctors, twenty nine teachers, eleven pharmacists, seven clerks, six defence personnel, sixteen fourth grade employees, thirty four in other services, four postal agents (who are mobilizing the people to deposit money at Post offices and getting their commissions from the postal department), seven co-operative society workers, seven mill workers and two contractors. In this village, besides the landholders, engineers, doctors, teachers, defence personnel, pharmacists enjoy a higher occupational status in descending order. Together with landholding, not below the rank of a clerk occupies a greater status in this village. However, the table shows that all the alluring jobs are occupied by the Komtis, Brahmins, Deras and Dhobas in a descending order.

Taking into consideration the entire population of the village, it may be observed that a very negligible percentage of them are engaged in different services. But it is also a fact that better means of communication educational facilities and the impact of urbanization and industrialization have opened new avenues and provided newer occupations to the members of various castes of the village. Even the people in lower castes prefer to take up new,

Sl. No.	*Caste*	*Engineers*	*Doctors*	*Teachers*	*Pharmacists*	*Clerks*	*Defence*	*4th Class servent*	*Other Services*	*Postal Agent*	*Co-operative Service*	*Mill Worker*	*Contractors*	*Total Service*	*%*
1.	Brahmin	02		10	01	...	01	...	04	...	...	01	...	19	12.42
2.	Komti	16	01	12	06	01	04	02	09	04	...	...	02	57	37.25
3.	Dera	02	...	03	01	02	...	...	03	...	07	...	...	18	11.76
4.	Keuta	...	...	...	...	...	...	01	01	...	...	...	...	02	01.31
5.	Kharuda	...	01	...	...	02	...	...	08	...	...	01	...	12	07.84
6.	Dhobi	01	...	02	02	01	...	02	...	...	...	01	...	09	05.88
7.	Dandasi	...	...	...	...	...	...	01	01	...	...	01	...	03	01.96
8.	Hadi	...	...	...	...	...	...	01	...	...	...	...	...	01	00.65
9.	Redica	...	...	...	...	...	...	01	01	...	...	...	...	02	07.84
10.	Kampa	...	...	01	...	...	...	02	01	...	...	03	...	07	04.58
11.	Barber	...	...	...	...	01	...	03	01	...	...	...	...	05	03.27
12.	Gudia	01	...	...	01	...	...	01	...	...	...	...	...	03	01.96
13.	Teli	...	...	...	...	...	01	...	...	...	...	...	...	01	00.65
14.	Khandayat	...	...	...	...	...	...	01	01	...	...	...	...	02	01.31
15.	Goldsmity	...	...	...	...	...	...	01	...	...	...	...	...	01	00.65
16.	Archaka	...	...	03	...	...	...	...	...	...	...	...	...	03	01.96
17.	Parcelia	...		02	...	...	...	...	01	...	...	...	01	04	02.61
18.	Kamma Brahmin	...	...	01	...	...	...	...	02	...	...	...	...	03	01.96
19.	Sundhi	...	...	...	...	...	...	...	...	...	...	...	...	Nil	...
20.	Barika	...	...	...	...	...	...	...	01	...	...	...	...	01	00.65
	Total	**22**	**02**	**34**	**11**	**07**	**06**	**16**	**34**	**04**	**07**	**07**	**03**	**153**	**100%**

though minor, jobs. They feel happy to work as mill-workers, teachers, shop-keepers, clerks, pharmacists, engineers rather than be exploited in their traditional occupations by the members of higher castes.

It is significant to note that the most economically predominant caste i.e., Komtis have also dominated in the 'service' sector, which they have adopted as an occupation. They have become the major beneficiaries in the existing system of education and urbanization. People of lower castes have had to struggle a lot to take the benefit of urbanization, education and industrialization.

(D) BUSINESS

As a result of modernization, business has become an essential part of the village economic life. The self-sufficient village economy on the basis of unequal exchange of relationships was affected by the British colonial rule in India. The British effort in India was to promote agricultural capitalism.[22] Hence, through the zamindari and raiyatwari system, individual proprietary right over land was introduced. Further, the rise of internal markets, assisted by the extension of roads and the expansion in foreign trade of agricultural commodities also helped the growth of market economy at the cost of the old self-sufficient barter economy of the village.[23] D.N. Majumdar remarks, "the status structure of our villages is in a fluid state. While still clinging to the traditional ways of eking out an income, the villager is today experiencing the impact of technology and competitive economy. Land is not in abundance, while the size of the family is on the increase....."[24] This new market economy has encouraged the people to adopt business as one of their sources of income. Hence the people of Nuapada besides keeping themselves engaged in traditional professions have also adopted other means of livelihood to improve their economic condition. Most of them prefer to have some side-business so as to have some extra income. It is quite disheartening to observe that occupational specialization which is associated with their castes is perhaps no longer feasible. For example, in Nuapada village, the castes like Dera, whose primary occupation is weaving, few of them now tend to undertake this business. The same is also the case with other castes. It is an axiomatic truth that "the business" enhances the economic conditions of the families who are actually engaged in trade or business. The Table 3.2 gives a clear idea about the business trend of the village.

Thus, it is evident from the Table 3.4 that the Komti caste has a strong dominance over the village economy as they have access to all kinds of business starting from opening a hotel to having a pan shop to selling medicines, etc. The other castes like Khadura, Dera, Brahmin, Teli, Barber, Khandayat and Goldsmith are also engaged in business on a low scale.

The new market economy has no doubt created a socio-economic change in the village, giving a free hand to all the sections of the village. To participate in the new economic system, even the lower strata of the village, who were previously exploited by the landlords, could be able to withstand such exploitation by resorting to different small and big businesses. It has also facilitated a better means of communication and transportation from Nuapada to other parts of the district. But, again here under the market economy, the advantage has been manipulated by a microscopic few converting the village economy from feudal orientation to capitalist trend. Because the common man in the village is still the worst victim of exploitation made by the big business people belonging to the predominant castes like Komtis and Khaduras. It is worth mentioning here that such castes by virtue of their economic strength had changed the castes structure in the village and have proved themselves to be more powerful than the higher castes like Brahmins (priests) and Khandayats (Warriers). So, one of the capitalists trends is that alongwith landlords the business magnates play a dominant role in the socio-economic and political life of the village Nuapada.

Another capitalist trend in the village is the development of the system of money-lending and exploitation by money-lenders. Money-lending is a product of the market economy which had developed in Nuapada during the British period. It was adopted as the easiest way of earning money by money-lenders. Money-lending is a product of the market economy which had developed in Nuapada during the British period. It was adopted as the easiest way of earning money by charging high interest on the amount given as loan. The borrowers have to deposit either gold or land as security with the money-lenders for the loan they have taken.

Sl. No.	Caste	Grossary Shops	Book Stores & Stationeries	Hotels	Pan Shops	Veg. Shops	Cloth Store	Aluminium Brass Shops	Small Mano Shops	Stationeries	Medicine shops	Photograph	Small Industries	Rice Mill	Swing Machine	Type Institute	*Other Business	Total
		1	2	3	4	5	6	7	8	9	10	11	12	13	14	15	16	17
1.	Komti	14	01	05	01	03	07	02	02	03	03	---	01	04	---	01	02	49
2.	Dera	--	--	01	01	01	05	--	--	--	--	--	--	01	--	02	07	18
3.	Brahmin	01	--	--	--	01	--	--	01	--	--	--	--	--	--	--	02	05
4.	Kharuda	01	--	--	--	--	--	02	--	-	--	--	--	--	--	--	15	18
5.	Dhobi	--	--	--	--	--	--	--	--	--	--	--	--	--	--	--	02	02
6.	Barber	--	--	--	--	--	--	--	--	--	--	01	--	--	03	--	02	06
7.	Gudia	--	--	04	03	--	--	--	--	--	--	--	--	--	--	--	--	07
8.	Teli	--	--	--	01	--	--	--	--	--	-	--	--	--	--	--	02	03
9.	Khandayat	--	01	--	--	01	--	--	--	--	--	-	--	--	--	--	--	03
10.	Goldsmith	--	--	--	--	--	--	--	--	--	--	--	--	--	01	--	02	03
11.	Others	--	--	02	--	--	--	--	--	--	--	--	--	--	--	--	--	02

*Other business includes Rice, Shyam Antenna connections (T.V.), Cycle repairings etc.

In most of the cases poor villagers because of high interest rate do not repay the money and ultimately forfeit their security deposits like gold and the land. No doubt, in recent years the system of banking and credit societies have come to the rescue of the debtors. But due to the cumbersome and tedious official procedure involved in the process of banking loan system and the inordinate delay caused deliberately or inadvertently in the release of money by the banks, villagers find no other alternative but run to the money-lender for borrowing money. As a result, not only the poor people are exploited but also the small businessman loose their credibility and join the rank of destitute.

In Nuapada village the big business people have got an organization to protect their own interest and continue their exploitation by dividing the poor people. This organization unfortunately has prohibited hoteliers, pan-shop owners, small shop-keepers etc. from becoming its members. Because they are treated as their clients who depend on their mercy for their livelihood. Their organization meets once on first day of every month and discusses matters of commercial interest.

In this meeting they decide they price structure, interest rate, etc. According to their decision the market rate of every commodity is decided and sold. Since they practise hoarding and black-marketing, they do not allow small businessmen to join their ranks. Thus, such an organisation set up by rich komtis protects and promotes the business monopoly in the village. As a result poor and low-income people become a victim to high price rise, shortage of food, etc. No doubt, to encourage the small businessmen like weavers, credit societies have.been established in the village whose work is to supply raw-materials and market the finished products. The establishment of this organization has not only saved the time and energy of the weavers in getting loan from the banks but also set them free from the clutches of Komtis *sahukars*. It has also helped in fostering a sense of unity among the class of weavers. But, unfortunately attempts have been made time and again by the organization of big business to sabotage the functioning of such an organization like credit society. Rich Komtis in the village try to create cleavages within such co-operative organizations. The intention is to give a severe death blow to the functioning of the co-operative societies and undertake the role of middlemen for earning money. Secondly, such business people know that once the weavers belonging to Dera community get united, they will be a threat to their socio-economic and political predominance of the business lords. But to their good luck they have become successful in such attempts as co-operative societies have developed snags because of lack of unity and sincerity. Besides, it is interesting to note that such business people support and oppose the creation of any new organisation or institution like schools, colleges, etc. keeping in view their economic interest. Thus, a minute observation on the functioning of market economy in the village indicates the trend of capitalist order.

Thus, it is evident from the above that the village economy of Nuapada leads to some necessary conclusions based on data and observation. Village economy, first of all, is not strictly agriculture in nature. It's traditional base has been replaced by a new market economy. Secondly, in spite of the land reform laws, feudalistic exploitation is still vivid in the village. Due to the initiation of the process of modernization, urbanization and industrialization, people have shifted their occupation from purely agriculture to that of business and jobs in different offices. But in both the sectors, one of the interesting findings is that a particular group of people in the village dominates both in the agricultural as well as service and business sectors. Replacement of traditional village economy by the market economy by the market economy has led to the creation of the producer and the labourer class, the exploiter and the exploited. No doubt, it has diminished the traditional higher caste predominance in the village, but it has not totally replaced the caste system. Komtis, who have a middle rank in the caste structure, continue to ascertain their caste identity by virtue of their economic supremacy in the village. So this study supports the Marxian doctrine of economic determinism. The people of other higher castes belonging to Brahmin and Khandayats play a less significant role in the village due to their poor economic predicament. Economically higher-ups in the village also decide the fate of educational and political institutions of the village. Thus, class determines the predominance of a caste in the village under study. Lastly, as mentioned above, village economy is tending towards a capitalist pattern, creating monopoly houses, producer and labourer conflict, hoarding and exploitation.

As pointed out above, since there is a close nexus between caste and clan in village politics, it is necessary to throw light on the social structure of the village.

References

1. B.M. Bhatia, "*Price Policy, Agriculture and Economic Growth*", IASSI Quarterly, Vol. II, No. 1, 1992, p. 59.
2. Sushila Mehta, *Social Conflicts in a Village Community* (New Delhi: S. Chand & Co. Pvt. Ltd., 1971), p. 139.
3. 'Mustadar' means the agent/officer of a village to collect the land revenue and deposit the fixed amount as rent with the Zamindars.
4. 'Sahukar' is a term used to mean a person of a Komti community who lends money to others.
5. Government of Orissa, Economic Survey—1991-92, p. 1.
6. B.R. Chauhan, A Rajasthan village, (New Delhi: Vir Publishing House, 1967), p. 148.
7. V. Shekerappa, Does Priority Sector Lending help the Poor ? Kurukshetra, July 1994, p. 8.
8. S.S. Sharma, Factions : Antecedents and Consequences—A Comparative Study in two Villages in Block in Western Uttar Pradesh, A report, 1985, p. 40.
9. Hanchett Suzanne Lorraine, Changing Economic, Social and Ritual Relationships in a Modern South Indian Village (Univ. Micro Films: International 1970), p. 21.
10. Ibid., p. 22.
11. Ibid.
12. Ranganath, "The Changing Pattern of Rural Leadership in Uttar Pradesh," Indian Academy of Social Sciences, New Delhi, 1971, p. 92.
13. K.K. Singh, "Rural Restlessness", Seminar, No. 299, July, 1984, p.15.
14. Dube, Op. Cit., p. 76.
15. Lorraine, Op. Cit., p. 136.
16. M.N. Srinivas, "*Future of Indian Caste*", Economic and Political

Weekly, Bombay, Annual Number, Feb., 1979, p. 241.

17. Lorraine, Op. Cit., p. 70.

18. K. Seshadri, "*Rural Unrest in India*", (New Delhi: Intellectual Publishing House, 1983), p. 28.

19. Ibid.

20. J.K. Mohapatra and u.M. Das, "*Agrarian Transition and Social Development in Orissa*", Indian Journal of Political Science, Vol. 54, No.2, April–June, 1993, p. 305.

21. S. R. Mehta, *Emerging Pattern of Rural Leadership*. (New Delhi: Wiley Eastern Pvt. Ltd., 1972), p. 30.

22. Daniel Thorner, *The Shaping of Modern India* (New Delhi: Allied, 1980), p. 239.

23. S. Thirumalai, "*Trends in Rural Change*" in A.R. Desai, (ed.), Rural Sociology in India (Bombay: Popular Prakashan, 1969) p. 691.

24. D.N. Majumdar, "*Fluidity of Status Structure in India*" in A.R. Desai (ed.), Ibid., p. 697.

4
SOCIAL STRUCTURE OF THE VILLAGE

A systematic study and critical analysis of village social structure, which has much significance in every sector of village life—social, economic, political and cultural—and which covers various aspects like the village as a whole, joint-family system, caste, status of women etc., throws much light on rural factional politics. An attempt has been made in this chapter to study how far or to what extent social structure of Nuapada village is responsible for giving rise to factions and factionalism.

India lives in villages. Hence much emphasis has bene laid on their development. Whatever may be the power structure and whoever may be in power, village is taken as a unit of action in the developmental programmes. No doubt, as a community it ensures its social solidarity and acts as a social stabilizer. The joint family system, one of the most important features of the social structure that has been slowly and gradually getting eroded in terms of its importance and significance, confers a status and prestige on those members who have adopted it. Unfortunately, over the years it has proved to be one of the greatest threats to the integrated family life. As the study reveals, it has given rise to bitter factions in the village. Caste, an important base of the social structure in Nuapada, has played a key role as an agency of social control and influenced the socio-economic and political life of the people of Nuapada. Besides, in view of the emerging political involvement of women in rural government and politics in different parts of the country, women groups have assumed a lot of significance, thereby constituting a significant part of the study highlighting the village social life.

Like other Indian villages, the village Nuapada, situated in Ganjam, which is one of the backward districts of Orissa, continues to be the basic unit of socialization, social control and social solidarity. Though marked by caste conflict between the Komtis and the Deras, and the family feuds arising out of the joint-family system, the unity of the whole village, as the study reveals, overrides on many occasions the separateness of each caste or caste factionalism.[1] Nuapada has a separate identity of its own and its people are influenced by the process of modernization. Inspite of this, the basic social orientation is shaped by the village itself. They (people) have love for customs and traditions, respect for the elders, regards for women, faith in the village deity, etc. These are some of the social values created and preserved by the village over the years. Those who defy or violate them are ostracized. It is interesting to note that in one of the festivals of the village i.e. during "Holi Yatra" (the festival which witnesses the people putting vermilion on every one's head) a barber played the mischief by rubbing the itching plants on the faces of others while embracing them. As a result, their faces got swollen with infection. This created a hue and cry in the village. The "Barapataka",[2] the village council, in a meeting condemned his action and imposed a fine of eleven rupees for violating the socio-moral conduct of the village. In another incident it imposed a fine of twenty one rupees on a person belonging to the Komti community for having stolen the electrical bulbs from different houses of the village. There are many such instances proving the effectiveness of village as an agency of social control. But the effectiveness of this role has been declining because of modernization, development of police administration in the village since 1984 and adoption of different legal measures. Of late, the youth of Nuapada are getting more and more exposed to values of modernization and sometimes take a defiant stand against the old values. For example, in 1985 a bank officer, Epari Tejeswar Rao, of the village decided to marry a widow of his own caste. No doubt, the laws do not prohibit it. But at the same time, it is not a common practice. To put it in other words, laws do not prevent it an customs do not approve it. Therefore, Rao's unexpected, though praiseworthy, behaviour invited strong protests not only from his own caste members but also the elders of the village. But, interestingly the youth of the village, irrespective of their caste background, whole heatedly supported the marriage. It may be observed here that Nuapada has been passing through a period of transition witnessing a conflict between the forces of continuity and of change. While the elders represent the former the modern youth of the village stand for the latter.

Social solidarity of the village has been ensured as the people have common faith in the village shrine, in the village deity and ceremonies which require the involvement of all the people irrespective of their caste affiliation. It is interesting to note that during the religious festivals the villagers, breaking the barrier of caste, gather at a particular place of worship to conduct the meetings regarding the finance and programmes of the festivals organized at an interval of every 3 to 4 years. It depends upon the decision of the "Barapataka" when to conduct and how to conduct them. But once a decision is taken all the villagers get involved to make the festival a success. Besides, when a person dies in the village, people belonging to different castes participate in the funeral ceremony directly or indirectly. During the time of any calamities or accidents, the entire village stands united. At the time of need or in case of any emergency, the village atmosphere gets surcharged with a strong feeling of unity and identification. Love for the village brings any amount of sacrifice on the part of the people who fight like bulls whenever the interest of the village is at stake. As said earlier, Nuapada is exposed to the forces of modernization because of its educational, transport and communication facilities and of its economic progress. Thus, village solidarity has not only established a community life, but also accelerated the process of development and modernization. It may be mentioned here that Nuapada for many years had remained under the estate of Badakhemundi, British system of administration was not directly applied to this village. So, it had its own system of administration prescribed by the rulers of the estate. Before independence, administration, both revenue and judicial, of the village was run by a 'Karan' and a 'Karji' respectively. The latter was the village 'Mukhia' (headman) who was appointed on hereditary basis, and he exercised both administrative and judicial power and was responsible for maintaining law and order in the village and deciding different cases of civil and criminal nature. If any one wanted to make any appeal to the king he could do the same only with his permission. On major cases like murder, stabbing, etc. he used to forward them to the king's court. Thus, he was both an administrator and dispenser of justice. 'Karans' were given the responsibilities of maintaining land records of the villagers. But subsequently during post-independence era, this Karji-Karan system was replaced by "Adalati Panchayat", an elected body consisting of five members of the village, which decided cases and settled disputes among the villagers. This became the foundation of a democratic-administrative structure in the village. With the introduction of three-tier system of panchayati Raj, the old Adalati Panchayat system was abolished. Following the introduction of a new judicial and Panchayat Raj systems, district administration and police administration, Nuapada village has lost its significance as an independent administrative unit. However, at present, it is the headquarter of Nuapada panchayat, which covers a number of villages including Nuapada and for its management it depends upon the state government. So, no more, Nuapada is having the same administrative identity as it had before. It is significant to note that the Panchayati Raj system, as has been observed by S.C. Dubey and F.G. Bailey, has strengthened the village solidarity. But interestingly it has been found that in Nuapada the panchayat system has created factions in village politics instead of promoting solidarity as is evident from the findings of the present study.

Joint-Family System

Constituting an important aspect for the social structure, consisting of parents and their married sons and their wives and children, or of brothers and their wives and children, joint-family may be large or small in size. In Nuapada, its size is small. It is a small unit in the sense that it usually consists of the persons as mentioned above. Because Grand father's father or his brothers or sisters are not found in any of the joint-families of the village. Normally when the grand sons become earning members, the joint-families get divided. No doubt, the system has its significance from economic point of view. It plays a dominant role as an agency of social control as members in a joint-family are guided by family norms. In a patriarchal family there is, obviously, a strong supervision and control over the social activities of the members. Joint-family system is normally regarded as an ideal as it has many plus points and advantages. But, unfortunately, in most of the cases the domestic quarrels and dissensions develop after the marriage of the grown-up sons who start thinking about living separately. After separation they start living as nuclear family, consisting of husband and wife and their dependent children. But because of the biological process, when the single family is expanded and all the members continue to live in their parental home the unit once again be classed as a joint-family.

In Nuapada village, the size of joint-families varies from caste to caste as is evident from the following table :

Table 4.1 : Caste and Family Size

Sl. No.	*Caste*	*Total House-hold*	*No. of Joint Family*	*Percent-age*
1.	Komti	70	41	58.40%
2.	Dera	79	45	56.00%
3.	Brahmin (including Kamma)	56	28	50.00%
4.	Keuta	34	11	32.50%
5.	Khadura	28	18	64.02%
6.	Dhobi	42	23	55.00%
7.	Dandasi	40	16	40.00%
8.	Hadi	13	09	69.00%
9.	Redika	12	07	58.00%
10.	Kampa	37	17	46.00%
11.	Barber	22	12	54.50%
12.	Gudia	12	08	66.00%
13.	Teli	09	03	33.00%
14.	Khandayata	14	09	64.00%
15.	Goldsmith	10	06	60.00%
16.	Mali (Archaka)	03	03	100.00%
17.	Parcelia	05	03	60.00%
18.	Carpenter	04	01	25.00%
19.	Karan	11	03	28.00%
20.	Sundhi	04	02	50.00%
21.	Barika	06	05	83.00%
22.	Jangam	03	02	66.00%
23.	Bauri & Others	23	10	43.50%
	Total	**537**	**282**	

The Table 4.1 shows that notwithstanding modernization and urbanization in Nuapada, Joint family system is still a common phenomenon because nearly 52% of the families have gone for it. It is found more in number among the lower castes than in the upper castes as is evident from Table 4.1. The reasons for this are not far to seek. Poor economic background and poverty force the downtroddens to remain together in a joint family. Since the members are economically dependent on one another, they don not feel the necessity of creating nucleus family and inviting more economic hazards. As said earlier, the joint-family system not only ensures a sound economy but also confers a status in the village. The joint-family, naturally, enjoys a greater proprietary status of wealth than the single or nucleus family. It is one of the important reasons for which certain joint-families continue to survive for a long time. This is more particularly so in case of the Komti community. It may be due to the fact that in this caste, the head of the family keeps a record relating to expenses incurred on each and every dependent from his very childhood up to the period of his earning. When he earns he has to repay the amount that was spent on him to the family. But, at the same time, it is significant to note that in this community joint-family system collapses more easily and quickly than what is the case in other communities. Because it is quite an easy job for the division of the parental property among the Komtis. But in other castes it is not the case. The property of the father is distributed among the sons only and married daughters are being given certain amount of his property which is proportional to their identification with the family. The individual earnings do not constitute a part of the parental property.

It is interesting to note that in case of other castes or communities the father (or the eldest son in case of his death) invariably takes care of his children (or brothers), spends money on them so that they can live and grow. And when they start earning money, they handover whatever they earn to their father (or elder brother). This they do until their marriage. Once this is solemnized, they stop making cash payments. Instead they bring necessary articles or provisions for the maintenance of the family. Everything is normal in the family as all its members lead a peaceful life. But, unfortunately, this is not a permanent phenomenon. Co-operation gives way to confrontation, peace to cold war, understanding to misunderstanding, decency and deliberation to distrust, dissension and disintegration, harmony to exchange of harsh words and finally unity to separation. It is significant to observe that in most of the joint-families belonging to almost all the castes, except the Komti community, conflict, confrontation, cold-war, etc. persist for a long time. This may be attributed to the fact that in such joint-families in these communities, the earning members are initially persuaded not to go for separation. But when it falls on their deaf ears the family feud becomes an open subject and the matter is referred to their relatives or the elder member of their kin groups for their interference, suggestions and advice so that the family does not disintegrate. But, unfortunately, the desired end is not achieved. Finally and ultimately, property, the root cause of family dispute, is ultimately divided according to the norms prescribed by the elders in presence of the family members. However, interestingly, the division of property notwithstanding, the family dispute goes on if some members are not satisfied with the way the property was divided. They nourish a grudge against those who acted as mediators in division of property. Such kind of ill-feeling also gets reflected at the time of elections. If one party supports a particular candidate, the other party blindly supports his rival or joins the opposition camp. However, with the passage of time, much of the bitterness of the dispute wears off and gradually cordially returns to the members of the same main family. In certain cases family ceremonies or the village festivals restore cordiality among them.

It has been rightly observed that "Rites connected with the major crisis of the life are great occasion for family reunions. Particularly in the event of death, old quarrels and misunderstandings are generally forgotten and all near-relations assemble for the last rites. In the rituals that follow the presence of all the branches of the family is regarded as obligatory, and the absence of any one on such an occasion is bound to be viewed very seriously."[3]

Joint family system in Nuapada is found to be both functional and dysfunctional. Not only does it create an atmosphere for political interactions but also plays an important role in giving rise to political factions. Because the members, though belong to the same family, have different party affiliations. They work openly in favour of their own party and contest the elections on different political party tickets. It does not, however, mean that their relationship is characterized by hostility, animosity and rancour-as is evident from the fact that they forget all their political differences the moment they step into the drawing room of their home. Interestingly, they sometimes discuss among themselves the political strategies of their respective political parties. That in some way helps the local units of the political parties to know about each other's strategy on different issues. It also promotes a friendly political interaction among different parties an prevents acrimonious feelings against each other. At the same time, it should be noted that the collapse of joint-families often gives rise to political factions in the village politics. If one brother supports one party, the other one becomes a natural enemy and prefers the opposite party. This happens because of the unpleasant situations that occur at the time of division of property. Thus, joint-family which is an important variable in the social structure of the village, is still found predominantly and plays a substantial role in social control, solidarity and better political interaction.

Caste

In Nuapada, caste is, as is the case in other Indian villages, an important unit of the village social structure as well as an important variable in village politics. Not only does it create social stratification, but also plays an active role in social control and social interaction in the village. Quite a large number of scholars have worked on one or another aspect of caste, which is more or less a unique phenomenon of the Indian society.[4] These studies have been made particularly by the American and European scholars with a great concern because of the rigidity of the caste structure. However, a new dimension i.e. caste under the impact of the growing forces of change has attracted the attention of social scientists, administrators and others.[5] Today, the trained social scientists, mainly those interested in social change, stress more on the innovation aspect. Because of various factors planned and non-planned, legal and voluntary, diffusional and evolutionary working of change in the structural and functional aspects of caste, there is a pressing need to study processes and reactions (as Srinivas has done) in the changing caste society.[6]

Under the framework of social change, the approach to the study of caste is more innovation oriented. Caste as a structural model and as an important functional group is highlighted. However, before making observations on the role of caste in Nuapada village politics, it will be pertinent to make a theoretical analysis of the origin, meaning and the role of castes in general.

According to Manu, the ancient Law-giver of India, the ancient Indian society was divided into four Varnas i.e., Brahmin Khyatriya, Vaisya and Sudra were created by God.[7] They performed different functions and had different rights and obligations. But, in due course of time, these caste started interacting among themselves at socio-cultural level. As a result, the rigidity of the caste structure or system got diluted. This was catalyzed and influenced by various social factors prevailing at different periods of time. This mixing and inter-mixing resulted in the origin of various social groups which assumed the present form of castes.[8]

It may be noted that the caste is an institution whose membership is governed by the principles of birth, endogamy, purity and pollution, distance, inter-dining and drinking, in that order.[9] But it should be mentioned that the caste-structure during Manu's time was never based on birth. It was one's role that determined his caste.

Weber attempted to understand caste as a system of social stratification. He pointed out that 'castes are strictly endogamous, hereditary groups arranged in a hierarchy of relative inferiority and superiority. Also that caste groups are characterised by a hereditary occupation so that the division of society into castes is roughly a functional division of labour...'.[10] About the nature of caste Hutton writes "Each caste is a social unit in itself. The customs by which it lives are generally different in some respects from those of other castes and are sometimes in marked contrast to those of any other caste at all. Persons of one caste do not marry in another caste. The extent to which persons of one caste will eat or drink with those of another is strictly limited by unwritten laws and everybody knows who is affected by them..."[11]

The trained social anthropologists and sociologists are no longer interested in origin but in the working of caste as a system of social stratification. The works made by many scholars provide an insight into the working of the caste system in its various aspects and in its relation with other aspects of social structure. Castes have been defined in terms of styles of life. They also constitute the status groups. Property and occupation enter as important elements in the style of life of a status group. Social honour in the caste system is very closely tied to ritual values. Thus, there arise restrictions among Brahmins on the eating of various kinds of food. Caste is, therefore, to be defined in ritual terms and this what makes it different from other systems of social stratification.[12] It is a hereditary endogamous usually localised group, having a traditional association with an occupation and a particular position in the local hierarchy of castes. Relations between castes are governed among other things by the concepts of pollution and purity and generally, maximum commensality occurs within a caste."[13] Castes, as status groups, may be defined essentially in terms of styles of life.

Thus, castes constitute the most universal social structure of Indian society and no society in the world is more highly structured or stratified.[14] Writing on the social structure of Hinduism, Pannikar (1961:29) observes—"The structure revolves round two fundamental institutions: the caste and the joint-family. Everything connected with the Hindu people outside their religion, is related to these two institutions. These, in fact, are the differentiating characteristics of Hindu life.[15]

The characteristics of caste, as is evident from the above, are as follows :

It is a system of social stratification; an endogamous and hereditary group; governed by social precedence, with a Brahmin at the head of the hierarchy; has distinctive styles of life and constitutes a status group; there are restrictions on feeding and social intercourse;—there are minute rules as to what sort of food or drink can be accepted by a person and from what caste; there is a lack of unrestricted choice of occupation; there is a functional division of labour.

Caste Structure in the Village

In Nuapada village there are 23 caste groups.[16] The settlement pattern of different castes in the village is accordingly to their social status. It affects their social interaction also. The pattern is that socially higher castes occupy the central place in the village whereas people belonging to low castes and untouchables live on its outskirts. Significantly a vacant piece of land demarcates these two territories.

It is a natural tendency that members of the same caste want to live together. It may be observed that social distance is still maintained or observed in Nuapada, although it is exposed to the forces of urbanization and modernization. However, such kind of feeling has undergone a radical change to a great extent. Localities are still arranged along caste lines. Streets are named after the castes, e.g. brahmin street, the Komti street, the weaver street, the washerman street, the fisherman street, the Kampa street, the untouchable street, etc. Arrangement of streets on caste lines illustrates the dominance of the caste system in the village.

As it has been pointed out earlier that caste is identifiable with occupational specialization. Different occupations carry different status in a village. Hence the caste and their traditional occupations have been dealt with. This is followed by a section on occupational shifts and social mobility in the sphere of interaction between castes. Inter-caste relations have been touched upon with a view to highlight an idea of their changing complexion. And lastly, some of the changes have been enumerated and discussed.

Brahmins

Among different castes the Brahmins hold the highest place. The Brahmin caste in the traditional sense is known for its learning, knowledge and priestly service. In Nuapada, of 56 Brahmin families, 29 of them are the permanent settlers of the village. Others are the immigrants who have settled there to serve in different government or semi-governmental institutions. Further, of 29 families (who claim to be the permanent settlers) three of them came from different places of the district (Ganjam) more than fifty years ago to serve as teachers. Over the years they have acquired lands, constructed their own houses. They are now men of means. The Brahmins are mostly Vaishnavites, the worshippers of Lord Vishnu. It is said that their ancestors at one time or other were either priests or acted as "Pujaris" by rendering services to Lord Vishnu.

It is interesting to note that in Nuapada four sub-castes of Brahmin are found: Danua, halua, Padhia and Sanjabi. Danua Brahmins are called so as they receive "Dana" or gift from others including Brahmins belonging to other sub-castes. The Halua Brahmins are the temple priests. They serve the God as well as the temple. They cook food for the God, look after the administration of temple, keep accounts of its income and expenditure. They cultivate the temple land withe their own bullocks. The Padhia Brahmins have their separate identity. They are either in charge of administration or act as teachers. Padhia Brahmins have their own landed property. Some of the lands they have are "Inam"[17] lands and as such they were free from revenues. They do not plough the land. They give their lands to the tenants on share cropping. Sanjabi Brahmins, the lowest in the ranks, plough their lands.

It may be noted that while some male members of some Brahmin sub-castes engage themselves, whenever necessary, in some form of agricultural work, their women folk normally abstain from doing such work. They remain themselves largely confined within the four walls of the house. Economic pressures, however, fail some to abide by the caste norms. A widow, helpless and poor, is rather forced by the situation to work in the field as an agricultural labourer to earn her livelihood. And whenever she does not get any work she does some menial jobs like stitching the leafs. Although there is a caste prejudice against the mánual labour, the Brahmin widow is bound to do it for her subsistence. It may be observed that economic constraints have led to occupational mobility among different castes.

The Brahmins, who undesirably claim themselves to be 'pure and high born' do not accept food from the hands of low caste people. Even there is no inter-dining among all the sub-castes. Though there is a lot of change in the value system following urbanization, modernization and industrialization, it is unfortunate that even the Sanjabi Brahmins remain aloof from other Brahmins. Other Brahmins—Danuas, Padhias and Haluas—do not attend the rituals performed by the Sanjabis.

Today the caste ideology no longer promises the livelihood to Brahmin families even if they pursue the caste occupation of priesthood. No doubt, the Brahmin caste occupies the top position in caste hierarchy. But no more they command that respect from other as they used to get the same earlier. Gone are those days when low caste people used to bow before them out of respect, love and fear. In day-to-day life, they are not treated as superior. The Komtis, infact, are much more vocal and assertive. They are now very dominant in every sphere—social, economic and political, though certain religious ceremonies are performed by the Brahmins alone. It may be mentioned that the elders or the old members of some Brahmins alone. It may be mentioned that the elders or the old members of some Brahmin families opt to perform the caste occupation of priesthood. Many of them are either in service or cultivate the land. Thus, gradually there is the occupational diversification of the Brahmins in the village. Those who secure jobs in nearby towns or elsewhere, do not want to come back to the village. They want to settle in the towns for promotion of education of their children.

The Brahmins of Nuapada take passive role in the political process of the village: partly because of their weak financial position and partly because they do not want to incur the displeasure of any one by joining any faction as they are serving as priests in the temples. But, however, the younger generation of the Brahmin caste takes interest in participating in the political activities of the village.

In Nuapada there is a 'Matha' (temple) known as "Balaji Matha", which is managed by a 'Mathadhisa' (Administrator) or 'Mahanta', a bachelor Brahmin. An unmarried person can only succeed him. He chooses a Brahmin child of his choice to manage the temple as well as its movable and immovable property after his death. This is approved later by the Endowment Board after his death. He is popularly called as 'Mahanta'. Lord "Balji", which is now called as "Balaji", is the most famous God in this village. Out of their devotion some people have donated some land to the temple. But gradually the Mahanta, who is also reverently called 'Guru' by the people belonging to the 'Sundhi' (wine-seller) community as he initiates them into the spiritual path, becomes the owner of the temple property.

It is significant to observe that Mahantas, who are supposed to play an important role in the sphere of culture and religion, have started evincing keen interest in politics as evident from the fact that for two times a Mahanta became the Sarpanch of Nuapada panchayat. But some times their sexual escapades, social life and political behaviour have contributed to the rise of factionalism in village politics, which is discussed in detail in the next chapter.

Komti

Ranked as the Vaisyas, Komtis are mostly engaged in trade, business and money-lending. In the field of business and trade they excel others and it has therefore, been very rightly said that they are born traders. In Nuapada, almost all the important shops are owned by them. It may not therefore, be wrong to say that business is their monopoly and no other caste can compete with them. It may be noted that in the absence of poor communication between Nuapada and other nearby villages the people of these villages used to depend exclusively on it for their business transactions. But with the improved communication facilities the situation has undergone radical change. Shops have opened in almost all the villages. As a result, the business interest of the Komtis has been adversely affected. In order to overcome this crisis and meet the new challenges, they have adopted various measures to keep their business intact. For example, some of them have shifted their shops to other villages, some changed the nature of their business, some become the whole sellers of different items. Communication development has, thus seriously affected the trade monopoly of the Komtis.

The Komtis, who are normally rich, are money-lenders. It is because of this, people call them "Sahukars" (masters). Under its customary purview, the system involved economic as well as social dimensions. Socially, a Sahukar has a strong hold over the families to whom he lent money. The borrowers are obliged to respect them. The latter give some money as loan to the people for buying bullocks and agricultural implements, or for performing or solemnizing festivals or ceremonies like marriage, etc. The loan is sanctioned against some security like land, gold, house etc. Poor, ignorant and illiterate peasants and workers borrow loan without knowing the fact that they have to pay a heavy interest. In certain cases accounts are maintained by the lender alone; the borrower simply puts his thumb impression on the account book, without understanding the entries. A mortgage is not insisted upon in all cases, but the rate of interest charged is not only exorbitant and high but also compounded. The Komtis also advance seed grain to the people. For this also they charge heavy interest. Some people from the nearby villages and particularly the Sauras (a scheduled tribe) of Batarada, Kamarakhali, Badua and Debipur villages take loans against a part of the crops. The creditor alone fixes the rates of crop product at the time of harvest when the debtor had to sell it off to him to adjust against the outstanding dues. Such rates were lower than those of the market price. All these practices have resulted in severe exploitation of the helpless farmers by the greedy Sahukars.

It is interesting to note that a Komti is "a born coward, but a shrewd business man. When he says something on oath, take it that he is telling a deliberate falsehood." 'He spares no ingenuity to save even a counterfeit coin. 'God do not penalize a Komti for telling lies, he is born to do that.' The stories of their cowardice are also many and quite interesting. "A Komti is a warrior in words, but a rat in deeds." 'If you strike him a second time, he will say, 'strike me a third time and I shall show you what it means to beat me'. You go on beating him, and all that he will do is to repeat his threats without having the courage to hit back even once.'[18] All this is true. But with the passage of time the situation has slightly improved as the younger generations of Komtis do not tolerate or digest any kind of humiliation and in some cases react immediately which leads to conflict. Of course, in many cases they too do not take any thing seriously even if it affects their business.

The Komtis, who reside in Orissa, are called Kalinga Vaisya. Unlike their counterparts in Andhra, they are non-vegetarian. However, they do not take fish or meat regularly. During festive occasion of their families like marriage, etc., they are strictly vegetarian and keep their houses very clean. Orthodox Komti women also bath before meals and eat food wearing a separate cloth as orthodox Brahmin women do. Economic superiority together with the ritual status enables the community to occupy the social status next to Brahmins in the village. They do not marry outside their caste. Inter-caste marriage is still a taboo and looked upon with contempt and derision. As they hail from the Andhra Pradesh they established their matrimonial relations with the Andhra Komtis. Of 70 households, 20 families have gone for such relations. They have 12 lineages. Seeing the economic conditions they have cross-cousin and uncle-niece marriages in the village itself.

In Nuapada the Komti caste has a caste organization. In order to strengthen the caste fund, one per cent of the 'dowry' is to be paid to the fund by the newly married persons. Now they have their own "pentho house" i.e. their "caste hall" which is meant to accommodate the people during marriage or at the time of death ceremony of the caste people. Some Komtis offer 'Dana' (gift of rice, dal and some vegetables) to the Brahmins daily. Four families of this caste provide four meals a day to the needy and poor people through the Satya Narain temple which is centrally located in the village and managed by the community itself.

Although they are traders, they do not neglect agriculture. They are the owners of fertile and irrigated lands of the village. It is quite significant to note that, of late they have started joining professions like medicines, law, engineering etc. and other government and non-government services. In other words, most of them have become job-oriented. They are financially sound and this economic power has given them a tremendous boost to play dominant role in village politics.

Dera

Deras, the weavers, are also known as 'Tanti' in other parts of Orissa. Like Komtis they also hail from Andhra Pradesh. It is, therefore, natural that they have interactions with Deras of that state through marriage etc. There are 31 families in Nuapada who have given their daughters and sons in marriage in Andhra. They have 14 lineages. In the village also marriages can take place among the different lineages. They do not prefer to have common dining with people of any other caste. They try to retain their own identity and want to lead homogeneous and secluded life. Interestingly, they do not take food from the Brhamins—nor allow the people of other castes to construct houses in their street. However, a few of them are forced to sell their houses to other caste members following their failure to repay the loan. Gradually other caste people are making an inroad into their territory. But the situation is changing fast because of their exposure to the forces of modernization and urbanization. As a result, the young Deras have not only started taking food with other castes but also inviting them to attend their socio-cultural functions. They have, of late, been taking food from the Brahmins, Komtis, Khaduras and of course very rarely from Sunari (goldsmith) and Barbers (Bhandaris). They do not attend any such ritual functions of lower castes particularly the untouchables.

Like Brahmins and Komtis, Deras also have distanced themselves from their traditional occupation. Those who are qualified seek jobs in different offices. Some of them are also engaged in various kinds of business. It may, however, be noted that most of them are bound by their traditional profession as they are not prepared to give it up. But, at the same time, it does not mean that they will forego their jobs, if at all they get them and stick to their profession. It is probably because of lack of opportunity to get any job that has forced them to carry on their profession. And they have no choice other than sticking to it. Deras are included in the other backward castes very recently. Weaving is their traditional occupation. They are generally poor. Of 79 families, 62 of them have no land. Because of poverty and backwardness, they have to depend on others including 'Sahukars' for financial help. They borrow money from them with heavy interest to purchase threads for weaving purpose. It becomes quite difficult on their part to repay the amount. As a result, their economic condition deteriorates further and further.

It may be mentioned that in the year 1951 for the first time a co-operative society was established for the purpose of providing raw-materials to the weavers as well as for marketing their products. Every member of the Dera community, particularly, a weaver can become its member by paying twenty one rupees as membership fee. These members elect the executive body of the society consisting of the president, secretary, manager and other members. They are elected for five years and become responsible for the management of the society. Such an organization has become very much beneficial for the weavers. Since 1985 the government has also extended financial assistance through this organization to the people for the social and economic rehabilitation of the weavers.

It may be mentioned that whatever clothes the weavers weave are to be sold to the co-operative society, which in turn, sells to different shops. As a result, the weavers are not getting their expected profit. It is quite marginal for them. Their labour is not properly rewarded. They work hard, yet they suffer. They feel that it is their fate. At the same time, it should be noted that their present economic condition is far better than what it was earlier, particularly prior to independence. Setting up of co-operative societies has gone a long way in protecting and promoting their interests and preventing them from being mercilessly exploited by the 'Sahukars'. Some weavers have been provided with powerlooms at subsidised rates and also have received financial assistance for electrification, construction of their houses etc. But because of nepotism and favouritism resorted to by the people at the helm of affairs in the co-operative the poorest section among the weavers not only suffers but also victimised. Resentment and dissatisfaction among them resulted in the formation of another society. The existence of these two co-operative organisations in the village at present has divided members of the Dera community both in social and political spheres. The situation takes an ugly turn when political leaders make attempts to make political capital out of it.

Keuta *(Fisherman)*

There are 34 Keuta families in the village. Their traditional occupation is fishing in the ponds, tanks and rivers and sell them in the market. It is their main source of livelihood. Hence, the tanks of nearby Gram Panchayats including this village are taken on lease by them. But this traditional occupation does not help them in meeting their demands and requirements. Hence, they are bound to choose some other professions, besides their traditional one. Poor and landless, they work as agricultural labourers during the crop seasons. Some of them have their own bullocks and plough the land on share cropping. It may be noted that only two members of this community have got opportunities to work as low grade government servants. They accept food from the clean castes like Brahmin, Komti, Khadura, Kampa but they cannot accept food from other scheduled castes of the village. The Dhobis, Dandasis, Barikas and Hadis used to take food from the Keutas. They have their own caste council which is hierarchical in nature.

Khadura

Khaduras, otherwise known as Kansaris in other parts of Orissa are shrewd and cunning businessmen and in this sphere rank second to the Komtis. Their traditional occupation is to sell Brass and Aluminium utensils. It is rather their monopoly. It is not only confined to their village but its domain extends to remote tribal as well as agency areas like Cheligada, Udayagiri, Turubudi etc. Of course, in recent years two Komtis have intruded into their business by setting up Aluminium utensil shops in the village.

The women folk of the Khadura community are engaged in stitching the leafs which are used as dining plates. In this area, Nuapada is famous for it. People from Berhampur town also come to this place to purchase the same. Of twenty-eight families, sixteen of them have the landed property in different villages. Hence, they also take interest in agriculture. But none of the members of this caste, either male or female is engaged as agricultural labourer. The educated and qualified persons are holding certain jobs in central or state or semi-governmental institutions. Traditionally they do not accept food from Komtis, Kampas and others except Brahmins. But today, barring the untouchables and scheduled castes like Keutas, they accept food from others and extend an invitation to them to participate in their socio-cultural function.

In the political field, they remain active and take decisions whether to support any candidate or not at the time of election. But, unfortunately, they are apathetic to and have little interest in any such developmental activities of the village.

Dhoba *(Washerman)*

There are 42 Dhoba families in the village. They are treated as impure caste because they clean the clothes of all the clean castes. They do not serve the Dandasis, Hadis and Barikas, who are the untouchables with the lowest ritual rank. Dobas are associated with the cleaning of clothes of women which they use during the menstrual cycle. All of them have consistently been pursuing their traditional occupation, although, except three households, all of them are at the same time agricultural labourers.

They have their strong caste organization, which regulates the area of their operation. Each washerman is allotted a particular 'Basti' or 'Sahi' (street) of the village. That washerman can only wash the clothes of the people belonging to that area. It is traditionally known as 'Jajamani' system where there is a formal relationship between the patrons and their clients in their respective area of functions. For their service, the Jajmans pay them on a yearly basis. Only married persons and couples are taken as units to estimate the amount of grain that one family has to pay to the washerman. A married person with his wife is considered to be a unit. A widow or widower is also considered to be one unit. For each unit, the family which receives Dhoba's service has to pay twelve Kgs. of paddy every year which is counted from one harvesting season to the next one. For the unmarried people of the family, the Dhobas do not charge any fee on the basis of custom. For the service-holders who are coming from different areas, the Dhobas charge Rs. 5/- for each menstrual cycle and the prescribed amount for washing the clothes of their dependent children of the employees.

The Dhobis have no land. Only three families have some land. Men and Women of the caste hire out their labour in the agriculture market. Some families have their bullocks and cultivate the lands on share-cropping. During off seasons, women work on daily wage basis in the construction works. Some go to the forest to collect fuel wood for sale in the village. The traditional occupation does not help in fulfilling their minimum requirements. They, therefore, choose other occupations too like tailoring, driving, carpentry, etc. Because of the reservation facilities provided to them in the government jobs, some tend to become engineers, pharmacists, clerks, peons, etc. in various governmental organizations.

Previously they were not admitted to the houses of the upper caste members. Nor were they allowed to enter into the hotels. But now the situation has undergone a change. But they are yet to find an entry into the houses of Brahmins.

It is significant to note that in the political sphere only three persons of this community are active. They not only contest in the panchayat elections but also mobilize their caste voters at the time of other elections in the village. They lead the untouchables of the village during the elections.

Dandasi

Dandasis are impure and untouchables, because of their profession of rearing country pigs living on stool and slush. Secondly, they eat pork and drink country liquor which down-grade their ritual status. There are thirty one Dandasi families in the village. Since they are landless, they are forced to work for others as labourer. Their traditional occupation is to vigil the village boundary and watch the crops. Accordingly, at the time of harvest, the land-owners pay some paddy or other products to them. But, due to expansion of their family, they fail to meet the requirements. As there is no such landed property provided to them by the villagers, now some of them are engaged as agricultural labourers. Others are working as daily wage labourers. They also sell fuel wood which they collect from forests. Previously they did not accept food from Dhobas. But today, they are accepting the same from them as well as Keutas and other superior castes. Yet they are neither accepting nor giving food to the Hadis, which forms the lowest caste among the untouchables.

Hadi

Hadis occupy the lowest position among the untouchables. There are thirteen Hadi families having seven lineages—among whom inter-marriage takes place. They have also matrimonial relations in other parts of the district. One Dhusa Ghadei is a service-holder and as such his financial position is sound. He is having some landed property and pucca building. All others are landless labourers. Their traditional occupation is drum beating. Interestingly, they also take the street of the Goldsmith on lease and through processing of dust and waste materials they collect gold. This enables them to earn something for their subsistence. They have not any share in the social values as they have been subject to social injustice and exploitation. They cannot enter into temples nor the hotels in the village. Disgusted and dissatisfied, they constructed their own temple known as "Trinath Mandir" within the complex where they are staying. But, unfortunately, this has given rise to a lot of resentment among the upper caste people as they wanted to construct a bus stand in that area. The latter insist that the temple should be shifted from that place to some other area. But Hadis are rigid in their stand i.e. not to shift the temple. The unfortunate thing is that it has given rise to a caste war between the untouchables and the caste Hindus. Hadis are the scavengers of the village. For their service, they get payment from the panchayat. They are now preparing handicrafts out of Bamboos and sell them in the market.

Redika

Of twelve Redika families in the village, only two of them have some landed property. The rest of them have enlisted their names in the labour class. Two are engaged in tailoring, one is postal runner and another is working in a cloth mill at Surat in Gujrat. Both men and women engage themselves in all sorts of work ranging from construction of houses to working in agricultural fields as daily labourers. Their financial position is not sound. In the socio-cultural life they do not have any role to play.

Kampa

Kampas are the agriculturists as cultivation of land is their main occupation. Of thirty seven families, nineteen of them are landless. Yet all of them, like other low castes, are invariably engaged in cultivating their own lands or of others on share-cropping. Most of them have their bullocks, plough and other agricultural implements. During transplantation and harvesting seasons, after finishing their work, they work for others on hired basis. But most of them are poor. Hence, agricultural work does not serve their purpose. As a result, some work as mill drivers, 'mestris' (masons) etc. Only three persons of this caste have jobs (two as teachers and a one as a peon).

Interestingly, Kampas have a regional organization which regulates the behaviours of the caste people staying in different villages. Because of their numerical strength, they have become an important factor in the regional politics. In 1986–87, their organizations witnessed a split because of their different political affiliations. Some of them formed an organization and named it "Pradhan Samaj" instead of keeping its title as Kampa Samaj. They felt that the work 'Kampa' indicated an inferior status in the society. Those who joined the organisation i.e. the 'Pradhan Samaj' came to be known as Pradhans, the higher ups and those who did not remain as Kampas. Thus, the Kampa caste split up into two: Pradhans and Kampas. Naturally, it has serious repercussion on their socio-political relations. A detailed analysis of it has been made in the chapter on factional politics in the village.

Barber *(Bhandari)*

In Nuapada, there are twenty two barber families. Of them,

only two of them have some landed property. The rest are poor, landless and depend for their livelihood on their traditional occupation i.e. to cut hair and nails and shave the beards of he upper caste people. It is because of this profession or occupation they enjoy a very low status in the caste hierarchy. Like other professional castes like Dhoba and others, barbers have also their caste organization which regulates their area of operation of its caste people. Each Barber household is allotted a particular street of the village to take care of by rendering his professional service. And in return he gets his salary mostly in cash. The *quid pro quo* is regulated by the 'Jajmani' system. Normally, each barber family gets ten kilos of paddy from each household allotted to them by their caste on hereditary basis. No barber is supposed to encroach upon the activities of another barber. Of late, a few of them have set up some shops in the village. Interestingly, untouchables like Hadis, Dandasis and Bauris are not allowed to enter to these shops. These Barbers also extend their services to the upper caste people living in nearby villages. During marriage or any such ritual ceremonies they use to go and serve them by helping them in taking their baths by cutting their nails, by supplying small pieces of wood for "homo" (Yajna) etc. and in exchange of their services they get both cash and kind. Traditional occupation has failed them to meet their demands and requirements. Hence, the women prefer to work as agricultural labourers. Besides this, some of them have adopted tailoring as profession. One has become a clerk and another a peon in the local college and still another serves as a dressing man in the local government hospital. However, the economic conditions of the barbers are not sound in the village.

Gudia

There are twelve Gudia families in the village. Only two of them are the owners of some landed property. Others are landless. Their traditional occupation is to prepare parched rice (Muri) and parched paddy (Lia). As the traditional occupation cannot satisfy their wants they have changed their occupation. Now, eight families are engaged in small business in the village. Four of them are having pan shops and rest are the owners of the small hotels. Still three families have their traditional occupation. The educated and qualified persons are engaged in government jobs. Significantly, the community has produced an engineer, a pharmacist and a postman. They also attend the functions and ceremonies of higher castes and prepare different kinds of sweets in and outside the village. Some women out of bare necessity are working as agricultural labourers during the harvest season. They accept food from the higher castes in the village.

Teli

There are nine Teli families in the village. They prepare the oil and sell it. But it may be noted that none of them is engaged in his traditional occupation. Only three families have around one and half acre of land for cultivation. Most of them are engaged as daily wage labourers. They have diversified their occupation and today it has been found that one family has a pan shop in the village, another has a mike set and two of them are the owners of small cosmetic shops. A member of this community is a police constable. The economic conditions of the Telis are not sound. In the social hierarchy they come next to Kampas.

Khandayats

There are fourteen Khandayat families in Nuapada. Of them five are not the permanent inhabitants of the village. Heads of these families are working in different offices. They have come from other parts of the district. Six families have some land. Most of the members of this caste are agricultural labourers. Two persons are engaged in small business and one is working as a peon in the local high school. In the social hierarchy they come next to Komtis in the village. They accept food from Brahmins, Komtis, Khaduras, Kampas etc. They are busy in their own affairs and as such they do not seem to evince any interest in the village politics.

Goldsmith *(Sunari)*

There are ten goldsmith families in the village. They make ornaments of gold and silver and sell them in the market. This they also do on orders placed by private parties. This is their traditional occupation. Except one family, the rest do not have any land. Now-a-days people prefer to purchase the golden/silver ornaments directly, from the Berhampur market. Hence, the people's rush to the goldsmith's house have been reduced. The latter, therefore, in addition to their traditional occupation, prefer to do the cycle repairing centres in the village. The women of this caste also used to work as agricultural labourers during the harvest season. A member of this community is engaged in the local nationalised bank and gets his wage as per banking system. His duty is to weigh the gold and to certify its purity on the basis of which the bank provides loans to the loanees.

Mali *(Archaka)*

There are three Archaka or "Mali" families in the village. Their traditional occupation is to look after the temple and serve its God or Goddess with devotion and dedication. They have attained proficiency in blowing conches in the temple and at the wedding ceremonies and other auspicious occasions of the clean castes. The land which is in the name of the temple is divided among the Malis. This was previously granted to them in lieu of their service to the Goddess temple. But, however, they cannot sell these lands to anybody. Besides this temple service, they also cultivate land with their own bullocks. It is pertinent to note that women of this caste, unlike those of other caste's, are not engaged in agriculture. It may be observed here that they attach more importance to agriculture. Some of them are also educated and qualified. Two of them are teachers in primary schools. One member after passing the matriculation started a "Palli Srota Mandali."[19] They discuss political affairs after listening to new items on radio. After the establishment of the college in the village in the year 1980, he got himself educated and now is a lecturer in a private college.

Parcelia

There are five Parcelia families in the village, whose traditional occupation is to prepare "Hooka" from the black leafs and sell them in market. Its size is like that of a cigarette. But its colour is black. Till today, they are engaged in their traditional occupation. Significantly, a particular family of this caste is very rich. The head of the family is a rich farmer having his own bullocks, servants, workers and agricultural instruments. He has two sons: one is a lecturer and the other one is not only a businessman but also an active politician. The family is not only having a flourishing opium business but also earns a lot of money through money-lending. It is, however, to be noted that the rate of interest charged on money-lending is quite reasonable. Hence, there is a mad rush on the part of the people to borrow money from the family. However, money-lending is limited to certain reliable parties only. Of course, money is leant against some security. Other families of this caste are landless. Besides their traditional occupation, they are also engaged in other activities. One of them is a clerk in Orissa State Electricity Board and another has become a police constable. It may be noted that the economic condition of the parcelias is not sound. Some of them have their matrimonial relations in Andhra Pradesh. They accept food from the higher castes in the village. On all such festive occasions of the village like pongal etc., some families of this caste distribute rice, clothes etc. among the Brahmins, poor and the beggars.

Kamma ***(Telgu Brahmin)***

There are only three Kamma families in Nuapada. They act as priests of Telgu families. In one family there is only one widow who has no children, in another its members (male) are working in government service while in the last family its head is still engaged in its traditional occupation i.e. priesthood even after his retirement from his government service as a school teacher. He performs all the rituals for the Komtis and Parcelias. On such occasions his services are highly indispensable. It may be noted that his sincere service has made him very popular in the village. That is why after his retirement from his service, the people elected him as the "Samiti" member of Nuapada Gram-Panchayat in the year 1992 as an independent candidate.

The Kammas have some landed property. But they have given their land to the tenants for cultivation on share-cropping. Since they belong to the higher caste they do not accept food from other castes, unless it is cooked by the Brahmins.

Karan

Of eleven Karan families, ten of them are "foreigners" as they are working here in different offices. Soon after their transfer or retirement they will leave the place. Only members of one family are said to be the permanent residents of the village. But it is said that the head of the family or his parents never belonged to this village. He came here as a Mohurior at the Revenue Inspector's Office in the village. Recently, he retired from the service. He has his permanent immovable property in this village. Karanas belong to upper caste and they have a decisive voice in the administration.

Sundhi

There are four Sundhi families in the village and their traditional occupation is to sell the wine. Three families are very deeply involved in it as it brings a good fortune to them." Although trade in country liquor is lucrative, it is socially condemned. Hence, the sundhis are considered to be a low caste. It is because of their profession no higher or middle caste people dine with them. However, the lower untouchables accept food from the Sundhis.

Swami (*Jangam*) : There are three Jangam families in the village. They are Telugu speaking people and act as the priests of the Dera community by performing all such "Sradhas" and rituals for them. Their traditional occupation is, however, temple service. They serve the Iswar temples of Nuapada village and are proficient in blowing conches in the temples. During the month of "Sagittarius" which generally falls in the month of December–January, a Jangam goes to the Dera streets in evening and blows the conch in high pitch thereby making a loud noise. The significance of this event lies in the beliefs that the priest invites the ancestors to bless the people of the Dera community in the village. This practice is still going on with much enthusiasm and interest. As they are the Sevayats of the temple, they get financial assistance from the temple. Besides this temple service, some members of the community are engaged in some other occupations like tailoring etc.

Carpenter

There are four carpenter families in the village. Interestingly, all of them are immigrants as they have migrated from nearby villages to seek and search after their livelihood. They get their daily wages by making wooden furniture. They get sufficient work in the village. A carpenter usually takes food from the clean castes only.

Barika

Barika is a lower caste rather a scheduled tribe. There are six Barika families in the village. All are landless and agricultural labourers. Only one of them is a mail career engaged in local post office. This is his part-time service.

Bauri :- Untouchables, landless, illiterate and poor, bauris work as daily wage workers either in agricultural lands for keep themselves engaged in the construction works. The women too are not only engaged in these works but also collect fuel wood from the Jungles and sell them in the village. They accept food from the Dhobas, Keutas and other clean castes and play a very insignificant role in village politics.

Caste Hierarchy

To trace the hierarchical gradation of the castes in a village is a very difficult task not only in Nuapada but also in other parts of India. The criteria used for the ranking of castes and their placement in a hierarchy are highly controversial. Some of the informants though belong to the lower castes, do not want today to be classed as lower and for that reason, do not regard their occupation as low, compared to the occupations of other castes of the same group. For instance, a Hadi is not prepared to consider his caste or occupation as inferior to that of a Dandasi or Bauri. Though all the castes like Hadi, Dandasi and Bauri belong to the category of lower caste, in actual practice, the former is much inferior to the latter. Under this complex situation the traditionally ascribed on hereditary status has been adopted as the sound principle of caste hierarchy. In India, castes are generally graded on the basis of occupation and ritual purity.[20] Hence, according to their occupation, commensality, practice relating to inter-dining, inter-personal behaviour, diet etc., the hierarchical arrangement of different castes in Nuapada is described in the table given below:

[Table 4.2] Hierarchy of Castes in Village Nuapada

[Caste rank level]

1.	Brahmin			Kamma		
2.	Komti			Swami (Jangam)		
3.	Khadura Dera	Parcelia Kampa	Karan	Gudia	Teli	Khandayat
4.	Redika	Mali				
5.	Barber Sundhi	Sunari (Goldsmith)	Carpenter			
6.	Keuta					
7.	Dhoba					
8.	Dandasi hadi	Bauri		Barika		

Thus, at the top tier of the caste hierarchy, there is the Brahmins, because tradition assigns it a predominant position. The untouchable castes like Dandasi, Bauri, Hadi etc. though originally left outside of varna system, are subordinate to all the castes. They have not any share in the social values. They were subject to social injustice and exploitation. They had to work for other castes. Due to recommendation of Mandal Commission some of the clean castes are included in the Other Backward Castes. These castes are Parcelia, Dera, Badhei (Carpenter), Barika (Bhandari), Gudia, Mali & Kharudas.

Caste Mobility

Caste mobility in Nuapada village is a marked phenomenon due to the introduction of the process of urbanization, westernization and industrialization and due to the process of sanskritization. Caste rigidity has been lessened but as mentioned earlier, Nuapada village has been passing through a period of transition. So, people with old values still observe the caste rules strictly whereas the present generation challenge such principles.

Different caste organisations exist in the village to defend the caste barriers and prevent the social mobility of the castes and to achieve their desired socio-economic goals. Unfortunately, they are mainly responsible for caste tension in the village. They have also brought cosmetic changes in the caste structure and have elevated their caste position in caste hierarchy. In other words, the caste hierarchical structure exists in the village without any meaning and relevance. That is why though according to caste hierarchical structure, Brahmins are at the top, but in reality, it is the Komtis who have replaced them in the socio-economic and political life of the village. It may be mentioned that caste organizations exists in the village only among the caste groups like Komti, Teli, Kampa, Barika, Redika and other untouchable castes like Dhobi, Dandasi, Hadi, Bauris etc. But the higher castes like Brahmins and Kammas do not have any organisation and have almost become secondary in the socio-economic and political life of the village.

Caste mobility in the village has led to the inter caste dining, inter-caste marriage and widow marriage system. It is, however, significant to note that such changes have been seriously challenged and vehemently opposed by the so-called vanguards and veterans of the caste structure. It may be mentioned that when the people belonging to different castes meet to dine together, people from lower castes serve food to the members of upper caste. A Sudra serves rice to a Brahmin. But as mentioned earlier, people with traditional values do not accept these changes and boycott such dinners. It is also observed that inter-caste dining is not applicable to the untouchables like Dhobi, Dandasi, Hadi and Bauris. But officers belonging to untouchables sit and dine together with higher caste people. It may, therefore, be concluded that castes today are no longer identified by their traditionally assigned occupations. Besides such inter-caste dining, the establishment of hotels and pan shops have also brought social changes. Even the people of lower caste (untouchables) go to the hotel shops of higher castes, take their tiffins and meals and came back without washing the utensils. No doubt, higher caste hotel-owners view the situation with contempt. But because of the laws made by the state government, which prescribe rigorous imprisonment for practising untouchability, they do not open their mouth. So, here a new trend can be observed in the village. Because of creation of laws like prevention of atrocities on Harijans the untouchables have become more assertive and challenging. In the year 1991 a case was filed by the untouchables against the Komtis for practising untouchability in the village.

It is significant to observe that inter-caste or inter-religion or inter-sub caste marriage is strongly resented, protested and vehemently opposed by the people in general and old-timers in particular. The public go mad on these issues and get easily provoked. Public opinion treats the issue with much contempt, suspicion and derision. For example, love and romance between a Danua Brahmin boy and a Sanjabi girl culminated in marriage. Since the girl belonged to a low cadre, the groom's parents and relatives took a strong exception to such kind of relationship. Ignoring their resentment, the boy went ahead in getting married to the girl. Disgusted and dissatisfied, they not only condemned the marriage but also ostracized them. This speaks of die-hard conservatism on the part of the old generation.

In another incident, a boy from the Dera community got married to a Christian girl. The couple were so much humiliated and the public opinion was so much bitter, harsh and against their marriage that they had to flee from the village after leading an ostracized life for some time in the village.

Previously, widow marriage was not allowed in the orthodox Hindu society as it was considered a social taboo. A widow was never allowed to remarry and was forced to lead an isolated, solitary life. Forcibly tonsured, compelled to put on a white sari and remove the bangles from her wrist, she was forced to lead a really humiliated and tortured life. But things have not significantly changed. Widow-marriage is not encouraged but, at the same time, it should not more be condemned as it used to be so earlier by the society. It is significant to observe that in case of Kampa and Dhoba communities the younger brother gets married to the widow of the elder brother. It has been accepted by their caste organizations. And it has been the practice since long. Other caste people, particularly the upper ones and belonging to the groom, have not accepted the widow marriage as an ideal. Lot of protests come from the groom's parents and relatives. This is what happened in Nuapada in the Komti community. In 1986, an educated youngmen, a bank officer, took a radical decision to marry a widow. Shocked with his decision, his parents strongly protested, admonised and criticized him. Notwithstanding all these, he went ahead and got married to the widow. Interestingly and significantly, the youth of Komti caste and some strongly supported him. As expected, some of the elders protested and boycotted the marriage. Even their caste organization imposed a fine of nine thousand rupees upon the young man. But he refused to pay even a single pie. Such incidents act as the indicators of social mobility.

Social mobility takes place when there is caste mobility as well as occupational mobility. Now-a-days, even the Brahmins have given up their traditional occupation and adopted agriculture as a means of their livelihood. The untouchables, because of reservation and banking facilities have also become the administrative officers as well as the business magnates. So occupational mobility among different castes in Nuapada is quite transparent. Since a detailed analysis has been made caste-wise in this chapter, showing the occupational changes, it is not necessary to mention here in detail.

Although, there is a general decline in the caste rigidity, in the village but due to the "Politicization of caste" and "caste politics", different caste organizations are gaining momentum. It is observed that caste has become an important factor in the factional politics of the village. Inspite of their social mobility and change, different caste groups are getting more organized in political sphere.

Cultural and Linguistic Groups

Nuapada, a bilingual and bicultural village, consists of two linguistic groups i.e., Oriya and Telugu. Though it is located in Orissa, it is nearer to the neighbouring state of Andhra Pradesh. Interestingly, majority of the population are the Telugu-speaking people, who not only have social links in Andhra Pradesh, but also culturally they are the inheritors of Telugu culture. That's why people belonging to Komti, Dera, Kamma, Parselia and Jangam observe some cultural functions of Andhra Pradesh like "Pongal"[21] Kadum[22] and Telugu New years day, etc. But Oriya-speaking people like *Brahmin*, *Khadura*, *Khandayat*, *Dhoba*, *Dandasi*, *Barber* etc. do not celebrate them as they have their own cultural functions like 'Dola Jatra'[23] 'Gamha Poornima'[24], 'Kumar Poornima'[25],etc. Some festivals like 'Savitri Amabashya'[26], 'Rath Yatra'[27], 'Pana Sankranti'[28] etc. are observed by both the linguistic groups. There are also many festivals like 'Makara Sankranti'[29], 'Kartika Amabasya'[30], 'Siva Ratri'[31] 'Durga Pooja'[32] during which the mode of observance of festivals differs between Oriyas and Telugus. Thus, Nuapada is divided culturally and linguistically. It may be mentioned that the 1992 Gram Panchayat elections witnessed a fight mainly between two candidates—One Telugu and another an Oriya—for the post of Sarpanch. Since two Telugu candidates were there in the race, votes were divided and this helped the oriya candidate to have an easy victory. It may, therefore, be concluded that language and culture create factionalism in rural government and politics.

Position of Women

The status of women differs from one caste to another. But the general trend is that they are less educated, self-dependent and less active in politics than their male counterparts. No doubt, the recent literacy drive made by the state government has made sixty per cent of them literates but that does not elevate their social position. Because they cannot read and write except putting their signature. The occupation of women depends on their education and caste background. Only ten of them are in different government or semi-government jobs, serving as teachers, clerks and peons. But women belonging to Dera Caste help their male counterparts in weaving, Komti women engage themselves in some business, Khaduras in stitching of leafs and other women belonging to lower castes serve as agricultural labourers. Politically, no doubt, women are becoming more active day by day, but in comparison with their male counterparts, their role is insignificant. In fact, the party affiliation of a woman in the village depends to a large extent, on her husband. Whenever he joins a particular political faction, his wife also supports him and follows his path. At present, there are only five women members in the Nuapada Gram Panchayat. Besides, there is a women organization known as "Mahila Samiti" in the village. A government sponsored organization, it seeks to provide assistance to the women destitute of the village. The women folk from among themselves elect one secretary who receives Rice, Dal, etc. from the Block in every month and it is her duty to distribute the cooked rice etc. to the needy of the village. Besides this, the 'Jayanti Pathagar', a voluntary organization of this village, has set up as well as supervises a "Balavikash Centre" (Child Development Centre), where one lady supervises the children who come under this programme. The labour class-women, who are going to the nearby forest to bring fuel wood leaving their children at home, do not take proper care of them. Hence a lady, who is engaged as care-taker of children of the centre, not only takes care of them but also undertakes various cultural programmes and feeds them the food provided by the organization. As a result, the labour class women are now free to go to the nearby jungle or to engage in other works as labourers to earn their livelihood.

Thus, emphasis has been made on the role of women in the socio-economic and political life of the village. They are no more the persona-non-grata in the social life of the village. Day-by-day they are emerging as a factor in both the social life and the political process in the rural politics.

References

1. C.C. Taylor, et al, *India's Roots of Democracy* (Delhi; Orient Longman), p. 37.

2. "Barapataka" is a term which denotes the assembly of different castes of the village to decide on any common issues.

3. Dube, Op. cit., p. 134.

4. A.C. Mayer, *Caste and Kinship in Central India.* (London: Routledge and Kegan Paul 1960); G.S. Ghurye, Caste and Class in India, (Bombay: Asia Publishing House 1950); Bailey, Op. cit., M.N. Srinivas, *Caste in Modern India and Other Essays*, (Bombay: Asia Publishing House, 1962); R.K. Choudhury, *Caste and Power Structure in Village India* (New Delhi: Inter-India Publications, 1987); *Andre Beteille, Caste, Class and Power*, (Barkely : University of California Press, 1965).

5. R.S. Mann, *Social Structure, Social Change and Future Trends* (Jaipur: Rawat Publications, 1979), p. 90.

6. Ibid.

7. The Common belief among Hindus is that the Brahmins proceeded from the mouth of Lord Brahma: the Kshaytriyas from his arms; the Vaisyas from his thighs; and the Sudras from his feet. John Muir, a distinguished Sanskrit scholar, devoled great attention to the origin of caste.

8. Choudhury, Op. cit., p. 62.

9. K. Ishwaran, Tradition and Economy in Village India (New Delhi: Allied Publishers Pvt. Ltd., 1996), p. 16.

10. Y.S. Subrahmanyam, *Social Change in Village India, An Andhra Case Study* (New Delhi: Prithviraj Publishers, New Delhi, 1975) p. 67.

11. See, N.K. Sukla, The social structure of an Indian village, (Delhi: Cosmo Publications) p. 48.

12. See, Subrahmanyam, Op. cit., p. 68.

13. Ibid.

14. Taylor et. al., Op. cit., p. 45.

15. Sukla, Op. cit., p. 48.

16. The caste groups in the village are (1) Brahmin, (2) Komti, (3) Dera, (4) Keuta, (5) Khadura, (6) Dhobi, (7) Dandashi, (8) Hadi, (9) Redika, (10) Kampa, (11) Barber, (12) Gudia, (13) Teli, (14) Khandayat, (15) Goldsmith, (16) Mali (Archaka), (17) Parcelia, (18) Kamma Brahmin (19) Karan (20) Sundhi, (21) Barika (S.T.), (22) Carpenter and (23) Bauri.

17. 'Inam' means the land which is donated by the king to the Brahmins and as such is free from revenues.

18. Dube, Op. cit., pp. 184–85.

19. Palli Srota Mandali is like an institution where the people assembled together to listen to Radio.

20. K. Ranga Rao, Village Politics: A Longitudinal Study (Bombay: Popular Prakashan), p. 26.

21. "Pongal" is a festival which falls usually on 13 to 16 January every year.

22. "Kadum" a festival of Telugu people is observed following the day of Pongal.

23. It falls on the full-moon day of Falgun (March). It is a famous festival of Lord Jagannath. Holi is observed the next day, which is a festival of fun and light heartedness.

24. Gamha Poornima is a festival which falls on the full-moon day of Sravan (August). It is the brith day of Lord Balabhadra of Balaram.

25. Unmarried girls offer puja to the early full-moon for a young and prosperous groom and happiness in life.

26. The Oriya married women undertake fast to please God on Death, Yama for allowing a long life to the husband.

27. It is the car festival of Lord Jagannath. On this occasion the three deities of Jagannath, Balabhadra and Subhadra are brought to the chariot one by one in process. Millions of prople gather at Puri to witness this event.

28. 'Pana Sankranti' falls usually on 13 or 14 April every year. The sun goes to equator and the duration of day and night becomes equal. It is a national festival in Orissa. The oriya year begins from this day.

29. The Sun God returns northward from the tropic of capricon towards the equator. It is observed as a winter festival.

30. It is also known as Kali Puja or Deepavali. It is a traditional festival with deep roots in mythologies of our country. Like other places in the country, it is observed throughout Orissa. People welcome the Goddess by offering galaxy of 'deepas' and enjoy the Fire Works on this occasion.

31. The 14th day of dark forth-night of Falgun is observed as Jagara Yatra. On this night the people of all age groups keep awake and offer lamp to Lord Siva. They fast throughout the day.

32. Goddess Durga is worshiped to ward off all the evils and dangers. It is a religious festival which starts from 1st day of bright fortnight of Aswin and spreads over to the 10th day.

5
VILLAGE FACTION LEADERS: A Profile

An Introduction

Studies of leadership usually begin with a profile of the leaders as it has a strong bearing and throws much light on their perception, orientation and role performance. Profile includes an examination of their traits, characteristics and socio-economic and political background. An enquiry into their political affiliation, linkage and interaction with the state level or central level leaders is necessary to understand the nature, scope and working of factional politics in a rural polity. To be more specific attempt has been made here to study the sex, age, marital status, family structure, education, occupation, income, land-holding etc. of the leaders and their Party affiliation, membership of political parties, habit of attending party meetings, involvement with Political parties, experience in village politics etc.

The word "leadership" has been differently used by social scientists, political orators, business executives, social workers and scholars employed in speech and writing.[1] It is an extremely complex term touching upon the various facets of social, political and economic life of rural communities. Among social scientists, the theoretical formulations of the leadership concept have continued to shift, focussing first upon one aspect and then upon another.[2]

Many social scientists have made attempts to approach the problem of leadership as a problem of classification of personality traits or the construction of a personality type. In some cases and in general to be more convincing, it is approached as a functional problem, viz., leadership is conceived of as a group property; the entire field or system of social relationships is taken into account for explaining the status and influence of a single leading individual. In fact, there is no such thing as a group without higher ranking and lower ranking, less influential members. For the social scientists, leadership and the presence of a leader in a group is a primary irreducible feature of group life.[3]

The term 'leader' is defined in different ways by different scholars. To put it simple, the leader is a person who holds an independent office to fulfill his personal desires, performs more important positive influential acts than any other member in the group, and finally, exerts a tremendous influence on goal-setting and goal achievement.[4] In a more specific way, he is a person who influences the activities of the group to which he belongs and plays a central role in defining its goals and in determining its ideology.[5]

There are a number of features in this definition which call for a further elaboration. First of all, it may be noted that the leader is part of the group. There is always a leader-follower relationship which underlies the concept of leadership and its effectiveness. Secondly, his role is central in the sense that his presence in the group is decisive and significant. All members of a group influence one another and in this sense, everybody has in himself a potential degree of leadership. What makes the leader a special type of member in the group is the value of his influence: significant at all times; decisive at critical junctures. Thirdly, his influence on the activity of the group may be direct or indirect.[6]

The term "leadership" has also been used to designate many different positions and functions:

i) it indicates a position in an organization or an individual who has been designated as leader by voluntary action of the group;

ii) it is a function of needs existing in a given situation;

iii) it consists of relationship between an individual and a group in the dynamics of human social behaviour; and

iv) finally in functional relationship leadership exists when a leader is perceived by a group as controlling means for the satisfaction of their needs.[7]

Leadership may also be defined as "an integral part of all inter-personal behaviour".[8] Ever since the inception of society there have been the leaders and the lead as it is the leader who makes the group activity a happy and satisfying experience for group members.[9] Leadership is an interpersonal influence exercised in a situation and directed through communication process towards the attainment of a specified goal or goals.[10]

Man by nature is power hungry. He wants to be powerful by acquiring power. As the leadership is instrumental in satisfying his lust for power, the leader who by the exigencies of the situation happens to capture a leadership position, develops a vested interest in it and strives hard to occupy the highest cadre of leadership by surpassing others. It is at this juncture that either the followers of the leader themselves feel that he, in spite of his inability to influence them and deliver the goods, is not ready to quit the leadership position or the rivals develop the psychology of being over-powered by the leader and thereby develop the fear of losing their leadership. Consequently, resistance is offered by his other rivals through a well-knit band of supporters operating in factions.[11] Thus, the leadership, inter-alia, is the main cause of factionalism which, in turn, limits the influence of leadership up to the level of factions only.[12]

Pigors says, "Leadership is a process of mutual stimulation which by the successful interplay of relevant individual differences, controls human energy in the pursuit of a common cause."[13]

Leaders are a part of the essential mechanism of groups. They are the product of situations. There cannot be a group without a leader. Sanderson and Polson have observed that: "Every group has within it the necessary leadership, whether acknowledged or potential. Every situation brings to the fore some leadership within the community."[14]

Oscar Lewis has pointed out that patterns of influence, or at any rate, communication, within extended family groups reach out to several villages.[15] H.S. Dhillon, on the other hand, discusses rural leadership so as to recognize its protean forms and its unreliability as a mechanism from extension work. They brought to light the varied roles of kin and caste-oriented factions in the decision-making process in rural India.[16]

A major attempt in the study of rural leadership has been made with the publication of Park and Tinker's edited volume, which includes a number of papers on various aspects of leadership in rural India.[17] Wood, has aptly pointed out that one factor is common to the countryside in the structure of rural India. Her illustration is: "A would-be or putative leader, who offers counsel or gives orders calling for a new practice or a changed practice on the part of his fellow villagers, will not be taken seriously for long unless he himself and his family follow consistently the changes required.[18] McCormack,[19] advances two arguments on the basis of his study and suggests that two general changes have increasingly affected Morsrelli and appear to be related to the growing importance of factional leadership in the village. One of these changes is the shift from a village economy based on subsistence farming and depending on free village group exchange labour among families to an economy in which cash farming with hired labour and outside employment are important. Secondly, the growth of factionalism appears to be related to increases in the extent of direct government interference in village affairs. Bachenheimer,[20] in his study on the leadership pattern, despite the outward looking groups in Padu. The increase in political awareness and the growth of political activities is due to changes which are sure to take place in future."

Thus, the leaders are the key figures influencing the decision-making process in the socio-economic and political affairs of the village[21] for, the villagers are not only very much influenced by other's opinion but also conscious of and sensitive to the opinions of their reference groups and especially of those whom they consider important and respected in the village. Sometimes their socio-economic background does not allow them to take independent decisions or right decision at right time. Right from childhood, they are influenced and guided by elders or other respected figures while taking decisions. Before acting on any matters, they always prefer to consult some one whom they consider as reliable and their own. Thus, they are mobilized by the leaders at the grassroot level and involved in a process of participatory development. Leadership is an important determinant of development, especially in a country like India, where it tends to operate on an informal level because of the primary and intimate nature of the patterns of social interaction. Furthermore, leadership not only facilitates development but also influences its direction. Thus, development based on social justice takes place when the leaders are responsive to the demands of a specific situation, but this largely depends on their social background, the capacity to absorb new ideas, and the skill to reflect and channel the aspirations of their followers.22

The development of a village will be related to the type of its leadership, since a more developed village will have more modern oriented leadership than the lesser developed one. Further, the favourable attitude of leaders towards the development activities as well as their participation in their activities will be the measure of modern oriented leadership in the villages.[23]

It is also said that leadership plays an important role in shaping the socio-political and economic life of the rural communities. It has been considered as an activity which influences the group-behaviour in order to effect co-operation towards some desirable goals.[24] It can also be viewed as a relation between an individual and the group built around common interests as directed and determined by the individual leader.[25]

The status and the role of the leader are, by all means, crucial in mobilizing the group to achieve the desired goal and thus, ultimately, affecting structural changes. In a changing social structure, from the traditional to the modern one, leadership is also prone to change.[26] The introduction of community projects, land reforms, de-centralized local administration and adult franchise, have brought forth the importance of leadership. It is believed that the success or failure of development plans may well depend upon the type of leadership available at the village.

Constituting, the core and nucleus of the faction, it is the leader around whom the group and its members revolve. The internal unity and co-operation that characterizes a faction may be said to be a matter of the relationship between the members and their leader. In other words, though the members of a faction may not be intimate amongst themselves, it would be enough if close relationship between the leader and the member was maintained.[27] When there are multiple factions the decision to join a particular faction depends on the members. But at the same time the leaders plays a vital role in enlisting their support or motivating them to join his group.

Srinivas[28] and Dube[29] have also added to the concepts and methods of study of the patterns of rural leadership. Srinivas regards the concept of "dominant caste" as crucial for the understanding of power relations in rural social life. Dube, after a careful analysis, finds that political power is concentrated in a few individual rather than diffused in the caste.

Pradipto Roy,[30] in his study on "The characteristics of Emergent Leaders", provides some features about the types of persons emerging as leaders in Indian villages and the modes of their operation:

a) people with more education participate more in the new social organization;

b) individuals with high income and a high level of living are more likely to become leaders in the new organizations;

c) members of large families are more likely to emerge as leaders;

d) age and caste do not seem to determine who will be leaders;

e) new leaders seem to have more contact with extension agencies; and

f) they are a little more secular-oriented than most village people.

It is evident from the above that a leader can be defined in various ways: he is the nucleus of a group or organisation; the key figure to influence the group thinking to take decisions and the group behaviour to implement the decisions. Qualities like hospitality, humility, politeness, sacrifice, etc., are much valued by villagers and their respect and appreciation automatically flow towards persons with these qualities.

However, because of increasing urban influence and the processes of modernization and industrialization, the Indian traditional village communities are experiencing fast change in their social life and social relations. Against this background it is found that there is the emergence of a new group of informal leaders in the village who play an equally important role like the formal leaders occupying official positions in the Panchayats and Co-operative Societies. But informal leaders, though do not hold any office, are still recognized as leaders because of their predominant role in the socio-political activities of the village. To substantiate this observation the role played by caste leaders in the village politics can be cited here.

It may be noted that leaders being ambitious and selfish, have a strong desire to acquire power and elevate their position in the society. They, therefore, utilize local bodies or co-operatives or any such decentralized organizations, since they serve as strategic power points, the control on which will help them in ascending to power at higher level.[31] However, to make specific observation an attempt has been made to find out their true identity in Nuapada in terms of their, sex, age, educational qualification, fairly, economic conditions, social background, pattern of leadership, political ideology, political affiliation, link with the district and state level leaders etc.

In this study, of 70 formal and informal leaders interviewed, seven are sarpanchas, six are defeated sarpanchas, fifteen are ward-members, ten are the members of the co-operatives and remaining thirty two are conventional and other types of leaders. The defeated leaders are those who are defeated in the panchayat and samiti leaders who have become leaders by convention and custom. On the other hand, the other types of leaders are the members of youth organizations, clubs and other village level organizations.

For the sake of convenience the chapter has been divided into three parts: the part-I covers the profile of faction leaders; part–II discusses the organizational affiliation, reason for joining politics, membership of the parties, habits of attending party meetings, involvement of faction leaders in political parties etc. and part-III highlights the linkage of the faction leaders with other level organisation.

II. Profile

a) Sex

Generally, it is believed that in a traditional society like ours, the overwhelming majority of the leaders are males. In most of the earlier studies also male dominance has been substantiated. K.D. Gangrade, in his study on "Leadership in rural India: A case of some villages in twelve states in India" observes that females comprise only 2 per cent among the formal leaders.[32]

In Nuapada too majority of the leaders are males as is evident from the following table.

[Table 5.1] Sex-wise Classifications of Leaders

Male		*Female*		*Total*	
Number	*Percentage*	*Number*	*Percentage*	*Number*	*Percentage*
66	(94.29)	04	(05.71)	70	(100)

Thus, the above table clearly indicates that the overwhelming majority (94.29 per cent) of the leaders are males while female members comprise only 05.71 per cent and all of them are formal leaders. It would appear that the preponderance of male leaders in the society is a reflection of the cultural tradition of the country which does not encourage women to take up leadership roles in politics and public life but expect them to play secondary and supportive roles within the family. The statutory representation of women in the Panchayati Raj and other bodies has now promoted the emergence of women leaders. No doubt, women members in the Panchayat are dominated by the elected male members, but the 73rd Amendment Act and Orissa Gram-Panchayat Act of 1992 have encouraged the women members to participate in the political processes of the village itself. One woman respondent has expressed her hope to participate, alongwith male members in the village politics.

b) Age

It may be noted that the average age of leaders in Nuapada is 53 years. It, therefore, appears that the rural leadership is largely monopolized by the old folk. The leaders have been classified under three groups viz. The young, the middle and the old. The leaders who are 35 years of age or less are considered as young, from 36 to 49 years as middle-aged and those who have crossed the age of 50 years are considered as old.

The Table 5.2 indicates the age group to which the leaders of Nuapada belong.

Thus, the Table 5.2 reveals that 8 leaders (11.43 per cent) are young, 18 (25.71 per cent) of them are middle-aged and the remaining 44 of them (62.86 per cent) are old, who are largely preferred to other two groups (as they out number the combined

[Table 5.2] The Age Group of the Leaders

Age Group	Number	Percentage
Young (Below 35 years of age)	08	(11.43)
Middle-aged (Between 36–50 Years)	18	(25.71)
Old (Above 50 years)	44	(62.86)
Total	70	(100.00)

strength of the first two groups) because of their experience, maturity, traditional outlook, old values and customs which are normally shared by the common people.

The study further reveals that leadership in rural Orissa is still dominated by the elders (62.86 per cent), but not by those who are young or middle-aged, who constitute only 11.43 and 25.71 per cent respectively. The present study corroborates the findings of Mehta that seniority in age is observed as an important qualification for getting into the Village Panchayat as the older people or those senior in age, are more experienced than the younger ones. They possess adequate knowledge and a knack of solving ticklish problems.[33] This finding is not, however, consistent with that of Panda's which concludes that both young and old have almost equal dominance.[34] It also goes against Harjindar Singh's finding that young persons are more capable than the middle-aged or old persons of becoming leaders or occupying leadership position. The young and dynamic leaders are preferred by the people to middle-aged or old ones.[35] But the correct picture of rural leadership is that it is distributed among all the three age groups.

(c) Marital Status

In Nuapada almost all the leaders (92.86 per cent) are married persons. Interestingly, nearly 69 per cent of them live in joint families-as is evident from the Table 5.3.

It may be mentioned that the traditional Indian joint family besides providing economic, physical and other securities makes it possible for some members of the family to be involved in various

[Table 5.3] Marital and Family Status of Faction Leaders

	Number		Percentage	
Married	65	70	92.86	100.00
Unmarried	05		07.14	
Single Family	22	70	31.43	100.00
Joint Family	48		68.57	

types of village work and undertake leadership responsibilities in social work and public life. But it does not mean that the leaders belonging to single family have no role to play. Their number in village politics is not insignificant. Twenty two (31.43 per cent) of them belong to the single family. Thus, the study supports the earlier findings made by Sirsikar (1970), M.P. Singh and R.P. Mishra (1973) that large-size households are a common feature among leaders in rural areas. It provides an opportunity to develop leadership qualities and leisure time to their members to devote themselves to political activities. But the nuclear type families do not provide enough time and the resources at the disposal of individuals to involve in leadership activities.[36]

(d) Leaders as Heads of the Family

It is interesting to note that 55 leaders (78.57 per cent) of Nuapada are heads of their families as is evident from the following table.

Table 5.4 : Distribution of Faction Leaders as Heads of their Family

Head of the Family		*Not Head of the Family*		*Total*	
Number	*Percentage*	*Number*	*Percentage*	*Number*	*Percentage*
55	78.57	15	21.43	70	100.00

As most of the leaders in the village are old and belong to the joint-family, the head of the family enjoys a superior status and gets all such information through their family members about the day-to-day affairs of the village. It supports the idea that elderly persons play a predominant role in rural politics which is still its marked feature.

e) Education

Education is considered to be an important variable to leadership. It enables the leaders to understand the issues and problems of the community and communicate their ideas to the people. An illiterate leader may not be able to comprehend all the rules and regulations. It is, therefore, interesting to study how far education plays an important part in the emergence of leadership. It is also equally important to findout whether illiterate persons can at all become leaders in the village. The following table presents a picture about the level of education of the leaders in Nuapdada village.

[Table 5.5] Leaders and their Level of Education

Level of Education	*Number*	*Percentage*
Illiterate	05	07.14
Primary	14	20.00
Middle and below Matric	21	30.00
Matric and aboive but below Graduation	21	30.00
Graduation and above	09	12.86
Total	**70**	**100.00**

It is evident from the above table that the literacy rate among the leaders is much higher than what it is at the national level. This amply proves that the rural socio-political scenario is undergoing a transformation. It is significant to note that 65 leaders (92.86 per cent) are literate and only 5 of them are illiterate. The study also contradicts the earlier view that higher the education among the leaders, greater is the faction. Because in this study people who are educated up to H.S.C. level, predominate the factional politics because of their numerical strength. The study proves beyond doubt that education is considered to be an important factor for acquiring leadership in rural politics.

f) Occupation

The following table gives an idea about the occupation of the leaders.

[Table 5.6] Showing Occupation of the Faction Leaders

Occupation	*Number*	*Percentage*
Cultivation	08	11.43
Service	02	02.86
Agricultural Labour	05	07.14
Manual Labour	05	07.14
Business	05	07.14
Multi-ocucpations	41	58.57
Other Occupations	04	05.72
Total	**70**	**100.00**

Leaders of Nuapada have been divided into seven occupational categories such as cultivation, service, agricultural labour, manual labour, business, multi-occupations and other occupations. The multi-occupational group includes the leaders who have various occupations like cultivation, business, services etc. and the other occupations include "Kulavriti" i.e. their traditional occupations like carpentry, selling wine, washing clothes etc. It is interesting to note that majority of the leaders (58.57 per cent) are engaged in multi occupations. About 80 per cent of the leaders are the cultivators. India being predominantly an agricultural country, agriculture is the most preferred occupation in rural areas. Next in ranking order come businessmen. Because among the multi-occupational group, we find that about 90 per cent belong to business group. The following table shows that 7.14 per cent of the village leaders attach much importance to business only.

It may be observed that in Nuapada the land-owners, who also control the business, hold the economic string and as leaders, they are in a better position to give benefits and prizes to their followers.

g) Income

It is a fact that money plays a vital role in the socio-economic activities of human life. Since rural factionalism is very much inter-related with these socio-economic activities, a study of the financial condition of the leaders in the village is highly essential. The following table throws light on their annual income.

[Table 5.7] Leaders and their Income

Annual Income	*Number*	*Percentage*	
Income up to Rs. 5000/-	08	11.43	
Between Rs. 5001/- — Rs.10,000/-	11	15.71	
Between Rs. 10,001/- — Rs. 20,000/-	15	21.42	
Between Rs. 20,001/- — Rs. 40,000/-	11	15.71	51.42
Above Rs. 40,001/-	25	35.71	
Total	70	100.00	

It may be noted that the financial condition of the faction leaders is not in bad shape. They may not be affluent, but at the same time they are not financially unsound.

In village standard an annual income up to Rs. 5000/- is considered poor, between Rs. 5001/- to Rs. 10,000/- It is not bad, between Rs. 10,001/- to Rs. 20,001/- as the higher ups. On the basis of this criterion, it is found that 11.43 per cent of the village leaders come from the poor family, 15.71 per cent from the middle class, 21.42 per cent from the higher middle standard and remaining 51.42 per cent from the higher ups. Thus, the study clearly shows that the higher income is considered to be one of the most important factors for holding leadership in the rural villages like Nuapada. But it does not mean that the leaders of the middle income group have no role to play. Their number in the village politics is also not quite insignificant as they constitute 37.13 per cent.

h) Land-holding

Land-holding is still attributed as an important determinant of leadership pattern in the village as is evident from the Table 5.8.

[Table 5.6] Showing Occupation of the Faction Leaders

Land-holding	*Number*	*Percentage*
Landless	26	37.14
Up to 5 Acs. of land	22	31.43
Above 5 Acs. and below 9 Acs.	03	04.29
10 Acs and above	19	27.14
Total	70	100.00

It may be noted that while 44 (62.86 per cent) leaders are having lands the rest of them (37.14 per cent) are landless. 22 (31.43 per cent) leaders land-holding size falls upto 5 acres, 3 (4.29 per cent) of them have lands from 5 to 9 acres and 19 (27.14 per cent) of them are the owners of 10 acres of land and above. It may be concluded that the land-holding plays an important role in shaping the rural leaderships. But, at the same time, it may be mentioned that land-holding is not the sole factor in this regard as more than one-third of them are landless. It may be noted here that the landless leaders are not poor. They are not interested in having lands as they give more importance to their business than to land because in their opinion business ensures more profit than agriculture. But, however, it may not be ruled out that land has certainly a prestige value, particularly in a rural community. Therefore, most of the leaders do not want to dispose of heir lands. Land-ownership is still regarded as a status symbol. The present study supports the earlier study made by Harjindar Singh that big land-owners are regarded as village leaders.[37]

(i) Caste

In a traditional society like ours caste still remains one of the most significant variables in establishing dominance in Indian villages. The notion of dominant caste introduced by M.N. Srinivas (1955) has been accepted by most of the survey researchers on rural leadership, rather uncritically. The studies of Iqbal Narain (1964), V.M. Sirsikar (1972), S.K. Srivastava (1965) have illustrated abundantly that leadership in Indian villages has been monopolized by the upper castes. Though S.C. Dube and others have offered criticisms, yet the notion as such remains undisputed in most of the empirical studies on rural leadership. Caste emerges to be one of the significant determinants of the pattern of leadership in Nuapada village.

The Table 5.9 shows caste-wise distribution of the faction leaders of Nuapada:

From the above it may be observed that majority of the leaders (41.43 per cent) in Nuapada belong to Komti caste. Next to them is the Dera caste (20.00 per cent). The Brahmins, though belong to higher caste, occupy the third position followed by Khaduras, Dhobas, Hadis, Dandasis, Goldsmiths, Parselias, Kampas,

Table 5.9 : Caste-wise Distribution of Leaders

Sl. No.	*Caste*		*Number*	*Percentage*
1.	Barber (Bhandari)	(O.B.C.)	01	01.43
2.	Brahmin (including kamma brahmin)	(U.C.)	08	11.43
3.	Dandasi	(S.C.)	02	02.86
4.	Dera	(O.B.C.)	14	20.00
5.	Dhoba	(S.C.)	03	04.29
6.	Goldsmith	(O.B.C.)	02	02.86
7.	Hadi	(S.C.)	03	04.29
8.	Kampa	(O.B.C.)	01	01.43
9.	Khadura	(O.B.C.)	04	05.71
10.	Khandayat	(O.B.C.)	01	01.43
11.	Komti	(U.C.)	29	41.43
12.	Mali	(O.B.C.)	01	01.43
13.	Parselia	(O.B.C.)	01	01.43
	Total		70	100.00

Bhandaris, Archakas (mali) and Khandayats. If we combine the scheduled castes (Dhoba, Dandasi and Hadis) they represent 11.44 per cent which is just equal to the Brahmin leaders. Thus, in Nuapada, most of the leaders belong to komti caste. The reasons for it are not far to seek as the people belonging to this community are rich and educated. They engage themselves in public services, business and other dignified occupations. Members of this caste play a vital role in the factional politics of the village to serve their social and economic interest. Next to Komtis, the Deras hold the second position. Had there been no weavers co-operative society, they would not have become the leaders. Because they are neither highly educated nor financially sound. Further, statutory representation in the panchayats and other co-operative bodies has provided for individuals from the Dera and Dhoba caste groups with greater access to leadership positions.

Motivational Factors for Joining Politics

Man is not only a social animal but also a political being by instinct. In other words, he is also by nature a political animal. By nature, instinct and inclination he is political. But, at the same time, it may be observed that he joins politics to achieve something in his life. Politics is an instrument that gives him power, prestige, position in the society, confers on him a status, makes him influential and brings him to lime light. It helps him in exercising his control over others, influencing and manipulating the will of others. Politics, which is the art of shaping and sharing of power, a game, an instrument in achieving one's end, motivates many to join politics. Factors like caste, region, religion, language, etc. or/ and motivations like acquiring or/and perpetuating oneself in power, development of the caste or community or region or religion—all these may be said to be playing a major role in influencing one to join politics.

The following table gives in detail the reasons why the leaders of Nuapada have chosen politics as a career :

[Table 5.10] **Leaders and Motivational Factors for Joining Politics**

Reasons	*Number*	*Percentage*
For development of the locality	03	04.29
For development of the caste	03	04.29
For the sake of prestige and power	01	01.43
For controlling other people	Nil	
For continuation of dominance of their leader	01	01.43
Without any reason	04	05.71
More than one factor	58	82.85
Total	70	100.00

It is evident from the above table that leaders have been motivated by different factors while joining politics. But significantly their number of percentage is much less as the Table indicates. Most of them (82.85 per cent) have, however, chosen politics as a career being influenced by several factors.

Party Affiliations

It may be noted that almost all the leaders of Nuapada are affiliated to one political party or another. Either they are the close supporters of political parties or have become their primary members and contest on their symbols. Since there are two important political parties (the Indian National Congress and the Janata Dal) in Orissa, who preside over the destiny of the State, there is not wonder that most of the leaders of Nuapada are associated either of the two parties.

But is significant to note that some leaders change their political colour frequently if it protects and promotes their interests. Defection, desertion, changing political violence etc. have become a part of our political culture. The following table discusses the political affiliation of he leaders of Nuapada:

[Table 5.11] Faction Leaders and their Party Affiliation

Parties	*Number*	*Percentage*
Indian National Congress	28	40.00
Janata Dal	11	15.71
Communist Party of India	Nil	---
Any other Political Party	Nil	---
No Answer	08	11.43
Changing party affiliation depending on the circumstances	23	32.86
Total	70	100.00

The Table 5.11 indicates that forty per cent of the leaders are the members of the Indian National Congress while 15.71 per cent of them belong to the Janata Dal. This might be due to the fact that the Congress is a very old party and the people still have their affiliation to it by retaining their faith in it. Since Independence, either the Congress itself or one of its splinter parties has often been in power in the State except from 1977 to 1980 and 1990 to 1995. About 23 (32.86 per cent) leaders, however, belong to opportunist group as they can change their political jacket depending upon the circumstances. Although eight of them (11.43 per cent) refused to give any answer, it is very difficult to believe that they are politically neutral.

As said earlier, most of the leaders belong to one party to another. This might be due to the fact that rural politics or panchayatiraj can not operate in isolation from the political framework of parliamentary system and political parties. In India, the latter have a great stake in rural politics and panchayatiraj institutions at the village, block and district levels. They are interested in awakening the rural masses, rallying them around their programme and ideological stand, if they have to succeed at the polls. They have to fight elections at the state and national levels. How can they think of winning elections, if they do not have a strong rural base ? To have it, they have to develop party organizations, at local level, cultivate and throw up local leaders and actively participate in the handling of local issues.[38] They are interested in getting their candidates elected to the office of the Sarpanch, or as Samiti members, so that for the assembly and parliamentary elections they can mobilize public opinion in the area in their favour on the basis of their achievements at the local level. Thus, political parties, which are national in character and have an ideological base, can provide better direction to village problems than parochial and short-sighted village factions.[39] Thus, political parties being reciprocal, the former try to keep good contact with the latter.

Attending the Party Meetings

Representative democracy has been introduced in India in the Post-independence era. As a result, each and every state has been divided into many constituencies for sending their representatives to the parliament and the state legislative assemblies. The citizens of India at the age of 18 years and above, otherwise not disqualified by the law of the state, are eligible to vote in the elections and choose their representatives for the popular bodies of Assembly and parliament. Political parties organize them on political lines and give them ideological training and political education on the basis of which public opinion is created and articulated; provide enthusiasm and political direction to the rural people who are otherwise apathetic to the political process; and impart political education through electoral campaign, propaganda, pamphlets, leaflets and political literature. The people are made aware of their problems and they know their own rights.

Political parties seek to acquiring power. They articulate as well as aggregate the interests of the people and champion them in the legislatures and outside and compete among themselves for power. The more powerful they are, the better placed they are to protect or promote the interests of the people. In order to gain more power, they need the support of the people. Hence, different political parties have been trying to woo as many villagers as possible to their side purely for their own electoral prospects. But it is not possible for any of them to establish direct contact with voters individually. Such connections have to be forged through intermediaries. This brings into focus the role of village leaders who act as the link between political parties and the villagers. They tend to be divided among themselves partly due to their own search for power and partly as a result of their identification with different political parties or forces which exert a tremendous influence on them. They attend various meetings organized by different political parties and also take initiatives to organize the party meetings in the village itself. This helps them and others to become more and more politically conscious. It is, therefore, of interest to know how many of them attend political meetings organized by various political parties. The following table throws lights on it:

[Table 5.12] Leaders Attending Party meetings

Attending Meetings		*Not Attending*		*Total*	
Number	*Percentage*	*Number*	*Percentage*	*Number*	*Percentage*
60	85.72	10	14.28	70	100.00

It may be noted that 60 (85.72 per cent) leaders attend political meetings. It not only shows their interest, zeal and enthusiasm in politics but also makes them, alongwith the villagers, more and more political conscious.

Experience in Village Politics

In the history of mankind, politics and man have probably emerged at the same time and wherever there is more than one individual, there is likely to be politics. In a narrower sense, the term politics refers to administration at different levels. But it is a comprehensive term covering many aspects of human life, and not limited to a particular aspect like government. Man by nature is selfish and ego-centric and has a natural tendency or desire, as said earlier, to exercise control over others to his own advantage. This is done through the medium (resorting to, taking recourse to) of politics, which at the village level is considered to be a demeaning exercise and this vulgar nature of village politics is aggravated by factionalism. Against this background, it is necessary to find out the leaders' experience or their involvement in village politics to find out whether more experienced leaders are more responsible for factionalism than the less experienced ones. It is an axiomatic truth that politics and factionalism go hand in hand in the Indian village and one can not exist without the other. The table given below indicates the experience or involvement of the leaders in village politics:

[Table 5.13] Political Experience

Years	*Number*	*Percentage*
Less than one year	Nil	
Up to 5 years	05	07.14
6 to 9 years	04	05.71
10 to 20 years	13	18.57
21 to 30 years	24	34.29
Above 30 years	24	34.29
Total	70	100.00

It is evident from the above table that involvement in politics or association with political parties is certainly a passport to becoming a leader or assuming leadership. In other words, it is the political experience or political background that plays a key role in the making of leaders and leadership is certainly shaped by politics. It is pertinent to note that 48 leaders (68.58 per cent) have more than two decades of political experience in village politics.

It may not be wrong to observe that political experience shapes the political orientations, attitude and culture of the leaders. The moment they step into the office they start either creating factions or join a faction which would satisfy their needs.

Association with Political Parties

It may be noted that rural leaders are closely associated with various political parties and party leaders as is evident form the following table. This association is mostly guided by the *quid-pro-quo* factor, as this helps both the parties.

[Table 5.14] Leaders' Association with Political Parties

Years	*Number*	*Percentage*	
Below 3 years	02	02.86	
3 years to 5 years	06	05.87	
5 years to 10 years	08	11.43	67.14%
10 years to 15 years	12	17.14	
15 years to above	19	27.14	
No information	23	32.86	
Total	70	100.00	

It may be observed that quite a large number of the faction leaders (67.14 per cent) of the village are actively associated with various political parties. 32.86 per cent of them are either passive supporters of different political parties or least interested in their affairs.

Association of 67.14 per cent of the respondents with the political parties is as old as three years or more than that. This is an indication of the involvement of the political parties in rural politics, though rural government and politics, is supposed to be non-partisan in nature. Leaders' long years of political involvement and association with different political parties leads to the conclusion that they are quite experienced in both party as well as rural politics.

Linkage with Other-Level Organizations

Leaders of Nuapada are not only associated with political parties or involved in local politics but also tied up with leaders of different organizations like Samiti[40] and district organizations[41] and those at state level.[42]

[Table 5.15] Leaders' Connection with Different Level Organisations

Different Organizations	*Response*					
	Yes		*No*		*Total*	
	No.	*%age*	*No.*	*%age*	*No.*	*%age*
Panchayat Samiti	50	71.43	20	28.57	70	100.00
District Level	12	17.14	58	82.86	70	100.00
State Level	36	51.43	34	48.57	70	100.00

The above table shows that a very high percentage (71.43) of the leaders have connections with the Panchayat Samiti Organizations.

This development or phenomenon may be attributed to the fact that after the implementation of the Panchayatiraj system in Orissa and India as well, the panchayat samitis are the local institutions and the village organizations and institutions are mostly partronised by these institutions. In a decentralized system of developmental administration introduced in Orissa since the sixties, the Gram Panchayat constitutes an important institution through which rural developmental activities are mostly taken up. The Gram panchayat is the first tier of the Panchayatiraj administration in India. It is the responsibility and the privilege of the panchayat samiti to act as an agent to discharge functions delegated to it by state or union government and passing the sub-agency in any of these functions in appropriate cases to the Gram Panchayat.[43] One of the main aims of the panchayatiraj is to take the developmental programmes to the masses and get their co-operation in implementing them with the support and co-operation of non-official leadership at the local level. As such the rural leaders have emerged and they try to keep constant touch with the rural local bodies. The leaders accordingly want to distribute the prizes and benefits to their followers. Thus, it is evident from the above table that Panchayat Samiti institution is of paramount importance to the leaders for strengthening their position at the village level.

Secondly, the leaders of the Panchayat Samiti namely, the Chairman, Vice-chairman and other members have a great say in deciding about different developmental works to be undertaken in a particular village. This is also of the important reasons that motivates, as mentioned earlier, leaders to keep good contact with the leaders of the samiti in order to get the benefits for themselves. Thirdly, direct election of the samiti members by the voters of the Gram Panchayat enables the leaders to come in close contact with them. Hence, their association is more inter-oriented, as they (samiti members) are supposed to be the co-villagers of the leaders. Through them they gain personal acquaintance with office bearers of the Panchayat Samiti. Further, its meetings are not always held at its headquarters. They are held in different villages under the jurisdiction of the samiti by rotation. This provides the leaders a scope to have personal acquaintance with the Samiti leaders. The extensive tours of the chairman, vice-chairman, samiti members along with the official persons like Block Development Officer, Gram Panchayat Officer, etc. in connection with the execution of different developmental projects in rural areas also help them to come in contact with them. It may, therefore, be concluded that rural leaders try to keep good contact with the Samiti level leaders to make their position firm in village politics as well as distribute the prizes and benefits to their followers.

The table further indicates that the rural leaders interact more with the state level leaders than with those at the district level. This is partly because at the district level, the Zilla Parishad has been replaced by the District Development Council or the District Development Advisory Board. The D.D.C., is purely an advisory body in the matter of developmental administration of the district. Secondly, the leaders of the district level organizations are mostly involved in politics at higher levels namely the district, or the state or the national level as the case may be. It is because of this reason, these organizations can hardly find time to meddle in the factional politics at the village level. Thirdly, the leadership at the district level is generally more urban in character. Hence, the rural leaders, whose outlook is more confined to the politics at the lower level, could not cope with the district level leaders, as they are unable to get immediate benefit from them.

Zilla Parishads and Panchayat Samitis were introduced in the State in 1961 statutorily by enacting the Orissa Panchayat Samiti and Zilla Parishad Act, 1961, on the basis of the recommendations made by Balwantrai Mehta Committee. As per the provision of the Act the non-official members of these institutions namely,

Panchayat, Panchayat Samiti and Zilla Parishad were to be elected. As a result, time and again, it became necessary to hold elections for filling of one casual vacancy or the other in these three institutions. And it is due to these elections, politics permeated into the rural life. Although elections give rise to different factions and cause much harm to the traditional cohesion and unity of the village, the village leaders try to take shelter under the shadow of leaders at higher levels and want to get some benefits for themselves: either to strengthen their position in the village or distribute the prizes or benefits to their followers. Since the district level organizations are unable to provide them any direct benefits, rural leaders' connections with those of the district have become quite minimal.

It is significant to note that the leaders of Nuapada do not interact much with the state level leaders. Though state and national politics centre round urban and semi-urban areas, rural politics cannot be said to be completely different. At the village level also the leaders try to keep contact with those state level leaders and sometimes act as their agents. But it is seen that only 51.43 per cent of them keep contact with the state level leaders. Thus, it is quite evident that the leaders' connections with those at the state level are secondary to those of the panchayat samiti.

Association with M.L.As and M.Ps.

Indian democracy within a short-span of time has become more participatory as there is an increase in the percentage of voters in different elections and also different socio-economic groups have been making a sincere effort to strengthen their position in the political process of the country. Politics in India is no more confined to the Centre only. It has broadened its sphere of action. Accordingly, leaders in the rural politics do not keep themselves confined to their own areas only. Infact, being the grass-root leaders, they help their political masters (M.L.As., M.Ps., etc.) in the electoral politics and also strengthen their own position in village politics by keeping contact with them. It may be observed that the emergence of Panchayatiraj leadership has multi-dimensional impact since the rural voters constitute the foremost political pillar in India.[44] Besides, another important aspect of this link between the rural leaders and the state-level leaders is the changing pattern of rural government in India after 73rd Amendment Act of 1992. Accordingly to this Act, Panchayatiraj is to function with full autonomy having its own sphere of activities. This has undoubtedly given more importance to rural leadership. But in view of the predominant role of the political parties in Indian politics, rural government and politics can never be free from their control.

In other words, in the Gram Panchayat elections the M.L.As decide the candidates and back them to victory through money and personal influence. As a result, rural leaders connections with the state and national leaders like M.L.A.s and M.P.s became purely "interest oriented". Because some times from the same party there are many candidates and each candidate tries to get the support of a faction in his party at the state level. In the fitness of things presented herewith, an attempt has been made to study the sources of linkage between the leaders of Nuapada on one hand and the M.L.As and M.Ps on the other hand. As M.L.As and M.Ps. are the peoples' representatives, they are supposed to have intimate contact with their constituents by making periodic visits to their constituencies, through organizing public meetings from time to time and so on. Hence, in this study, both sitting and defeated M.L.A.s and M.P.s. are taken into consideration while analysing the linkage pattern of the leaders of Nuapada with them. The following table speaks of the details thereof:

[Table 5.16] Leaders' Association with M.L.As. and M.Ps.

Causes	*M.L.As.*		*M.Ps.*	
	Number	*Percentage*	*Number*	*Percentage*
- Personal	09	12.86	07	10.00
- During Election	09	12.86	53	75.71
- During visit to the constituency	44	62.86	04	05.71
- As a member of the same party	02	02.86	02	02.86
- Other sources	02	02.86	---	
- No knowledge on any relations	04	05.71	04	05.71
Total	70	100.00	70	100.00

The table shows that only 4 (5.71 per cent) leaders of Nuapada do not have any relation with or any knowledge about the members of the Assembly or the members of parliament. This may be because of their ignorance or political apathy. But vast majority of them (94.29 per cent) interact with these leaders or have links with them in one form or another.

It may be noted that while majority (62.86 per cent) of the rural leaders come to know about the M.L.As. only leaders when the latter visit their areas similarly, 5.71 per cent of them come in contact with the M.Ps. on their visit to their localities. No doubt, both the M.L.As. and M.Ps. are the peoples' representatives and are supposed to have intimate contact with the them. But it does not seem to be the case as they (M.Ps.) hardly visit their constituencies. However, an M.L.A. visits his constituency more often than an M.P. This may be because a parliamentary constituency is far more extensive than that of an Assembly. It is because of this an M.P. is not as well known to the people of his constituency as an M.L.A. is. By making frequent visits to his constituency before and after the election, the latter is more familiar with the rural leaders. This helps him to make his position more stable than an M.P. in electoral politics. The study, thus, reveals that the more one visits the area, the more he becomes popular and intimate with the people. This ultimately strengthens his political base.

An interesting finding is that majority of the leaders (75.71 per cent) come to know about the M.P. at the time of election only, which provides a platform to them to interact with the M.P. Once the election is over, the relationship between them abruptly comes to an end. It may be noted that nearly 13 per cent of the leaders come to know about the M.L.A. at the time of election only. Because of his frequent visits to the constituency an M.L.A. is able to establish a very good rapport with the leaders and gets their support in elections. The quid-pro-quo relationship between them helps a lot in securing their ends—political, social and psychological. The rural leaders feel proud of being henchmen of an M.L.A. This gives them a feeling of satisfaction. The leaders vie with one another to come close to the M.L.A., try to cultivate good understanding with him when he visits them. About 62.86 per cent of them come in close contact with him, while he visits the constituency. Interestingly, only 12.86 per cent of them know him personally while 10 per cent of them have very close contact with the local M.P. A very few of them (2.86 per cent) belong to the local M.Ps. or M.L.As political party.

Leaders' Help to M.L.As and M.Ps. in Strengthening their (M.L.As and M.Ps.) Political Base

The rural leaders play a major role in strengthening the political base of the local M.Ps. and M.L.As. They not only influence their vote banks but also sometimes they themselves constitute the vote banks. The leaders campaign for them, try to ensure their victory in the elections, help them in under taking local problems and implementing developmental activities. Their help, co-operation and support go a long way in ensuring political victory of the M.L.As and M.Ps. The following table discusses the nature of help rendered by the leaders of Nuapada to the local M.L.A. and M.P.

[Table 5.17] Nature and Extent of Help given by the Leaders to the Local M.L.A. and M.P.

Nature of Help	*Help given to M.L.As.*		*Help given to M.Ps.*	
	Number	*Percentage*	*Number*	*Percentage*
Help in the election compaigning	58	82.86	63	90.00
Help in the developmental activities of the area	08	11.43	Nil	
Other type of help	01	01.43	02	02.86
Not applicable	03	04.28	05	07.14
Total	70	100.00	70	100.00

The above table shows that 58 leaders (82.86 per cent) of Nuapada extend such help to the local M.L.A. at the time of elections. The percentage of respondents extending help to them in connection with execution of various developmental works in the area is much low, being 11.43 per cent only. Three of them (04.28 per cent) do not extend any help to the M.L.A. In other words, they do not bother about it.

It is important to note that about 90 per cent of the leaders of Nuapada help the local M.P. by joining, supporting and organizing his election campaign. But it is very sad to note that he hardly helps them in implementing developmental projects in the village. This shows that for a M.P. electoral prospects are far more important than actual execution of developmental activities in the area. Since the activities of the leaders of Nuapada are confined to their village only and, as such, can hardly have any impact on the political matters outside the boundaries of those villages, the elected representatives (both M.P. and M.L.A.) are mostly not prone to note taking any help from village leaders in matters of politics. Thus, it is evident from the Table 5.17 that more help was taken from them by the M.Ps. and M.L.As. during the election campaign than in formulation of policies or execution of programmes. This clearly indicates that the latter are guided more by their narrow and selfish interest i.e., their own electoral prospects are more important than actual developmental work in their areas.

It has also generally been observed that during elections, the M.L.As. as well as the M.Ps. approach the panchayati raj leaders for support. The latter also depend on them for their survival. They seek their help in getting some rural development projects sanctioned for their area.

Leaders Getting Help from their M.L.A. and M.P. to Make their Position firm in Village Politics

It may be noted that in an inter-personal relationship the representatives (M.L.A. and M.P.) and the rural leaders help each other for serving their mutual interests. Since this help is bound to be a mutual process or affair it is necessary to examine how far they (leaders) see the help of their M.L.A. and M.P. The Table 5.18 gives a detail picture in this regard.

It is evident from Table 5.18 that 74.29 per cent of the village leaders are getting various kinds of help from the M.L.A. at different times on different occasions.

It may be noted that like many other State Governments, the Government of Orissa (during 1990–95) also took a decision to place five lakhs rupees at the disposal of each M.L.A. The amount is to be spent on developmental activities of his constituency. Therefore, the faction leaders try to get some benefits for the

[Table 5.18] Leaders getting Help from M.L.A. and M.P.

Nature of Help	*Getting Help from M.L.As*			*Getting Help from M.Ps.*		
	No.	*%age*		*No.*	*%age*	
Electioneering	02	02.86	74.29	02	02.86	27.14
Village development	08	11.43		05	07.14	
Personal	02	02.86		Nil		
Other types of Help	04	05.71		Nil		
More than one from the above	36	51.43		12	17.14	
Help not taken	18	25.71		51	72.86	
Total	70	100.00		70	100.00	

protection of the interests of the village. Secondly, as discussed earlier, the relationship between the M.L.A. and the rural leaders counts much in the village level politics, as it is a matter of great prestige on the part of the leader to be branded as the close men and followers of the former.

It is also seen that about 25.71 per cent of the leaders do not seek any help from the M.L.A. in order to strengthen their position in politics. But as already mentioned in Table 5.16, about 95 per cent of them associate themselves with him on different occasions to further his objectives. As compared to this the percentage of leaders getting such help by way of reciprocity comes to about 74 per cent. Thus, it shows that the M.L.A. is more dependent on leaders but not vice-versa to promote to fulfil their respective objectives.

References

1. R. Tannenbaum, I. Weschler and F. Massil, *Leadership and Organisations*: (New York: Mc Graw-Hill Book Co., 1961), p. 23.
2. Ibid.
3. B. Jeorges "Leadership and Social Change", in J.W. Airam (ed.), *The Nature of Leadership*, (Bombay: Levani Publishing House, 1969), p. 75.

4. Richard T. Morris and Malvin Seeman: "*The problem of leadership: An interdisciplinary Approach*, American Journal of Sociology, Vol. 56, No. 2, p. 151.
5. See, S.J. Filella, "*The Psychology of Leaderhip*" in Airan, Op. cit., p. 56.
6. Ibid.
7. Irving Kricker Bocker, "*Leaderhsip: A Conception and Some Implications*" in C.G. Borwne and T.S. Danville Coha (ed.) *The Study of Leadership* (The Inter-State Printers and Publishers: 1958), pp. 10–11.
8. L. Petrullo and B.M. Bass (ed.), *Leadership and Inter-Personal Behaviour* (New York: Holt Rinehart and Winston, 1961).
9. O. Tead, *The Art of Leadership* (New York: McGraw Hill Book Co., 1936), p. 68.
10. Tannenbaum, et al, Op. cit., p. 24.
11. Surendra Singh, "*Leadership and Factionalism*" Eastern Anthropologist, 31: 3, July–September 1978, p. 305.
12. Oscar Lewis, *Group Dynamics in a North Indian Village*, (New Delhi: Planning Commission, Government of India, 1954), p. 33.
13. See, Harjinder Singh, *Village Leadership: A Case Study Village Mohali in Punjab*, New Delhi: Sterling Publishers Pvt. Ltd., 1968, p. 12.
14. Ibid.
15. Lewis Op. cit., p. 102.
16. See, Parmatma Saran, *Rural Leadership in the context of India's Modernization* (New Delhi: Vikas Publishing House Pvt. Ltd., 1978), p.11.
17. Richard L. Park and I Tinker (ed.) *Leadership and Political Institutions in India* (Princeton, N.J.: Princeton University Press, 1959).
18. Evelyn Wood, "*Pattern of Influence within Rural India*" in Park and Tinker (ed.), Op. cit.
19. William McCormack, "*Factionalism in a Mysore Village*", in Park and Tinker, Ibid.
20. R. Bachenheimer, "*Elements of Leadership in an Andhra Village*", in Park and Tinker, Ibid., 1959.

21. Sushila Mheta, *Social Conflicts in A Village Community*, (New Delhi: S. Chand & Co., Pvt. Ltd., 1971), p. 63.
22. K.D. Gangrade, *Leadership in Rural India: An Analysis of Some Trends*, in Alfred Desouza (ed.), *The Politics of Change and Leadership Development* (New Delhi: Manohar 1978), p. 165.
23. Shiv Rattan Mehta, *Emerging Pattern of Rural Leadership*, (New Delhi: Wiley Eastern Private Ltd., 1972), p. 115.
24. Satinderjit Kaur et. al., "*Role of Village Leaders in Rural Upliftment*", Kurukshetra, September 1993, p. 11.
25. Ibid.
26. Ibid.
27. Fukunaga, Op. cit., p. 169.
28. Srinivas, Op. cit.
29. S.C. Dube, "*Dominant Caste and Village Leadership*" paper read at the seminar on "*Trends of change in village India*", held at central institute of study and Research in community Development (Mussourie, India, 1961).
30. Roy, Op. cit.
31. Seshadri, Op. cit., p. 111.
32. K.D. Gangrade, "*Leadership in Rural India: A Case of some Villages in Twelve States in India*", in Alfred De-Souza (ed.), Op. cit., p. 169.
33. Mehta, Op. cit., p. 80.
34. Panda, Op. cit., p. 119.
35. Singh, Op. cit., p. 68.
36. C. R. Bada "*Emerging Pattern of Rural Leadership*", Indian Journal of Public Administration, 23(3) July–September, 1977, pp. 810–811.
37. Singh, Op. cit., p. 70.
38. C.P. Bhambri, "*Political parties and Panchayati Raj: Some theoritical Considerations*" in M.V. Mathur and Iqbal Narain (ed.), Panchayati Raj Planning and Democracy (New Delhi: Asia Publishing House, 1969), pp. 313–14.
39. Ibid., p. 317.

40. The term Panchayat literally means council of five. This refers to the "Panch Parameswar" which means that God is speaking through the five. Though, it is so, the body is not limited to this number. Generally a Panchayat may be formed either taking only one big village or many small villages where population is 2000 or above. It is the 1st tier of the Panchayati Raj institutions in India. The panchayat samiti is the second tier of the panchayati raj institutions. It's office is located at the Community Development Block head quarter and its Jurisdiction is coterminus with the Community Development Block. The Chairman of the Panchayat Samiti is elected by the elected samiti members of the Gram Panchayats under its jurisdiction. As per th Amended panchayatiraj Act in Orissa, each and every adult citizen, who is otherwise not disqualified is eligible to participate in electing one sarpanch to the Gram Panchayat and the Samiti member to the Panchayat Samiti. The Samiti member is a popular representative at the Panchayat level. Although Samiti members are elected representatives for the panchayt samiti, they are eleigible to partake in the discussions and deliberations at the Gram panchayat meetings without having right to vote. Similarly, the sarpanchs, under the jurisdiction of the Panchayat Samiti, are the ex-officio members of the samiti having no voting right.

41. Under the de-centralized set-up of administration as recommended by Balwantray Mehta Committee and the introduction of the three-tier system of Panchayat Raj Institutions in Orissa in 1961, the Zilla Parishada is the district-level organization. Fortunately or unfortunately, it was abolished in Orissa in 1968 and replaced by the District Development Advisory Board. The Board was created vide Government of Orissa, planning and Co-ordination Department order no. 16, 336 dated 14.11.1970. The following persons were the members of the District Development Council (1) District Collector (Chairman) (2) Members of the Legislative Assembly from the district, (3) Members of the parliament from the district, (4) Chairman of the panchayat samities, (5) Chairman of the Municipalities, (6) President of the Co-operative Bank, (7) President of the Land Development Bank, etc. For details see Gram Panchat Manual, Government of Orissa.

42. State level leaders, in this study, includes the Ministers, and leaders of the state level party organisations.

43. Narmadeshwar Prasad, "*Panchayati Raj–Problems and Reorganization*" in M.V. Mathur & Iqbal Narain (ed.), Panchayati Raj: Planning and Democracy.

44. P.C. Mathur, *Political Corollaries of Panchayati Raj* in M.V. Mathur and Iqbal Narain (ed.), Op. cit., p. 335.

6
LEADERS' AND VILLAGERS' PERCEPTIONS ON FACTIONAL POLITICS

The role performance of rural leaders is considerably influenced by their attitudinal orientation. In order to ascertain this, a questionnaire was administered to them. The main objective is to study their attitude towards factional politics: how they feel about it, how they react to it, what factors they hold responsible for it, whether they consider it functional or dysfunctional, would they like to involve themselves in it or take measures to prevent or promote it. Besides the leaders, 118 villagers were also administered a questionnaire to elicit their opinion on different aspects of factional politics.

It is pertinent to note that politics of Nuapada village, as that of any other village, is faction-ridden and it is unfortunate to observe that leaders, who are in power by occupying office in rural government, make themselves involved in factional politics. It seems they encourage it, promote it and by all means are a party to it. They do not hesitate to openly mobilize their supporters against other factions. It is, however, significant to note that most of them (87.14 per cent) are strongly opposed to factional politics as is evident from their answers to a question: "Should the village politics be faction-ridden?" But in reality there is a wide gulf between what they preach and what they practise.

Those leaders, who favour factional politics in the village, argue that it checks the monopoly of a particular group in the village politics and forces the ruling group to expedite the process of development in the village and think in terms of village development for its own existence in village politics. Some progressive factions mobilize the villagers against the conservative groups to bring socio-economic changes in the village rapidly. Due to social diversities in Orissan villages some respondents feel that factional politics has become an inevitable part of the village political process.

The leaders, who are very much averse to factional politics, observe that the village Nuapada as a community has its unity in the midst of diversity. But over the years this has been gradually eroding with the rise of factionalism. It has also created bitter feelings among the villagers who belong to different uncompromising factions. It retards the developmental process as formulation and implementation of the developmental schemes in the village becomes difficult because of animosity and conflict between factions. It may be pointed out that earlier most of the posts in the rural government were being filled up through unanimous choice of the villagers. Only in rare cases elections were conducted and the people used to oppose the candidates who contested for any post against their wish. But with the rise of factional politics, election has become almost inevitable and different factions are backed by different political parties. As a result, "the politics of consensus" has been replaced by "the politics of challenge and contest."

Factional politics in Nuapada is partly attributed to the introduction of the Panchayati Raj Institutions. It has become a debatable issue. The village leaders who support the argument are of the opinion that over the years these institutions have become highly politicized, dividing the villagers, creating factional groups among them and providing an infrastructure for full manifestation of factionalism. Active involvement of political parties in the village politics has further deteriorated the situation by sharpening the political rivalries.

The leaders who do not agree with the argument that the village politics has been debased by the Panchayati Raj Institutions are of the opinion that factions are not new to the Indian villages as they existed even before the creation of the Panchayati Raj. They are endemic in most of the Indian villagers and it would be incorrect to say that they are the product of the Panchayati Raj Institution. With the greater political participation and the influence of modern mass media, villagers have become highly ambitious as their desires and expectations have gone up.

The Indian society is caste-oriented as it not only plays a dominant role in socio-political aspect of human life but also provides a functional base to the Indian village life and determines the socio-economic and political attitudes of the people. It has also, so to say, become an important determinant of factional politics in Nuapada—since 60 per cent of its leaders agree with this observation. They are of the opinion that factions are organised on the basis of caste. The predominant caste creates factions for its political and economic benefits as well as for the continuation of its dominance so that other castes will not get an opportunity to be in power. The economically strong caste also dominates politically, as is the case with the Komtis of Nuapada.

But some leaders do not believe that caste is responsible for factional politics. They believe that the increasing political awareness of the people and their participation in village affairs has diminished the importance of caste in factional politics. The economically predominant caste has no more an upper hand in the rural government. The role of the political parties in the village politics has become more important in organizing factions than the caste system.

As said earlier, Nuapada was known for its unity in the midst of socio-economic diversities. But unfortunately, it no more exists as the village life has been seriously affected by factions, discord and conflict. The village is divided, villagers are divided and the leaders are also divided. It is significant to note that 92.86 per cent of the leaders are of the opinion that the village life is marred by factions. This is a fact of village life. Because their argument was that factional politics in the village centres around personal and political ambitions of the leaders who, therefore, do not hesitate to adopt all the unfair means to divide the villagers.

The village life in Nuapada is not peaceful as it has been threatened by factions and it is commonly believed that they also give rise to violence.

When the leaders in Nuapada were asked about it, majority of them (71.43 per cent) believed it to be so. It is they (Factional leaders) who create group rivalries in Nuapada for their own benefit.

Interestingly, they blame one another for it and hold others responsible for the same. But unfortunately most of them use their muscle power in asserting themselves in the village politics. One faction some times threatens another faction or other factions to maintain a low profile. Rejecting this argument some other leaders argue that factional politics does not create violence because violent occurrences in the village are mostly sporadic and are not in politically organized form.

Rural government and politics is supposed to be non-partisan in character as it is not to be influenced by any political party. But there is a vast gap between theory and practice. Political parties are very much active in village politics. Most of the village leaders owe their existence to them. 57.14 per cent of leaders strongly believe that factional politics promotes indiscipline.

Political parties and their leaders are, undoubtedly, responsible for evils like corruption, group-rivalry, violence, false propaganda, in the national and state politics. Therefore, most of the leaders (88.57 per cent) are of firm conviction that political parties should be kept away and not be allowed to have any say in village politics. What they feel is that evils of the party system may pollute the rural government and destroy the feeling of oneness and commonness among the villagers. However, a few of them (11.43 per cent) do not adhere to this view. They argue that the party politics should permeate the village life and influence its government. Because they think that party in power in the State (or for that purpose at the centre) will give more support to the developmental projects and the schemes of the village, if its leaders also belong to the same party.

Panchayati Raj leaders have come to enjoy certain measures of influence among the people in the rural areas because of their day-today contact with them and also because of the fact that they try to alleviate or improve the conditions of the people. Their power of patronage and also their power to implement certain programmes have given them an influence and a capacity to create an image for themselves among the rural masses. Panchayati Raj Institutions initiate and undertake developmental works and activities by mobilizing resources and the people at the local level.

In the post-independence era rural government has been more emphasized in India. It has been institutionalized to bring socio-economic changes and development in different spheres of village life. Another objective has been to make democracy participatory, mass-based and de-centralized. In other words, basic to primary objectives of rural government are development and establishment of grass root level democracy. It is significant to note that majority of the leaders (68.57 per cent) are of the opinion that the rural government has proved itself to be highly functional to the community as it has done a splendid job not only by implementing developmental schemes but also involving the people in all these works. On the other hand, 21.43 per cent of them believe that it has harmed the people and their interests by inducting party politics indirectly into the village life, dividing the village in to many factions, encouraging group rivalry for capturing power and corroding those age-old and traditional values that once upon a time sanctified the village life. As a result, the villagers have now become acquainted with the art of corruption and manipulation as are prevalent in urban government.

It is significant to note that leaders have, as it appears from the above analysis, their own perceptions which are, to a great extent, shaped by various factors including their socio-economic and political background. The Table 6.1 discusses in detail the perceptions of the leaders.

[Table 6.1] : Leaders' Perception on Factional Politics

	Yes		No		Both		No Answer		Total	
	No.	%age	No.	%age	No.	%age	No.	%age	No.	%age
1. Should the village politics be faction ridden ?	03	4.28	61	87.14	02	2.86	04	5.71	70	100
2. Can the factional politics be attributed to the Panchayati Raj Institutions?	61	87.14	09	12.86	..	..	..	..	70	100
3. Do you think that caste is an important determinant of factional politics in the village?	42	60.00	22	31.43	..	..	06	8.57	70	100
4. Does factional politics divide the village?	65	92.86	05	07.14	..	..	..	..	70	100
5. Does it encourage violence?	50	71.43	04	05.71	16	22.86	..	..	70	100
6. Does it promote party indiscipline ?	40	57.14	15	21.43	..	..	15	21.43	70	100
7. Do you favour a non-party system in rural government?	62	88.57	08	11.43	..	..	..	..	70	100
8. Do you feel that factions obstruct the developmental process in the village?	30	2.86	40	57.14	..	..	..	..	70	100
9. Has the rural government harmed the people rather than solving their problems?	15	21.43	48	68.57	..	..	07	10.00	70	100

II

A lot of discussion has been held and much concern expressed by the people belonging to cross-section of Indian society relating to factional politics as a growing phenomenon in Indian political scenario. It has not only affection national and state politics but also the rural politics. Causes responsible for factional politics are too many, but broadly speaking they may be classified under five categories: (i) personal and psychological, (ii) social, (iii) economic, (iv) political and (v) institutional.

It may be noted that power, prestige and personal interest are very important factor responsible for factional politics. Leaders create factions for the sake of their own position which would confer on them power and prestige. It is this narrow and selfish interest combined with mutual jealousy that foment factionalism as is evident from the Table 6.2(A).

Table 6.2 (A) : Factors Responsible for Factionalism Personal and Psychological Factors

Sl. No.	*Factors*	*Very important*		*Important to some extent*		*Not at all important*		*Total*	
		No.	%	No.	%	No.	%	No.	%
1.	Power and Prestige	40	57.14	13	18.57	17	24.28	70	100
2.	Personal interest/benefit	30	42.86	12	17.14	28	40.00	70	100
3.	Jealousy	08	11.43	15	21.43	47	67.14	70	100

Social life and structure of the village play an important role in the village politics. Hence, eight important causes of factionalism were listed to elicit the responses of faction leaders which can be evinced form the Table 6.2(B).

Caste as a factor in encouraging factionalism in rural politics comes first because the village political scenario largely depends on the nature and functioning of caste system. So long as, there is a dominant caste in the village without being opposed by other communities, there is no conflict. But some times the internal conflict mars or destroys the unity with in the predominant group and the internal strife continues and spreads further. It may,

Table 6.2 (B) : Social Factors of Factionalism

Sl. No.	*Factors*	*Very important*		*Important to some extent*		*Not at all important*		*Total*	
		No.	*%*	*No.*	*%*	*No.*	*%*	*No.*	*%*
1.	Caste feeling	25	35.71	27	38.57	18	25.71	70	100
2.	Linguistic groups	20	28.57	07	10.00	43	61.43	70	100
3.	Anti-social	08	11.43	04	05.71	58	82.86	70	100
4.	Education	23	32.86	18	25.71	29	41.43	70	100
5.	No Education	04	05.71	06	08.57	60	85.71	70	100
6.	Sex	04	05.71	02	02.86	64	91.43	70	100
7.	Mass Media	19	27.14	32	45.71	19	27.14	70	100
8.	Impact of Urban politics	32	45.71	18	25.71	20	28.57	70	100

therefore, be observed that "the weakening of dominant caste and the collapse of its internal cohesion was clearly the root cause of the activities of the faction."[1] It is significant to note that most of the leaders (74.28 per cent) of Nuapada agree that caste plays a very vital role in the factional activities of the village.

Besides caste, language also sometimes promote factionalism. Nuapada is bi-lingual as it consists of Oriya and Telugu-speaking people. Though, the latter constitute the minority, sometimes they get organized as a faction and play their role in village politics. A significant number of respondents (38.57 per cent) agree that such linguistic groups create factions in the village politics. Anti-social elements like the muscle men, drunkards and the hooligans are gradually making their presence felt in rural politics. Sometimes they also encourage factions. But in the present study a negligible percentage of respondents agree that such elements have anything to contribute to factional politics.

In Nuapada, there is also a dichotomy between the educated and uneducated participants in politics. The study reveals as majority of the respondents (85.71 per cent) feel that it is the educated leaders with minimum education up to M.E. standard are involved in factional politics. They feel that uneducated leaders do not create factions nor are they involved in it.

Sometimes sex is considered as a factor in creating factions in the village. This has been observed by the scholars like Lewis in his study on Rampura. Factions may develop around: quarrels over the inheritance of land, adoption of sons, house-sites and irrigation rites, sexual offences, murder and quarrels between castes. The people of Rampura have a popular saying that Dharas (factions) revolve round wealth, women and land.[2] Earlier, in Nuapada, sex was responsible for factions. However, majority of the leaders (91.43 per cent) do not consider it of having any bearing upon factional politics.

In modern times, Mass media, which include news papers, magazines, radio and television, etc., have undoubtedly influenced the political thinking of rural people. Wide spread education and exposures to mass media, particularly the electronic one, have made the villagers "educated" in true sense of the term and play a major role in shaping their political orientations, influencing their attitudes towards politics. In other words, importance of media in guiding the political destiny of the people cannot be ignored. Fagen observes "the existence of national mass media, with all that they imply in increased message capacity, speed and pervasiveness, changes in a basic way, a system's potential political communication.[3] In our study majority of respondents (72.85 per cent) consider mass media as an important factor in factional politics. Because, as we have stated earlier that the factional politics at the centre and state level has a greater impact on village politics. For example, when there was a split in the Congress at the centre, one led by Indira Gandhi and another by Devaraj Urs, in the village under study, leaders were also identified on that basis. So, it may be concluded beyond doubt that the mass media, which carry messages to the doorstep of the villagers, act as an important agency in influencing the political thinking of the villagers.

Like mass media, urban impact is an inevitable part of the external influences on rural life. With the improvement of communication facilities and the interaction of socio-economic forces this impact has become prominently conspicuous. It has been rightly observed : "Many villages all over India are becoming increasingly subject to the impact of urban influences. The nature of urban impact, however, varies according to the kind of relation a village has with a city or town."[4] Lambert is right when he says that "Urban returners bring with them many elements of modern ways of life and habits from the cities to the villages."[5] Since the village Nuapada is well connected with the urban centres of the district 45.71 per cent of respondents agree that urban politics is a very important influential factor in the rural factional politics. It may be noted that leaders of the village visit the urban centres, come in contact with the different leaders, interact with them, seek their guidance and suggestion and to a great extent are influenced by their advice. They also change their life style and mode of behaviour, and modify their political strategies to gain the favour of the villagers and influenced their political behaviour.

Thus, in this study, we can conclude that social factors like caste, mass media and urban politics have an important bearing in the factional politics of the village Nuapada.

Table 6.2 (C) : Institutional Factors of Factionalism

Sl. No.	*Factors*	*Very important*		*Important to some extent*		*Not at all important*		*Total*	
		No.	*%*	*No.*	*%*	*No.*	*%*	*No.*	*%*
1.	Panchayati Raj Institutions	48	68.57	14	20.00	08	11.43	70	100
2.	Co-operative Societies	26	37.14	32	45.72	12	17.14	70	100
3.	Social Institutions like Schools, pathagars etc.	20	28.57	28	40.00	22	31.43	70	100

The co-operative institutions or organisations are highly necessary for rural development. So leadership of any kind is analysed in relation to new organisations like the statutory panchayats, co-operative societies, the schools, etc.

The panchayat is one of the very important institutions in the rural area and its objective is to make democracy distributary and decentralized. However, Panchayat institutions have brought about a number of changes in the traditional, social and political structure of the village. It has been observed that" as a result of introduction of schemes of rural development and Panchayati Raj Institutions in place of traditional micro-structure new factions based on divergent membership have emerged on the rural scene reflecting the dynamics of the people as well as the forces of change.[6] This observation supports our study on Nuapda village in which majority of leaders (68.57 per cent) have considered Panchayati Raj Institutions to be one of the most important factors in the factional politics of rural government.

Co-operative Societies, instruments of socio-economic changes of rural area have been formed with an objective to make the villagers free from exploitation. But they have been misused by those who manage it as they try to extract maximum benefit out of them. Since they have become the sources of pecuniary benefits, leaders associated with these bodies encourage factions. An overwhelming majority (82.86 per cent) of leaders agree that co-operative societies have become centres of factionalism. But compared to Panchayati Raj Institutions, they are much better and least dangerous in polluting the village atmosphere.

With a view to spread education in rural areas some new social institutions like schools, college and pathagaras (libraries) have come up in Nuapada village. No doubt they are the centres of learning but unfortunately, at the same time, not free from the political opportunism. Especially with the flow of governmental assistance to them, rural leaders have become more keen to associate with them so that they can promote their interest. Therefore, there is a tussle among them to exert control over these institutions so as to project themselves as effective leaders. In the present study, though only 28.57 per cent of them think that such institutions enjoy a place of important in the society, a majority (68.57 per cent) of them consider these institutions to be playing an important role in encouraging factions in rural politics. (The details have been discussed in Chapter 7).

[Table 6.2 (D)] Political Factors Promoting Factionalism

Sl. No.	*Factors*	*Very important*		*Important to some extent*		*Not at all important*		*Total*	
		No.	%	No.	%	No.	%	No.	%
1.	Political Ideology/Issues	29	41.43	22	31.43	19	27.14	70	100
2.	Party Affiliations	44	62.86	18	25.71	08	11.43	70	100
3.	Mass Participation in Politics	36	51.43	20	28.57	14	20.00	70	100

Ideology is derived from a number of sources like political issues, statement of public policies, religious ideas, aesthetic judgments and even from specific social practices. Thus, an ideology becomes a strong way of abstracting, conceptualising and evaluating the social environment. Brown[7] arrives at some useful generalization regarding the concept of ideology. To him, it provides answers to important questions and defines approaches to them, involves commitment to a recognised position and makes the individual aware of the society and culture. The response to ideology is personal although its basis is social. Accordingly factional alignments are formed whenever there is any controversy over any issues or ideologies. That's why a person may join one or the other faction group irrespective of his caste or clan. Beals8 observes that a faction exists because of a particular dispute and its membership changes when it is over. Thus, he characterised factions as non-enduring groups that are basically interest-oriented. In this present study, majority of the respondents (72.86 per cent) viewed that political ideology or issues sometimes also create factions in the village.

In the rural government and politics, political parties have started playing the guiding role by virtue of their importance in the district, state and national politics. So rural leaders are affiliated to one party or another as their future is determined by it to which they belong. In Nuapada village, majority of leaders (62.86 per cent) have said that party affiliation creates factions in the rural government. Members belonging to different parties are opposed to one another and this gives rise to factions. Sometimes in equal representation of political parties in rural government also creates factions.

In the general political scenario of India, growing political awareness and participation is an undenying truth now. Accordingly in rural politics also peoples' participation is increasing. Structurally Panchayati Raj Institutions have been given more importance and their representative character has been broadened by making special reservation for the representation of scheduled castes, scheduled tribes and women. This restructuring has taken place after 73rd and 74th constitutional amendments. The present study reveals that majority of the leaders (80 per cent) agree to the view that political consciousness among the people also cause faction in the village.

[Table 6.2 (E)] Economic Factors of Factionalism

Sl. No.	Factors	Very important		Important to some extent		Not at all important		Total	
		No.	%	No.	%	No.	%	No.	%
1.	Conflict between rich and poor	05	07.14	04	05.71	61	87.15	70	100
2.	Land-ownership	20	28.57	18	25.71	32	45.72	70	100
3.	Unemployment	04	05.71	21	30.00	45	64.29	70	100

Panchayati Raj has, undoubtedly, increased the pace of political consciousness among the people in the rural areas.

Economic factor is an important dimension of rural politics. It has been noted earlier that the Nuapada village consists of people belonging to different economic groups. It is quite interesting to note that scholars like Massaki Fukunaga are of the opinion that economic factor is not an important cause of factionalism in a village.[9] But contrary to this observation, it has been found in our study that conflicting economic interests play an important role in creating factions. So a few questions were asked to the leaders on this aspect. Under economic category four factors are included: conflict between rich and poor, land-ownership, business conflict and unemployment. Though the village is divided between the rich and the poor sections, only 12.85 per cent of the leaders view it as an important cause where as 87.15 per cent of them do not think so. It is because poor people, inspite of poverty and scarcity of resources, do not have sufficient strength to get themselves organised. As a result, they do not create any faction. Land-ownership is a very vital factor in rural politics. Scholars like Lewis argue that "one of the fundamental causes of factions is the insecurity of village life with its scarcity of land and limited resources."[10] Baljit Singh further narrows it down: "clearly land is the issue that causes the major factional split among the dominant factions. Around the land problem, lie the discard, an extreme disorganization of the village people...."[11] In this study majority of the leaders (54.28 per cent) are of the opinion that land-ownership is an important cause of factional conflict in Nuapada village which consists of different business groups. Such business cover a wide area like weaving of clothes, grocery shops, money lending, rice mills, medical shops, etc. Some business people also play the role of middle man and exploit the small business groups. When leaders were asked to give their opinion on this aspect, only 49.51 per cent of them opined that business conflict often creates factions. It is pertinent to note that since most of the village leaders are engaged in business they are not ready to confess that the conflicting business interests create factions. But, undoubtedly, it is the case—as is evident from what is happening in practice. In Nuapada, the Dera community is a divided, a faction-ridden class or community.

Unemployment is a growing phenomenon in Orissian villages. As a result, more and more number of unemployed people find politics as a vocation of their life. But this does not create factions as is evident from the opinion of 64.29 per cent of the leaders.

Villagers' Perceptions on Factional Politics

Here a sincere attempt has been made to study as well as make an analysis of perceptions of the people of Nuapada on various aspects of factional politics as well as on the role performance of the leaders. Accordingly, 118 members of the village were chosen on the basis of random sampling and selected on 4:1 ratio (households of the village) excluding those of leaders. A questionnaire was administered to them.

The study reveals that most of the villagers (69.49 per cent) are strongly averse to any kind of factional politics as they 87.29 per cent) are convinced that it has not only created division among them but also posed a threat to their life and property and destroyed the peaceful atmosphere of the village. It has also made their life more complicated.

As mentioned earlier caste plays a dominant role in village life. It is both functional and dysfunctional. A majority (78.81 per cent) of the villagers do not agree to the view that it creates factions. This is in sharp contrast to the opinion of the leaders (60 per cent) who firmly believe in the opposite. A lay man believes that factions is the product of patron-client relationship and it rests more on economic consideration than on caste.

Development is an important aspect of the rural government at present. Because through the latter only, as has been felt by the

Government of India, that development in the rural area can be possible. But unfortunately, the developmental process of the village has been retarded because of factional politics. An overwhelming majority (80.50 per cent) of the villagers very strongly believe this. This is, however, in sharp contrast with the opinion of their leaders (57.14 per cent) who do not think that faction hinders the development process.

It may be noted that the people of Nuapada feel that their leaders think first about their own interest and try to build up their own image. As a result, faction emerge and they stand poles apart. It is because of this common interest of the village is often sacrificed. It is this narrow and selfish interest that has spoiled the image of village leaders as well as impeded or retarded the developmental process of Nuapada.

After independence the importance of rural government in India is very much felt. Because everyone has realized that unless there is involvement of the people in the developmental process, rural areas can not grow. But how far this creation of rural government has helped the people to solve their problem is a matter of concern. Interestingly, more than 50 per cent of the respondents are of the opinion that the rural government has failed to deliver its goods, belied their hopes and aspirations, created a sharp division among the leaders and the people, and made the former highly politicized. Instead of concentrating on developmental activities, the leaders give top priority to their political survival in the village government and politics. It may be noted that the existing representative rural government was preceded by what was known as mass assembly or "Barapataka". In that system every villager was a member, participating in welfare activities of the village. But it is very sad to observe that both the decision-making process and the developmental activities are influenced and controlled by some self-centered rural elites. Fifty percent of the people think that the rural government has divided the people and polluted the village life. 83.05 per cent of the villagers believe it to be so. They feel that after the establishment of the Panchayati Raj system political parties have not only emerged as the key factors in the system but also created factions among the rural leaders. Here, both the leaders and the common people agree with one another by sharing the identical views. It is because of this more than 86 per cent of the people of Nuapada favour a non-party system and their village government should be absolutely free from any party politics as this would go a long way in preserving the basic ideals of village life.

In rural Orissa, political consciousness of the people is a growing phenomenon as is evident from their participation in the political process on a wider scale. But, at the same time, this has given rise to factions. 64.41 per cent of the villagers feel so about this. It is sad to comment that the growing unemployment has forced quite a large number of unemployed youth to choose politics as their career and they have made it a means to achieve their selfish ends. This further motivates them to hobnob with different political leaders and act as a stimuli for the creation of factions.

Factionalism has become a marked feature of national and state politics in India. In most of the urban centre of political activity there is faction. And this has a direct impact upon the rural government and politics as is evident from the opinion of the villagers. Rural leaders keep contact with their urban counterparts, interact with them and in the process they are influenced by the attitudes of urban leaders.

As said earlier, the village Nuapada is quite a busy place as it is the centre of business activities. So business people, as mentioned earlier, generally dominate the village politics. This is also what the people of Nuapada believe.

Though Nuapada is a business centre, it is like other villages in Orissa predominantly agricultural in nature. Land-holding is a part of agricultural economy. But consolidation of land in a few hands has given rise to many problems in the village, including factional politics. However, only 26.27 per cent of the villagers feel that there is any linkage between land-holding and factions. There is hardly any conflict that centres round land-holding. In the year 1975, after the rigid implementation of Land Ceiling Act by the Government of Orissa, Nuapada village for the first time saw, following a call given by the Communist Party of India, a revolt by the tenants against the landlords. But subsequently the latter by virtue of their economic strength, could ride over the situation and brought the tenants again under their control. So land conflict is a rare phenomenon in Nuapada village and hence is not considered by the villagers and their leaders as a factor to create factions.

As mentioned earlier in this Chapter, violence is making a vengeance entry into the political life of rural Orissa and Nuapada village is no exception to it. Sixty seven per cent of the people are of the opinion that factions create violence. They have seen how leaders have taken recourse to violent measures in achieving their goal or teaching a lesson to the enemies. The Table 6.3 reflects the perceptions of the people of Nuapada on various issues revolving around factional politics.

References

1. Fukunaga, Op. cit., p. 171.
2. Quoted in Nagla, Op. Cit., p. 17.
3. R. Fagen Richard "*The Components of Communication Net Works*", Politics & Communication (Boston, Little Brown: 1966), p. 42.
4. M.S.A. Rao, "*Urbanization and Social Change*", in Urban Sociology in India" (Calcutta: Orient Longman, 1974), p. 500.
5. D. Lambert Richard, "*Some Impact of Urban Society Upon Village life*", in Roy Rurner (ed.), India's Urban Future (Bakerley: University of California Press, 1962), p. 117.
6. Nagla, Op. cit., p. 36.
7. L.B. Brown, "*Ideology*", London: Cox and Wymen Ltd.: 1973, pp. 173–79.
8. Alan Beals "*Leadership in a Mysore Village*", Park and Tinker (eds.), Op. cit., pp. 427–37.
9. Fukunaga, Op. cit., p. 9.
10. Lewis, Op. cit., p. 148.
11. Baljit Singh, "*Next Step in Village of India*", (Bombay: Asia Publishing House, 1961), pp. 10–15.

[Table 6.3] Villagers' Perception on Factionalism

	Yes		*No*		*Both*		*No Answer*	
	No.	*%*	*No.*	*%*	*No.*	*%*	*No.*	*%*
1. Should the village politics be faction ridden ?	11	09.32	82	69.49	15	12.71	10	08.47
2. Does factional politics divide the village ?	103	87.29	10	08.45	--		05	04.24
3. Is Caste an important determinant of factional politics in the village ?	22	18.64	93	78.81	--		03	02.54
4. Does factional politics obstruct the developmental process of the village ?	95	80.50	18	15.24	--		05	04.24
5. Has the rural government harmed the people rather than solving their problems ?	60	50.85	43	36.44	05	04.24	10	08.47
6. Is the faction a product of Panchayati Raj system ?	98	83.05	08	06.78	--		--	
7. Do you favour a non-party system in rural government ?	102	86.44	16	13.56	--		--	
8. Does participation of people in the political process create factions ?	76	64.41	38	32.20	--		04	03.90
9. Can factionalism in rural politics be attributed to the impact of urban politics ?	84	71.19	29	24.58	--		05	04.24
10. Does it occur because of conflicting interest of different business groups ?	68	57.63	40	33.90	--		10	08.47
11. Does consolidation of land-ownership give rise to factions ?	31	26.27	87	73.73	--		--	
12. Are factions responsible for violence ?	80	67.80	25	21.19	10	08.47	03	02.54

7
FACTIONAL POLITICS AT WORK

The phenomenon of factionalism with its impact on almost every aspect of the social, political and institutional systems in the twentieth century, has generated much academic interest. It is a great epidemic which has been rooted in almost all institutions such as schools and colleges, clubs and libraries, panchayats and co-operatives and in different political and non-political institutions. Even one can feel and mark its foot print at market places, tea-stall, hotels, bus stops and so on. In one form or the other it has always been there in the community, but in the modern society its ramifications are greater than ever before so much so that faction has become an integral part of the modern society.

As mentioned earlier, factions constitute an important and inseparable part of the village social organisation. As a basic element of social structure, individuals interact with one another and are involved in the network of social relationships and mutual obligations. Sometimes these individuals and their groups work in co-operation with one another while on other occasions they may function in situations of conflict. One group of individuals working in conflict with another group may be said to constitute a faction. In other words, the conflicting tendencies among group members results in factions. They are formed by different groups in order to pursue their interests, goals etc. Where a community is divided into many non-structural interest groups and each of them striving to achieve its goals, it may be said to have many factions. The study of factions attains a special significance in helping to understand the village power structure.

It is needless to over-emphasize that factionalism hinders the growth of homogeneous feeling amongst the members of society and thus obstructs its alround development. Its effects are all the more harmful and pernicious in rural areas where traditionally there has been a spirit of heterogeneity on account of castes, classes, social customs and so on. It is here in the rural areas that the deleterious effects of factionalism are severely felt and become more pronounced. Though, it is not possible to completely uproot it from the society, it is, however, not difficult to keep it at a distance any danger to the society. This can be done with the help of various methods, out of which the most important ones are (a) removing its causes and (b) controlling its effects.

In order to identify the causes and effects of rural factionalism, it is necessary to examine how it is working in Nuapada village. While dealing with these, two major sociological aspects of factions—organizational and operational—are to be highlighted. To have a complete overview of the structure and functioning of factions in the village, both the aspects must be taken into account simultaneously. Here, the causes refer to the organizational aspect and the effects to the operational aspect of the faction in the village.

Some scholars like Lewis (1954), Nicholas (1965), Firth (1957) and others in their studies have laid more emphasis upon the organisational aspect of factions, though they did not neglect the other aspect. It is observed that all the castes in the village are divided into groups called factions, which "are held together by corporative economic, social and ceremonial relations."[1] Depending upon the numerical strength they may be further classified into major and sub-factions. Major factions, in so far as the distribution of power is concerned, represent broadly identifiable cleavages in the community. Sub-factions are small groups constituted by the people who join together, not necessarily for a long period, to fulfil their aims after which they may dissolve or may continue as such. Some of them remain unaligned but, in such situations, when hey choose to function separately, their influence in the community power structure is limited. Most of the them, therefore, align themselves with one or the other major factions, without losing their identity.[2]

There may be a few people with greater resources and power at their command who, on that basis, may also be able to exert a certain amount of influence over others. But they would not be recognized nor would they overtly assert themselves as "leaders".

What Berreman (1963:283) observed in Sirkanda village is that "—there is generally no recognised leadership in the village,—. No man is in a position to tell others outside his family what to do. Villagers found it hard to conceive of an influential leader".[3]

Articulate leadership is an important determinant for the successful functioning of a faction. Leaders of both the major and sub-factions draw strength and help from different sources and different people in the village. It has been found that the people in the village helped their leaders because they were "Kinsmen", some were "economically dependent on their leaders", some "backed their neighbourhood head men", others helped on the ground of caste relations whereas still another group of people helped their leader hoping that they could defeat their enemy.[4]

The operational aspect of factionalism covers the study of conflict between factions and has been emphasized by the scholars like Epstein,[5] Siegel and Beals[6] and Pocock.[7] To them, factions appear and become operative and active at the time of conflict. Rest of the time members of the factions may help one another but the real expression of factionalism is not apparent in the social interaction by the people. Writing about the conflict, Epstein has asserted that "it is not the number of factions that is important, but rather the way hostilities between the opposing factions are expressed. In any one dispute there can be only two opposing factions."[8]

Having considered both the organizational as well as operational aspects, an attempt has been made to give a complete view of the factions operating in Nuapada and study the following aspects:

- Origin, growth and recognition of factions in the village.
- Caste dominance and Factionalism.
- Organisation of factions in the village.
- Panchayat Raj and factions.
- Assembly elections and factions.
- Educational institutions and factions.
- Co-operatives and factions.

- Sex and factions.
- Cultural associations and factions.

Origin of Factions in Nuapada

In Nuapada, factionalism is popularly known as groupism and factions as parties or the groups. Factionalism might have existed here earlier also, but it could be traced back to a period between 1926–1930. Its origin may be attributed to a dispute between the Dera community supported by Rajaguru Mahanta Sri Kaibalysa Das Babaji, a religious man (Mathadhisha of a "Matha" i.e. temple) and the Komti activists on the issue of staging a drama. The members of the Dera community though poor, were very much interested in organizing and staging the dramas in the village. Mahanta also evinced a keen interest in these activities. So he would come to their rescue by providing financial assistance to them. He was their patron, God-father, friend, philosopher and guide in true sense of the term. He encouraged and promoted art and culture in the village. With his ungrudging help they constructed a house known as "Akhada Ghar" (where rehearsals are being made before staging a drama). They staged a drama. Tickets were sold. It was a stupendous success and made a good profit. Successful enactment of dramas, staged one after another, fattened the purse of the Dera community. They, therefore, created a 'fund' and deposited in it whatever income and profit they earned from staging the dramas. But unfortunately the Komtis wanted to bring this 'fund' under their control. It may be noted that a village committee was constituted with some office bearers like secretary, treasurer, etc., to handle the fund. The Komtis without having made any contribution to the organization and enactment of the dramas, wanted to control the 'fund' by assuming the office of either the secretary or the treasurer. Mahanta organized the Deras and encouraged them to protest and oppose such kind of move (by the Komtis) as it was the Deras who by dint of their hard work had created this 'fund' and the Komtis had nothing to contribute to it. Since they were never associated with the village dramas, they were not allowed to keep the fund with them. Since then the Komtis were organized to go against the Deras as well as the 'Mahanta', the source of inspiration for the Deras. Thus the seed of factionalism was laid in Nuapada in as early as late 1920s. The era of factionalism began with distrust, opposition and hatred.

Evolution/Growth of Factional Politics in the Village

It is interesting to note that during 1938–1940 when the group rivalry between the Deras and Komtis was too much severe and bitter, the 'Mahanta' eloped with a beautiful girl, named Naseri, from the 'Bhandari' caste. It may be noted here that, she was the 'kept' of T. Narseya, one of the richest persons of the Komti caste. He frequently visited her as he had extra-marital, relationship with her. Naturally, he was highly provoked when he came to know about this elopement. The matter was brought to the notice of the Commissioner of Endowment Board. To teach the 'Mahanta' a lesson the Komtis gave money and wine to Redikas (labour class people) and asked them to harass and humiliate him ('Mahanta'). As a result he felt deeply insulted. But without keeping quiet, he also organized the Deras to avenge his humiliation. Gradually the village witnessed the emergence of factions: the 'Mahanta' and the Deras on one side and the Komtis and Redikas under the leadership of Tumulu Narseya on the other.

This was the beginning of factional politics in Nuapada. This was intensified following another social feud while took place between the two communities—Deras and Komtis. In Nuapada, earlier there was no latrine facilities. Whenever the people wanted to attend the call of nature, they used to go to the river Bahuda as its bank was converted into open latrines. An interesting incident took place in 1941. Gala Fakir, a rich man of the Dera community, went to the river bank to answer the call of nature. And while he was busy, his water jug was stolen by a Komti, Adi Narayan. Angry and annoyed, embarrassed and insulted, Fakir returned home and narrated the matter to his fellow brothers. To take revenge on Adi Narayan, they went to the Komti street and stabbed Adi Narayan and after that they went to the police station which is about 5 kilometers away from the village. They bribed the police and won them to their side. All the appeals made by the Komtis to the police to take stringent actions against their Deras, fell on their (police) deaf ears. The Deras got scot free. Disappointed and frustrated, the Komtis could not reconcile with the situation as their ego was terribly hurt and wanted to take revenge on the Deras at any cost. Therefore, they secretly met and engineered a plan. They firmly believed the Deras could not be taught a lesson so long as they remained united. This unity was to be broken into pieces at any cost. Hence, they provided some financial assistance to some poor and needy members of the Dera community with a view to win them to their side. Further, they also threatened not to lend money to those who would go against them. They succeeded in their attempts through coercion and manipulation. Besides these, certain conditions also favoured the Komtis. It may be noted that Gala Fakir, a Dera, had a tremendous influence on the members of his community as he was very rich and lent money to them. Since he charged heavy interest on the loan amount, the people were not happy with him. Further to add fuel to fire, with his influence and money-power he succeeded in ostracizing a person of his caste, who kept a Christian lady. This enraged the victim who with the support of a few member of his caste, challenged Fakir. The result was the division of Dera community into two hostile groups and all the efforts made by the 'Mahanta' to keep it united ended in a dismal failure. The group that opposed Fakir was supported by the Komtis. Since them, these two warring groups of the Dera community have been at loggerheads, disrupting the peaceful atmosphere of the village and often causing law and order problem in the area. Significantly, a faction of the Dera community was supported by the Komtis led by Sunkuru Jagannath who also headed a faction of his community.

A faction is generally formed when certain issues become controversial or disputed. It exists as long as these disputes continue to be there in the society. It has, therefore, no historical permanence. Events and incidents also give rise to factions. A faction gets dissolved the moment a dispute disappears. But the story does not end here since disappearance of a dispute gives rise to another dispute. In other words, when one dispute ends, another dispute arises and in that condition the faction gets re-formed. It has happened in the case of Dera community several times in Nuapada village.

Recognition of Factions

It is pertinent to note that an informal and close discussion with the villagers throws much light on village factional politics. But in the beginning they pretend to be highly united and organized. However, this pretentious posture of the unity soon starts collapsing and crumbling like a house of cards on establishing a good rapport with them. Cleavages cut across the community at various levels. It is interesting to point out here that whenever an outsider or officer visits the village or wants to stay there, leaders of the village meet him and highlight its goodness. Thereafter, they advise him not to meet some people as they are dangerous fellows.

They tell him "whenever you require any thing, kindly seek the help of so and so. Or you may inform me so that I will instruct somebody to make your stay more comfortable." This clearly indicates the existence of different factional groups. Further, one may observe some stereo-typed features about such groups and the people involved there in the village. Some of the comments villagers make about these factions are as follows :

"The Komtis have dominated the village since ages."

"They will never allow others to grow."

"Everybody in the village thinks of himself as a leader."

"There is no unity among the Oriyas."

"Panchayat People manipulate everything for their own interest."

"Politics has spoiled the atmosphere of the village."

It is factional politics that was responsible for delay in providing street lights as well as in the construction of the bridge over the river Bahuda.

Caste Dominance and Factionalism

In some cases, factions are organized along the caste lines. So, in a village different castes make groups of their own which may be called as small factions. Sometimes, they are aligned with major factions. A leader of a particular faction recruits the members and strives to increase its strength so as to become numerically stronger than the other faction(s). This certainly helps him to command more respect, prestige and influence in the community and the village.

On the basis of this criterion, it may be said that numerical strength is an important element of dominance of a group. M.N. Srinivas has propounded that numerical strength, economic power, political power, ritual status and western education help a caste to acquire and exercise its dominance over others. A pertinent question arises here i.e., what is or which is the dominant caste ? In fact, only those caste can wield dominance which are numerically large, organized and united and the strength so gained is used for the whole caste as a unit.[9] In Nuapada, as said earlier, Deras constitute the largest segment of the population, followed by the Komtis. But with their economic and political power they (Komti) are the most dominating community as they command positions of control and leadership. All other castes regard them as their natural leaders.

It is significant to state that this dominant caste maintains its supremacy and control over the village affairs as long as it has not been severely challenged by other groups. It is also an admitted fact that castes having more members are generally split into rival groups involved in rivalry, and leg-pulling to negate each other's influence. This phenomenon has assumed greater dimensions following the introduction of Panchayati Raj system in India. Kothari (1963) has pointed out that since candidates of the same caste contest against each other, the caste as a factor is losing importance and political factions and personal ambitions cut across caste loyalties. The same is the case in Nuapada also. As a result of internal split, the unity of the Komti caste is lost. Internal strife still continues and has spread its tentacles, eating thereby the vitality and strength of the community. No doubt, weakening of the cohesive force that once kept the dominant caste united and organized, and the resultant split, of the community provide an opportunity to the middle and lower caste groups to increase their influence and power in village politics. But it is not the case in Nuapada. Because the factions or rival groups of the dominant caste (Komti) strive their best to perpetuate at any cost their dominance. At least on this issue they are strongly united. The Dera community, which is numerically superior to that of the Komti, is divided into two rival groups and one of them has close links with one of the Komti factions. It is pertinent to note that a patron-client relationship exists between these two communities.

Factions are, therefore, created in the village, and it so happens that members belonging to a particular caste may align with one of the factions of another caste and in the process, multi-caste alliances come into existence, which are generally the foci of power rather than the caste as a whole. It may be noted that these alliances are clearly visible during panchayat elections. Gould (1963) in his study of a village in Uttar Pradesh has pointed out that traditionally powerful men were defeated in the panchayat elections at the hands of a leader of low caste because of his numerical superiority. Srinivas[10] has observed that with the introduction of the Panchayat system, the low caste people have become conscious of their role in the village power structure. Rastogi[11] is of opinion that factionalism comes to the fore at the time of Panchayat elections and that co-operation is at the low ebb on such occasions. From these studies it can be observed that power structure in the villages is undergoing a sea-change; loyalties cut across the caste boundaries; leaders of low castes are coming to power because of their numerical strength; new alignments are taking place with the introduction of universal franchise; and traditionally powerful men are losing their ground. Factionalism has, thus, become a part of village politics. On the basis of these studies it can also be said that in different spheres—whether in exercise of power or dominance in elections or in decision-making process of developmental activities or in articulation of leadership, the intra-caste unity is questioned. This is more so during the Gram-Panchayat elections in Nuapada, particularly in 1984 and 1992. In all panchayat elections except these two held in 1984 and 1992, leaders could succeed because of the dominant caste support. In Nuapada village the economic or numerical dominance of a particular caste is an index of panchayat leadership. The Komtis, though numerically smaller in comparison with the Deras, dominate village politics because of their economic dominance and land-owning status and even more so on account of their tenant relationship with the labourers.

Organization of Factions in the Village

The origin of factional politics in Nuapada can be attributed to the failure of "consensus" in organizing cultural activities in the village. But subsequently it centered around various political issues, perceived differently by different factions having different political affiliations. In the present study, the Komti caste as a whole vis-a-vis other castes may be termed as faction 'A'. The Komtis have their own organisation which regulates their social life. Every month they meet together to resolve their differences. But gradually because of several factors including differences of opinion and urbanization and modernization, intra-caste factions within faction 'A' have come up. It is, however, significant to note that so far the existence of intra-factions has not affected the predominance of this caste over others in the village.

Faction 'B' comprising the Deras, the weaving class constituting the majority of the population, came into existence under the leadership of 'Mahanta' Sri Kaibalya Das Babaji, a religious leader with an interest in the cultural activities of the village. Since the faction 'A' tried to dominate all the village activities, he, alongwith the Deras, challenged the dominance of the Komtis. As he was rich, he provided financial assistance to this faction. It may, however, be noted that in the absence of the 'Mahanta', the faction 'B' over the years lost its unity and strength as there was no one to guide it, advise it and provide effective leadership.

The conspiracy hatched out by faction 'A', frequent absence of the 'Mahanta' in the village, lack of understanding among the Deras, their squabbles over petty issues, etc., led to the split of the Dera community into two factions which can be termed as major factions 'C' and 'D'. The 'Mahanta', could not succeed in keeping the community united despite all his sincere efforts. He failed to resolve their differences. Besides these major factions, small factions also exists within small castes, having affiliations with major ones. Factions were also formed alongwith the kinship line. Besides, as said earlier, narrow and selfish interest also gave rise to intra-caste factions in the village. The Table 7.1 mentions about the existing factions in the village and their leaders.

It may be noted here that despite strong unity and cohesion, factions developed within factions 'A' when it split up under different circumstances. Faction 'A' was formed under the leadership of Tumulu Raghunath, who was ignored by his fellowmen in the caste council. Humiliated, he wanted to teach a lesson to the entire community by providing secret information to the police on the activities of his caste people. He acted as the agent of the police. Notwithstanding bitter opposition from his own community, he formed his own group, with the support of the poor, downtrodden, oppressed and exploited people of the village. Under his leadership came up the union of coolies "Khalasi Sangh" and the

Table 7.1

Major Factions	*Sub-Factions within major faction 'A'*	*Leaders*
'A'	—	Tumulu Eghnesu, T. Krishna Murty, Epari Lingaraju, Sunkuru Jagannath, Katakata Ram Murty, T. Narseya, Silla Sankar Narayan, Silla Sudarshan and others.
	a–1	Tumulu Raghunath
	a–2	Barat Rama Rao
	a–3	Epari Tejeswar and his brother E. Simanchal
	a–4	Tumulu Nageswar
	a–5	Epari Abbayi
'B'	—	Mahanta Sri Kaibalya Das Babaji
'C'	—	Gala Fakir now represented by his son Gala Chineya
'D'	—	Khadi Chandra, Bodedi Ganeshu, Manimi Bighnesu, Sunupu Baleya, Batala Abbayi.

"Dusthajan Samaj". All these activities helped him to challenge the predominance of he major faction 'A'. As a result, his faction had a serious tussle with the latter, thereby seriously affecting the functioning of the social and academic institutions of the village. For example, he (Raghunath) was asked by the Governing Body of the Nuapada College to collect donations from different sources for its development. And for this service he was given a commission. But, unfortunately, while collecting donations for the college from the people, he misbehaved with some, abused them, coerced them and threatened them with dire consequences unless they obliged him. He also fabricated certain charges against them and brought the same to the notice of the police. As a result, the litigations started. Victims, harassed and humiliated, resented against the malicious behaviour of Raghunath. The situation was however, pacified following his removal from his position by the Governing Body of the College. Raghunath was also socially ostracized by his community when his daughter-in-law committed suicide in a suspicious manner. His own caste people, who were so much angry and annoyed with him, did not even agree to carry the dead body to the cremation ground. Rather they wanted to exploit the situation to their advantage. It is pertinent to note that the faction led by Raghunath ceased to exist following his death. His son T. Chandra Mohan, paid a sum of five hundred and one rupees as fine and joined the mainstream.

The origin of the sub-faction a–2 can be attributed to the process of implementation of Land Reforms Act by the Government of Orissa in 1975. When it was strictly implemented, most of the land-owners belonging to the major faction 'A' were affected. At that time B.Rama Rao was the Sarpanch of the village who had a good rapport with government officers. So the affected members requested him to do some thing for them. But he did not pay any heed to their requests. He even remained indifferent towards his political master S. Jagannath. Aggrieved, the latter tried to put the Sarpanch into trouble and this finally led to the creation of another sub-faction a–2. Another cause was the distribution of fertilizer. Since Rao was in-charge of the Co-operative society, which distributed the fertilizers among the farmers, Jagannath asked for the same at a cheaper rate. But Rao refused to oblige him as it would go against the principle. This further aggravated the factional hostility between the two.

The rise of sub-faction a–3 was due to a conflict between the forces of change and those of continuity. Epari Tejeswar Rao, who stood for change, wanted to introduce certain reforms in the society by abolishing blind beliefs and superstition challenging the social barriers, he went for marriage with a widow. This decision, naturally, was not acceptable to conservative forces represented by a major faction 'A', which laid a condition that the marriage would be acceptable to the community if Tejeswar Rao paid a fine of Rs. 9116/- to the caste council. But Rao, along with his young friends, who also belonged to his own caste, rejected this proposal. As a result, a sub-faction was formed to challenge the major one. However, with the interference of the State Council of the caste the matter was resolved. Marriage was accepted by the community and Rao paid a sum of five hundred and one rupees as donation but not as fine to the local caste council. In spite of this, the sub-faction a–3, led by Epari Simanchala, elder brother of Tejeswar Rao continues to exist in village politics. Conflicting business interests and lust for political power are the major factors responsible for conflict between these groups.

As mentioned earlier, some times conflicting personal interest also creates factions. It was the main reason for the creation of faction a–4 under the leadership of Tumulu Nageswar, who originally served as a mechanic in Sonepur College of present Sonepur District. He lost his job for his insincerity and irresponsible conduct. He returned to Nuapada and as he had no other job he chose politics as his career. But he could not endear himself to his own caste people as he was arrogant. He did not get any support from them. Since he was egocentric and narrow in his approach he was hated by many. Besides, to protect his personal interest he always went on changing his political affiliations. In 1980, he supported Chinamani Dyan Samantara who successfully contested the Assembly Election. But when no loan under self-employment scheme was sanctioned to him by the M.L.A. In 1985 general election to the Assembly he asked his people to support the Janata Dal candidate, Usha Rani Devi but not Samantara. Usha Rani Devi lost the election and Samantara won the race. Despite this, Nageswar opposed Samantara and even made demonstration with black flags during the latter's visit to the village. This cost his job (he was working as a clerk in Jayanti Pathagar of the village) as he was not in the good books of the M.L.A. and was also arrested by the police. In 1990, the election scenario changed and Usha Rani Devi, came out victorious. Since faction a–4 was affiliated to her, it tried to extract as much benefit as possible and, in fact, got maximum contracts for various developmental works. Since his work was found to be sub-standard, the Block Development Officer, refused to sanction the amount and surprisingly he was supported by the M.L.A., Usha Rani Devi. As a result, Nageswar felt offended. This was compounded when he could not succeed in his attempts to transfer certain officials who were opposed to him. The M.L.A. did not support him. Frustrated and disappointed, he directed all his anger and hatred towards the faction 'A' and attributed all his failures to the functioning of the latter. It may be noted that personal trait and character of a person promotes, aggravates and influences the curse of the factional politics of a village.

The sub-faction a–5, small in size and led by Epari Abbayi,

cuts across communities like Komti and Dera. Abbayi, an opportunist, a fence-sitter, is well known for his diplomacy as well as for changing his political affiliation too frequently. His faction, therefore, does not command much respect and has, lost the confidence of the people as well as of the political parties.

The second major faction i.e., the faction 'B', as mentioned earlier, was organized under the leadership of Mahanta Sri Kaibalya Das Babaji during the period 1926–30. Its origin has been discussed earlier in detail. This faction had a peculiar organizational set-up. The Babaji, a Brahmin, took its lead though it consisted of the members of the Dera community only. He was almost an outsider. Though he used to remain absent in the village, he was extremely popular among the people because of his personal contributions and strong opposition to the monopoly of the major faction 'A'. The popularity of faction 'B' went up when it took steps to establish and promote a college in the village. While other factions, apprehending danger, shirked from taking any responsibility to take the lead in this direction, it came forward with maximum drive and initiative to fulfil a long-cherished desire of the people.

It may be noted that like the Komti caste the Dera community was also not free from internal conflict. Misunderstanding, selfishness, lack of any broad outlook—all these caused the split of the major faction 'B', resulting in the formation of major factions 'C' and 'D'.

During 1938–1950 intra-conflict as a phenomenon was highly conspicuous in the Dera community. Things, however, improved with the establishment of a weavers' co-operative society. But the members could not forget their past activities, hostile attitudes towards one another. Animosity and hatred characterized their relationship. Although in the years 1969, 1989 and 1996 they got united to perform the Thakurani Yatra—a common cultural festival of the village; they fell apart soon after the festival was over. A detailed discussion is also made later in this chapter.

Factions Among Other Castes

Like the Deras and Komtis, other castes are also divided into small interest groups i.e., factions. Interestingly, some people from these castes and groups align themselves with the major factions on grounds of friendship. Most of these alignments are interest-oriented. Castes with a large population have been found to have more factions. Castes having small population join one or the other major faction. Normally they do not split up into smaller groups. The following table shows different castes being split into different factions and their alignment with the major factions.

Table 7.1 : Factions among Different Castes

Caste	*Leader*	*Align with Major Faction*
Barber (Bhandari)	Sarathi Dakua	B and D.
Brahmin	Raghunath Tripathy	B. (Occasionally)
	Somanath Padhy	B and C.
	Surendra Nath Panda	B.
Brahmin (Kamma)	R. Janaki Rao	A, B, C and D (Opportunists)
Dhoba	Sridhar Sethi	A, B and C.
	Dandasi Sethi	B and C.
Goldsmith	Kumari Achary	B and D.
Gudia	Raghunath Sasamal	A.
	Ladu Kishore Sasamal	A and C.
Hadi	Murali Patro	A and D.
	Dhusa Ghadei	A and D.
Kampa	Babu Pradhan	B.
	Zadi Pradhan	A and C.
Keuta	Bharat Behera	A and B.
Khadura	Hrusikesh Nayak	A.
	Lingaraj Mahaptra	B.
	Siba Nayak	A, B
Mali	Lingaraj Rana	A and B
Oriya (Jani)	Anada Jani	C and B (Occasionally)
Parcelia	K. Krishna Rao	A, B and D.

Panchayati Raj and Factions

Panchayati Raj System, introduced in India with the twin objectives of democratic decentralisation and peoples' participation in planned programmes, aimed at strengthening the foundations of democracy by linking the Gram Sabha with the Lok-Sabha in

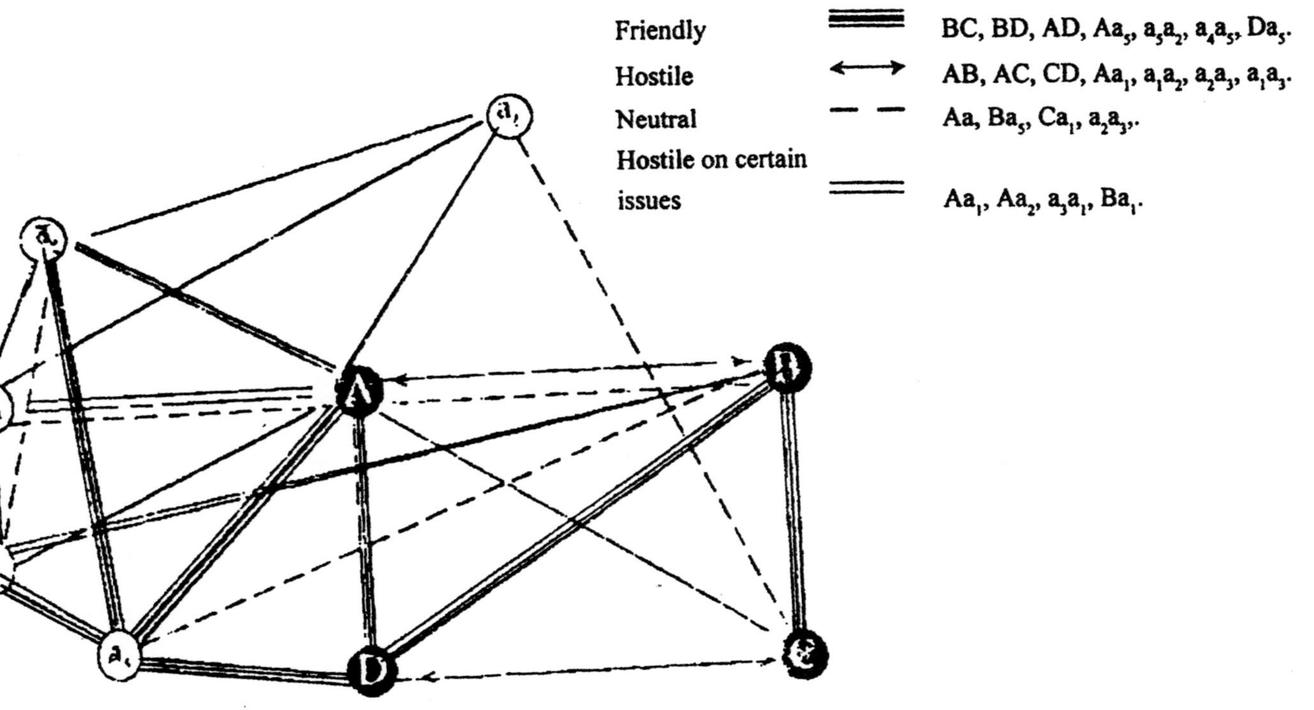

Diagram Showing the Alliance of the Different Factions in the Village

an interconnected system of democratic administration. No doubt, participation of the people at the grass-root level and their own personal involvement in the democratic process are highly essential for the successful functioning of a democracy. They also promote a sense of identity as well as a feeling of oneness among them. But it has miserably failed in its efforts at social mobilization and in getting co-operation from the people to the extent it is necessary for the effective implementation of the nation-building programmes. Elections to the local bodies are of great importance for the village people. But personal enemity and animosity narrow feelings of casteism, language, economic status and groupism with their concomitant vices generate bitterness among the contesting candidates and their supporters. Therefore, the institutions of Panchayat Raj have become riddled with factionalism, casteism, and the nasty game of politics has been carried to the door-steps of the villagers.

Factional activities present a new dimension in the context of elections in the democratic political structure. While the factions tend to get themselves involved with the political parties at the state and the national levels, they form the main foci of power conflict in the village panchayat elections.

The Orissa Gram Panchayat Act was passed in the year 1948 and because of certain defects it was amended in 1950. However, within a few years of independence–in 1951–community development programme was introduced by the Government of India with a view to expediting the rural development. But this programme, mostly run by outsiders, failed to elicit the spontaneous popular participation and involvement. Hence, this generated rethinking on the part of the government and prompted to introduce Panchayati Raj in order to remove this lacuna. Panchayati Raj, a product of the Balwantrai Mehta Committee report was, however, not introduced all over India at the same time. In Orissa, it was started in the year 1961. In course of time, it brought about significant changes in the attitude of villagers. The importance of Panchayats for the people of rural India has been perpetually growing. With the exception of revenue, law and order, and judicial matters, the Panchayats are expected to perform practically all the administrative, Municipal and developmental functions. As membership of a Panchayat means a share in power and the consequent enhancement of one's prestige in the village, it occupies a very vital position in village politics.[12]

The Panchayati Raj, as originally conceived, involved three tiers. At the top of the structure was the Zilla Parishad at the district level, the Panchayat Samiti at the middle and the Gram-Panchayat at the grass-root level. This system was meant to introduce self-government at the local level, encourage popular participation in governmental as well as developmental activities and give a share to Gandhian ideal of self-government. It was hoped that it would be free from party politics so that the villagers would remain mostly united in an ideal environment congenial to united efforts for development. But with in a short time those pious hopes were shattered into pieces and heated political battles, little different from other arenas of politics.

In the initial phase the people did not have much idea about the power potential of the Gram Panchayats. These new statutory bodies in rural areas looked quite innocent and were hoped to augment health, education, construction of roads, and digging of wells and other aspects of village development. Hardly had any one an idea that they would turn out to be store houses of power, prestige and money. In course of time, it became evident that the Gram Panchayat provided ample scope for manipulation and misappropriation.

In fact, over the years the Panchayats have become tempting grounds for individual manipulators to feather their nests. Further, they have provided opportunities to political parties to strengthen their bases at the grass-root level. Even though, they have been statutorily forbidden to directly enter the Panchayat politics, they found it almost impossible to resist the temptation of going there. According to Sarvodaya ideal, 'Politics' and 'Panchayati Raj' are anti-thetical terms. The former disrupts and divides, while the purpose of the latter is to promote development through consensus and unanimity.[13] Hence, it has been suggested that political parties which inevitably carry the germs of 'politics' should be excluded from the operation of the Panchayati Raj.[14] But, however, after sometime the Gram Panchayats became hot-beds of politics, and the hunting grounds of manipulative and power-hungry politicians, as well as of political parties and factions.

In 1961, the year in which statutory Panchayat was introduced in Orissa, Nuapada was a part of the Digapahandi Panchayat Samiti. Earlier it was also the Panchayat head quarter. Initially, the Nuapada Gram Panchayat comprised of 31 villages. The area of its operation was very vast.

It is significant to note that successive Gram Panchayat elections from 1948 onwards took place peacefully without much factionalism in the village. The village ward members used to be elected without any opposition. This was possible because of Sunkuru Jagannath's sincere efforts. He discussed the matter relating to election of ward members with the people. The choice of candidates was unanimous. The election atmosphere witnessed consensus and unanimity but not contest and conflict, co-operation but no confrontation; debate and discussion but not disharmony. Such a peaceful atmosphere of panchayat election devoid of any factionalism prevailed for sometime. The people had come together with a spirit of unity and unanimity atleast for more than one decade (upto 1970). Certainly it was an unusual and unique phenomenon for an Orissan village.

It has been rightly observed that instead of de-centralizing political and administrative powers, the panchayats rather assist to centralize the powers in the hands of those who are socially and economically dominant and whose influence extends upto the state and central governments.[15] It is seen that in Nuapada, right from the inception of the village panchayat, the elections are manipulated by the rural elites. Further, because of the economic predominance, the Komti caste was not only able to field a large number of candidates but also assumed the leadership role as is evident from the Table 7.3.

The Panchayat bodies were superseded during the periods from 20-07-59 to 29-01-60, 01-04-68 to 31-03-69, 19-02-81 to 15-02-84, 27-12-89 to 11-07-92 and placed under the government control. During these periods the village level workers (VLW) were posted as Sarpanchs. Since March 1995, the VLW has been functioning as the Sarpanch of Nuapada.

Thus, the Table 7.3 indicates that after the establishment of statutory panchayats (1961) the office of the Sarpanch was occupied by the Faction 'A' upto 1985. Although before 1961, 'Mahanta'

Table 7.3

Sl. No.	*Name of the Sarpanch*	*Caste*	*Period*	
			From	To
1.	Sunkuru Jagannath	Komti	Aug. 1953	10-05-54
2.	Rajaguru Mahanta Sri Kaibalya Das Babaji	Brahmin	11-05-54	23-11-55
3.	Gala Chineya	Dera	24-11-55	20-07-59
4.	S. Jagannath	Komti	29-01-60	31-03-67
5.	Tumulu Mohan Rao	Komti	01-04-67	31-03-68
6.	Tumulu Mohan Rao	Komti	01-04-69	23-06-70
7.	Barat Rama Rao	Komti	24-06-70	18-02-81
8.	Barat Rama Rao	Komti	16-02-84	15-09-85
9.	Ananda Jani Naib-Sarpanch in Charge	Oriya (Jani)	15-09-85	16-11-85
10.	Mahanta Sri K.B. Das Babaji	Brahmin	17-11-85	26-12-89
11.	Ananda Jani	Oriya	12-07-92	25-03-95

Sri Kaibalya Das Babaji (Faction-B) and Gala Chinneya (Faction-C) occupied the office, in 1954 and 1955 respectively they were in fact, supported by their rich friend S. Jagannath, a leading member of the Komti caste. Secondly, as the territorial jurisdiction of the panchayat was also very vast, people of the surrounding villages also favoured them because of their strong assurance of undertaking developmental activities in those villages. In those days, the Sarpanchs were elected Babaji and Chineya. Thirdly, other Komti fellows of the village were not aware of the power potential of the village panchayat.

It may be noted that as a result of the delimitations of the Gram-Panchayats, the Nuapada Gram-Panchayat became a part of the Chikiti Panchayat Samiti during 1962–63. The Government of Orissa vide its notification no. 3765, dated 11-03-1966 bifurcated the Panchayat and as a result the Nuapada Gram-Panchayat comprised of ten villages including Nuapada itself. Significantly, many candidates wanted to contest the election to the office of the Sarpanch. Even for the office of ward-members people filed their nominations and were prepared to contest the election. Though, the Panchayats were represented by women as well as

Scheduled Caste members, in most of the cases they were ingnored on the important issues pertaining to the general welfare of the villages. The dominant castes with their high profile out numbered the Scheduled Castes so far as their representation in the Panchayats was concerned.

In 1970, Barat Rama Rao, a young, energetic and qualified person belonging to the Komti caste, contested for the office of Sarpanch. He was supported not only by different factions of the village, but also by some of the educated people of nearby villages. Interestingly, Tumulu Raghunath, who also hailed from the same caste and was the leader of the faction a-1 filed his nomination for the office of the Sarpanch despite the fact that he did not have any base at the Panchayat level. Famous for litigations in the village, he was popularly called 'liar' and the people did not have any faith in him. Therefore, they did not extend their help to him at the time of election. Besides, they were very much averse to him as he was the leader of the untouchables. Therefore, the members of the Komti community supported Rao. As a result, he not only won the election but also because of the ogod will and support of the people he won the subsequent elections and remained in the office of Sarpanch upto 18 February, 1981.

It may be noted that the Congress Government of Orissa in 1981 dissolved the Panchayati Raj bodies. Though, election to the different Gram-Panchayats took place in January 1984, during the intervening period i.e., from 1981 to 1983 he (Rama Rao) was addressed as the Sarpanch by the villagers. This shows his popularity among them. In 1980, General Election to the State Legislative Assembly was held. He supported Chintamani Dyan Samantra who successfully contested as an independent candidate from the Chikiti Assembly Constituency. He cultivated a very good relationship with him (Samantara). Taking advantage of this, he started misguiding him by providing false information against some leading members of the factions—A, B and C.

As stated earlier, factors like personal enemity and differences of opinion with S. Jagannath (a member of faction 'A') on issues like implementation of land reforms, supply of fertilizers and dissociation fromthe prominent leaders of faction A and B on various developmental activities including setting up of a college in the village were mostly responsible for Rao's isolation as well as emergence of factions in village politics. However, this could not bring any set back to his political career and fortune.

When the Government of Orissa announced that the election to the local bodies would take place in the month of January 1984, the people as well as the factional leaders became alert, serious and active and began to applroach the M.L.A. for his support for their cause in the Panchayat election. Many unknown faces also appeared in the political scene, who wanted to try their luck. Just on the eve of the government notification for election to the local bodies, the villagers' irrespective of their political affiliations began to hink of the construction of a bridge over the River Bahuda and in this connection they held several meetings, collected funds and proceeded to Bhubaneswar to place their demand before the authorities through the M.L.A. They got a strong assurance from the concerned Minister that their demand would be fulfilled. To see that their demand was not ignored and steps were taken to realize it, meetings were held regularly by the villagers to discuss the issue. Their attendance at these meetings was quite encouraging. Because whenever there was any problem confronting the whole village, they came forward to face it with courage and solve it with conviction. This showed their unity, strength, determination and courage. Once it was decided that a meeting would be convened to discuss the construction of the bridge and secretly a decision would also be taken about the unanimous choice of the Sarpanch (The election to this office was to be held in January, 1984). But when this matter was leaked out most of the leaders and their supporters did not turn up to the meeting. Inspite of poor attendance, those who attended it proposed that Silla Sudarshan Rao should be the unanimous choice for the office of Sarpanch. Soon after this meeting, one of the factional leaders, Kaibalya Das (Faction—B), informed the proceedings of the meeting to the M.L.A. over phone, and the latter was not happy with the decision as he did not like him personally. Therefore, when Silla Sankar Narayan, elder brother of Sudarshan approached the M.L.A. to seek his support for his son, S. Badri Narayan, who wanted to contest for the office of Sarpanch, the M.L.A. happily assured him of all his help, support and co-operation. Rama Rao (Faction a–2) who had been the Sarpanch of the village panchayat from 1970 also wanted to fight for the same office. Apparently he was very close to the M.L.A.

It may be noted that when Badri Naryan filed his nomination, Sudarshan withdrew his candidature. It is interesting to note that in 1984 Gram-Panchayat Elections all the four candidates who contested for the post of Sarpanch announced that they were nominated by the Congress–I M.L.A., C.D. Samantra. And the village was drastically divided into separate groups ignoring differences fo the social, economic and cultural as well as caste feelings. It was their personal interest, narrow approach and selfish outlook that divided the village community and other factors—social, economic, cultural, etc. had little impact on it. Altruism was sacrificed at the altar of narrow selfish interest and development of the village as a whole was thrown as a subject to the wind. It seemed as if everyone was under the strong grip of jealousy and protection and promotion of self-interest.

Representatives who are voted into office, function under the constant supervision of the people, because all their actions are subject to their scrutiny. Politics has also become more accessible to the humbler section of the society. The elective element of the Panchayati Raj has become more organized in terms of institutions that are quite close to the people and the possibilities of their feeling of affinity for the working of these institutions are greater. Hence these have resulted in the emergence of more competitors in the formal political setting,[16] as is evident from the following discussion.

In the 1984 Gram-Panchayat Election four candidates were in the race for the office of the Sarpanch. They were:

(1) Silla Badri Narayan (Komti)

(2) Barat Rama Rao (Komti)

(3) Sapata Mohan Rao (Dera)

(4) Hari Sethi (Dhoba, S.C.)

It may, however, be noted that the contest for the office between Badri Narayan and Rama Rao was keen and tough as both were considered to be strong candidates by the villagers. The former was supported by most of the important members of the village. They were: S. Jagannath, S. Sankar Narayan, 'Mahanta' Sri Kaibalya Das Babaji, Gala Chineya, Silla Sudarshan, Somanath Padhy, T.N. Murty and Epari Simanchal. They sincerely wanted that he should win the game at any cost.

It may be noted that Barat Ram Rao is called as the old mouse as he is shrewd and cunning with a tremendous foresight. As he was not acceptable to many important personalities of the village because of differences of opinion with them on several issues, he left the place. He felt that separation might help in bridging the gap between him and leaders who opposed him. The leaders might also forget him. As a result, they might not be that hostile, have had he continued to stay in the village. He left for Berhampur and stayed there for six months till the election which was held on 23 January, 1984. Interestingly, till 21st he was not seen in the village. Immediately, till 21st he was not seen in the village. Immediately after his return, he met Epari Abbayi (of faction a–5) and Raghunath Tripathy (leaders having close link with the M.L.A.), offered his unconditional apology to them and appealed to them for help. He also told them that the M.L.A. would certainly back him and that's why in the eleventh hour of the election he came for canvassing among the people. Since Abbayi and Tripathy were opposed to Badri Narayan, they extended their support to him. He was also supported by his rich friend Kandeti Krishna Rao of Parcelia. With their support as his strength, Rao started his hectic compaigning, going from door to door, approaching the women voters in particular. He lay prostrate before them and requested with his folded hands to bless him for his success in the election. His humility and polite behaviour had a tremendous impact upon the women voters. They assured him of their strong support and unstint co-operation. It is pertinent to mention that unity, co-operation, cordiality, fellowship, harmony, etc. that once characterized the Komti caste were lost in this electioin, as both Badri Naryan and Rama Rao belonged to this community. It is significant to observe that when the candidates of the same caste contest against one another for the same post the caste as a factor loses its importance as political factions and personal ambitions cut across caste loyalties.

The Nuapada gram panchayat was bifurcated again in 1983 vide government notification no. 17965 dated 20-10-83, where by it comprised of only three villages, namely, Subalaya Sasan, Brahmin Nuapada and Nuapada. Subalaya Sasan is inhabited by Brahmins only. Most of them are primary school teachers. Rao met them and solicited their support to win in the election. He also influenced them through the Sub-Inspector of Schools. Lastly, he wanted to mould the voters of B. Nuapada where 98 per cent of them belong to 'Gola' (shepherd) caste. The village, in fact, was a vote bank for all the candidates. The villagers had a great respect for the M.L.A., Samantara. Therefore, those influential members of the village, who supported Badri Narayan, requested the M.L.A. to visit the village and request the voters to support Badri Narayan. Though he was not favourably disposed towards him, he visited the village with much reluctance on 22 January, 1984 and asked the people to support Badri Narayan. After staying for a short while in the village, he left for Bhabaneswar. It was strongly believed that his appeal and convassing would certainly bring a good dividend to Badri Narayan and there would not be any problem for him to win the election. Soon after his departure, Rama Rao, along with his close friend Krishna Rao, went to the village and showed the villagers a letter written by Samantara where in it was mentioned that Rao would be the most suitable candidate for the post and he (M.L.A.) would be very happy if the villagers elected him as their Sarpanch. It is significant to note that the letter was a fake one as is evident from Krishna Rao's disclosure in a personal interview with the researcher. He confessed that as there was no other alternative, to motivate the people to support Rama Rao, they were forced to resort to such dubious means. But, undoubtedly, the letter threw the people of B. Nuapada into a state of utter confusion. Both Rama Rao and Krishna tried their best to convince them that had the M.L.A. been a true supporter of Badri Narayan he would have definitely come to the village much earlier to convass them to support Badri Narayan. He visited them at the last moment to satisfy those important members who supported Badri Narayan. But inwardly he did not like him. Hence his letter to them. They also provided them enough liquor. Influenced by the letter and liquor, the people changed their minds and decided unanimously to cast their votes in favour of Rama Rao. The very next morning i.e. the election day when the supporters of Badri Narayan went to the village, they saw a drastic change in the attitude of the people.

Besides Badri Narayan and Rama Rao, there were two other candidates in the race for the office of Sarpanch. S. Mohan Rao, a Dera by caste and Hari Sethi who belonged to Scheduled caste were not popular in the village. The latter was not even liked by the people of his own community. It is pertinent to note that because of patron-client relationship, caste as a factor could not influence the voters as was expected. People particularly belonging to the washerman community supported other caste people like Badri Narayan and Mohan Rao more than Sethi as is evident from the voting result.

Rama Rao won the election by a slender margin of votes. His victory was certainly a great setback to badri Naryan who was over-confident of his victory. He and his supporters lost their faith in the M.L.A. who, in their opinion, ditched them, deceived them. They, therefore, nurtured a grudge against him. They also took a vow to teach him a lesson at the time of need. Factional politics, thus, gained a new momentum, in Nuapada.

It is very significant to note that though Rao won the electioin, he was scared of the people, felt insecure, apprehended danger to his life from their side. Therefore, very often he left the village and used to spend his time else where, preferably at Berhampur with his father-in-law. As a result, there was a great dislocation in the panchayat work. Panchayat meetings were not help regularly and whenever held majority of the ward members did not turn up as they belonged to different factions of the village. Many developmental activities were stalled. The administration was thrown into turmoil and utter confusion.

But Rama Rao was in no way personally affected. Rather he was elected to the office of the vice-chairman of the Panchayat Samiti with the support of Samantara. Arrogant, power-drunk and irresponsible, he had little respect or love for anybody in the village. His own cousin brother, Barat Bhadranchal, a ward member of the panchayat, also became hostile to him. When the situation became so bad, so intolerable and reached its climax, ward members opposed him and passed a no-confidence motion against him. Eight out of eleven ward members of the panchayat submitted a petition to the Sub-Divisional Officer, Berhampur on 25-06-1985 stating that since they had lost their confidence in Rao, a date might kindly be fixed to pass a non-confidence motion against him. When the matter became serious and political atmosphere tense, Samantara invited the ward-members to resolve the crisis through discussion and negotiation. Samantara, who had already by then become the Deputy Speaker of Orissa Legislative Assembly, was disappointed and felt very much offended when no body except S. Sabreya turned up to meet him. Sabreya had a detailed discussion with him about the activities of Rao as Sarpanch and the opinion and impression of the ward members about the Sarpanch. Since, he was a supporter of Rao he did not believe what Sabreya told him. Since emotion and affection blinded him, he completely lost sight of reality. In other words, he was not pragmatic.

It was, therefore, not unnatural when he asked the S.D.O. not to accept the demands of the ward-members. The S.D.O., kept quiet and did not take any action on their memorandum on the plea that it did not contain anything that warranted for such a drastic action. Aggrieved and disappointed, they rushed to the Pattapur Block to bring a copy of the memorandum submitted by the members of the Pattapur Panchayat Samiti, to the S.D.O., on the basis of which permission was given to them to pass a no-confidence motion against the Sarpanch. In the same line the ward members of Nuapada also prepared a memorandum and submitted it to the concerned authority. In the mean time the Chairman, the Block Development Officer and the Gram Panchayat Officer of the Chikiti Panchayat Samiti came to Nuapada to discuss the matter with the aggrieved ward-members. The discussion eneded in failure. Permission was given to them to pass a no-confidence motion against the Sarpanch. It was decided that on 22 August, 1985 the fate of Rao would be decided. Rao did his best to divide them by creating a rift. But he could not succeed. He felt that his days in office were numbered. It is interesting to note that on 20 August, just two days before the passing of a no-confidence motion against Rao, all the eight aggrieved members went to Berhampur and remained in an unknown place. On the D-Day, they went to the Nuapada Gram Panchayat Office by a taxi. The G.P.O. asked them whether they were in favour of no-confidence motion or not. Out of nine members present, eight of them were unanimous in their opinion that they have lost all their trust and confidence in Rao. He was, removed from office—by rival factions. He handed over his charge to Ananda Jani, Naib Sarpanch on 15 September, 1985. For the first time in the history of Nuapada Gram Panchayat, a Sarpanch was forced to quit his office ignominiously.

With the notification for the fresh election to the office of the Sarpanch, the village politics took a new turn and factioinalism assumed a new dimension. Removal of Rama Rao from the office of Sarpanch by the ward-members supported by Komtis, distanced the latter (Komtis) from the M.L.A., Samantra. Annoyed and unhappy, Samantara nurtured a grudge against the Komtis. The latter were also apprehensive of being victimized by the M.L.A. in form of vigilance raids on their business houses. They feared him and hated him. Thus, hatred and fear prevented them from selecting or sponsoring any candidate for the office of the Sarpanch. Except the group led by T. Nageswar, all of them supported the 'Mahanta' because they were well aware of the fact that he had a very good understanding with Samantara. They also did not want to further embitter, their relationship with the latter as this might be harmful to their interest.

Besides the 'Mahanta' there were three more candidates, namely, (i) Kandeti Krishna Rao, (ii) Hrusikesh Nayak, (iii) Hari Sethi, in the fray. Rao was also the favourite candidate of the local M.L.A., and close friend of Rama Rao, the former Sarpanch. Since the Komtis were apprehensive of the the 'Mahanata's' withdrawl from the contest at the last moment, they decided to extend their support to H.K. Nayak, a Khadura by caste and th eblue-eyed baby of Jagannath Pati, a former M.L.A. of the area. It felt that in case the 'Mahanta' withdrew his nomination, it would not support Rao, a Parcelia who belonged to the rival faction led by Rama Rao.

It may be observed that Raghunath Tripathy, a retired teacher and supporter of Samantara, was unhappy with the Mahanta as he was once humiliated by the latter. To keep the 'Mahanata' out of the race he insisted that Ananda Jani, the then Naib-Sarpanch, should contest the election. Dr. Bamadev Panigrahi, the ten Medical Office enjoying the patronage of Samantara, however, strongly recommended the name of 'Mahanta' for the office of Sarpanch, because there was none other than him, to challenge the dominance of the Komtis. K. Krishna Rao, a supporter of Samantara, withdrew his nomination as he felt that this would enable the 'mahanta' to win the election.

Mahanta was declared elected as he got an absolute majority of votes as is evident from the Table 7.4.

It may, therfore, be said that in this election, the 'Mahanata' was the unanimous choice of theh people. Factions irrespective of

[Table 7.4] Voting Pattern and the Support of Different Factions in 1985 Panchayat Election

Sl. No.	*Candidates*	*Caste*	*Votes Secured*	*Supported by*
1.	'Mahanta' Sri Kaibalya Das Babaji	Brahmin	1010 (Elected)	Factions A, C and D except faction a–1, a–4 & some followers of other factions
2.	Hari Sethi	Dhoba	97	Faction a–1, and Murali Patro, Dandasi Sethi.
3.	Hrusikesh Nayak	Khadura	89	Faction a–4 and his own caste members of his faction.

their differences of opinion supported him. H. K. Nayak was supported by Nageswar. Raghunath, leader of the untouchables, supported Sethi. But most of the members of the washerman community to which Seti belonged, favoured the 'Mahanta' not because of the patron-client relationship, but because of their sweet relations with his other supporters.

Politics is a power game and political actors play it with all seriousness with all the resources available with them. As has been rightly said, in this game no one is one's permanent friend or permanent enemy. Today's best friend can be tommorrow's worst enemy. It is one's interest that forces one to accept one and treat him as his friend or foe. In other words, one's interest is always permanent but not his friends and foes. It is probably because of this, politics does not follow a fixed route. It rarely moves in a straight line as it has very often taken a zig-zig route frequently changing its course. The same is the case with the factional politics of Nuapada. Devoid of consistencey and uniformity, it has become one of the most unpredicatable phenomena.

In 1985 panchayat election in Nuapada the Mahanta was elected as the Sarpanch with the support of the M.L.A., C. D. Samantara. But the honey-moon period between the two could not last long. Soon differences cropped up between the two. They differed on the issue of appointment of some one as the librarian of the Nuapada College. Ego clash and misunderstanding between the two cost Samantara his job. He lost the 1990 election because of strong opposition from the 'Mahanta' and his supporters who played a very significant role in the 1990 electoral politics of the Chikiti Assembly Constituency.

In December, 1989, the Government of Orissa dissolved the village panchayats and in a notification declared that elections to these bodies would be held on 30 May, 1992. With the approach of this election, leaders of the Nuapada panchayat became very alert and vied with one another to get the support of Usha Rani Devi, the then local M.L.A., who could not decide whom to support and whom to oppose. She was not decisive. At last she, however, decided that some one should be "selected" as the Sarpanch by the people in her presence in the village. On reaching there, she was invited by the supporters of Anand Jani and K. Krishna Rao to B. Nuapada village for discussion. She turned down their request and asked them to come to Nuapada.

Interestingly, factions led by T. Nageswar and Hrusikesh Nayak selected different spots in the village for discussion with Usha Devi. On her way to the village she got all such information from her supporters. Therefore, instead of going to any spot selected by any faction, she went straight to the Balaji temple and invited all the leaders and their supporters to come to this place to discuss the matter relating to the 'selection' of a candidate as Sarpanch. She did not allow to have a prolonged discussion and nominated Anand Jani as sarpanch and Ramesh Chandra Padhy as Samiti Member. As per the Amendment (1992) to Orissa Gram Panchayat Rule, like Sarpanch, a Samiti member is to be elected by the adult citizens of the panchayat. This system has been adopted for the first time in Orissa. Therefore, the candidates for both the offices were nominated by the M.L.A.

Soon after the meeting was over, most of the Komtis, being dissatisfied, got united and unanimously took a decision to support Hrusikesh Nayak, a Kadura by caste and a dissident member of the Janata Party. Interestingly C.D. Samantara ignored the Komtis by not choosing any one from their community for the said posts. This he did to avenge his defeat in the 1990 Assembly Election. He held the Komtis responsible for his defeat. He, therefore, nominated Mupunu Bairi (a Dera by caste) as Sarpanch and Gazi Bairi (a Gola by caste) as the Samiti Member.

The election witnessed the emergence of many new faces joining the race. Though, five candidates contested for the office of Sarpanch, it was, in fact, a tringular contest involving Anand Jani, M. Bairi and H.K. Nayak. Besides these three, T. Nageswar (a Komti), who was not in the good books of both Usha Devi and Samantara, and Hari Sethi (Washerman by Caste) were in the fray. Forgetting all their past differences, the Komtis got themselves united and adopted all measures to make Nayak, victorious in the electioin. Ananda Jani was elected to the office of Sarpanch by securing 608 (42.58 per cent) votes. The Table 7.5 gives a picture about the candidates and votes secured by them in the panchayat election held on 30 May, 1992.

It is significant to note that for the first time in the history of Nuapada Gram Panchayat election a non-Komti without any support from the Komtis of the village got elected to the office of the Sarpanch. This is due to the fact that at village level politics, particularly in recent times, Sarpanchas are elected mainly with support of the M.L.A. Nuapada is not an exception. Since 1980, the local M.L.A. has been playing a key role in the election of Sarpanch. He has a decisive voice in the electoral process of the panchayat. People's easy access to him has helped him a lot in manipulating the election to his own advantage. Secondly, there was the Janata wave. Hence, the non-Komtis who belonged to Janata Dal favoured Anand Jani. Thirdly, he got maximum support from theh people of B. Nuapada. For the first time in this election the people of Nuapada turned a deaf ear to the requests of the Komtis to support Nayak, despite their patron-client relationship with most of them. Fourthly, he extended his support to Ramesh Chandra Padhy, a contestant for the office of Member of the Panchayat Samiti and in return got his support. Fifthly, one of the Dera factions led by Chineya also supported him.

T. Nageswar was not in the good books of Usha Devi. Therefore, his candidature was vehemently opposed by her. Angry and annoyed he filed his nomination as an independent candidate. Because of his political activities and flexible character neither the Janata Dal nor the Congress supported him. The people of his own

Table 7.5

Sl. No.	*Candidates*	*Castes*	*Party Affiliation*	*Supported by*	*Votes Secu-red*	*Rema-rks*
1.	Ananda Jani	Oriya	Janata	Usha Devi (M.L.A.), People of B. Nuapada S. Mohan Rao, Sridhar Sethi, Lingaraj Rana, K. Krishna Rao, Bharat Behera, Raghunath Tripathy, Siba Nayak, Ramesh Chandra Padhy	608	42.58% (Elected)
2.	T. Nageswar	Komti	Independent	His own group	38	02.66%
3.	N. Bairi	Dera	Cong.(I)	C.D. Samantara (Ex M.L.A.), Batala Abbayi, Sarathi Dakua, B. Rama Rao, T. Harishchandra, S. Nag Bhusana, S. Mohan Rao, Kumari Achari, Bodedi Ganeshu, M. Bighnesu, G. Chineya	338	23.67%
4.	Hari Sethi	Dhoba	Ind.	Dandasi Sethi, Murali Patro	45	03.15%
5.	Hrusikesh Nayak	Khadura	Ind.	Jagannath Pati (Ex. M.L.A.), S. Sankar Narayan, S. Sudarshan, Babu Pradhan, Lingaraj Mahapatro, Zadi Pradhan, S. Badri Narayan, S. Sabareya, E. Simanchal	319	22.34%
	Invalid Votes			80	05.60%	
				Total	**1428**	**100.00%**

community (Komti) also opposed him because of his rude behaviour and unfair dealings.

M. Bairi (a Dera by caste), was another choice of Samantara. But, unfortunately, his relationship with the members of his own community was not good and cordial. Besides, he was branded as a gambler. This certainly created a barrier between him and his own caste people who never took him into confidence. His own character, attitude and dealings proved to be his worst enemies. He was incorrigible and a personality without any credentials and credibility. His defeat, therefore, was not a surprise to any one.

Hari Sethi (a 'Dhoba' or Washerman by caste) was also supported by Samantara. But it was not easy on the part of a member of the scheduled caste to win the election, since the upper caste people would not support him. Besides, he was a hoodlum, rowdy, and drunked. Members of his own caste even did not like him. Therefore, he secured only 45 votes in the election.

H.K. Nayak was supported by the Komtis. They provided funds for his election. But his own caste people living in his own street did not support him because he was supported by the Komtis. Votes of his caste were divided. His defeat was certainly a blow to the prestige of the Komtis as they incurred the displeasure of the state level leaders. The elected sarpanch became their enemy and ignored all their demands.

It may be noted that despite the Janata wave, out of eleven ward-members, five were from the congress and two were independent members. The latter were 'fence-sitters' and opportunists. Therefore, though Jani was elected as the Sarpanch, he could not take any decision independently. His hands were tight as he always had to consult the M.L.A. to undertake any developmental activities in the village. He felt so helpless scared of the Komtis that he did not take any step to collect the fees towards the street lights. Neither was the amount borne by the panchayat nor had he courage to ask the Komtis to pay the same alongwith others. As a result, the people had to go without electricity for a long time. Jani's problems were compounded, when the local M.L.A. Usha Devi did not pay any attention to the developmental activities of the village. She did not grant any amount from her discretionary fund to the village development fund. Therefore, developmental activities were either stalled or could not be launched. It may, therefore, be concluded that even when backward sections of the village have captured a panchayat, defeating the traditionally dominant sections, they have failed to achieve anything because of non-cooperation and opposition of the defeated interests. The class-conflict approach at the village level is likely to help least those very sections of the community that stand most in need of it.[17]

It is immaterial who won or who lost the panchayat election in 1992. By no means it would be unpalatable to observe that the election and its consequences heralded a new era in the electoral process of the panchayat. It gave a tremendous blow to the traditional authority to a considerable extent. The process of reducing traditional authority has certainly led to the emergence of new leaders.[18]

The politics of Nuapada took a different turn in the election of a member to the Samiti. In Orissa, as per the amended provision of Orissa Gram Panchayat Rule of 1992, every Gram Panchayat should elect a Member to the Panchayat Samiti on the basis of universal adult suffrage. So, when the government of Orissa announced the date of election of the Members of the Panchayat Samiti five candidates filed their nomination belonging to different castes and supported by different political parties as is evident from the Table 7.6.

Table 7.6

Sl. No.	*Candidates*	*Caste*	*Party Affiliation*	*Vote Secured*	*Percentage*
1.	Gazi Bairi	Golla	Cong(I)	413	26.56
2.	Puspita Patnaik (W)	Karan	Independent	204	13.12
3.	Ramesh Chandra Padhy	Brahmin	Janata	220	14.15
4.	Ramesh Choudhury	-do-	B.J.P.	83	5.34
5.	Ravi Janaki Rao	Kamma Brahmin	Independent	516	33.18
	Invalid Votes			119	7.65
			Total	**1515**	**100.00**

G. Bairi, a new comer to the political field, was supported by Samantara of the Congress (I). Since he did not have any reputation in the Panchayat area, he lost the election to R. Janaki Rao. Only a few voters from his caste and the supporters of Samantara cast their votes in his favour. He secured 26.56% of votes.

Puspita Patnaik is one of the organisers of the Youth Mahila Congress at Block level. Being a woman candidate, she, however, could not get all the votes of women as the women voters of the congress were divided. Her personal contact (her husband is an employee of a Nationalized Bank in the village) helped in securing 13.12 per cent of votes.

Ramesh Chandra Padhy, an unknown and unfamiliar face and quite new to politics, was nominated by the then M.L.A., Usha Devi on the recommendation of Ananda Jani. He failed to get the support of the people as he was not popular among the voters. It may be noted that though he was assured of Jani's support, the latter was not that serious in his commitment as he hardly approached the people to request them to support him (Padhy). His supporters' votes were, therefore, divided as they cast their votes according to their own choice. Thus, it is evident from the election that people not only cast their votes on party basis but also take into consideration the factors like personality of the candidates seeking election, the caste to which he belongs, his socio-economic background, etc.

Ramesh Choudhury, a young fellow was supported by the Bharatiya Janata Party. The district level leaders of the party joined Choudhury's campaign and solicited the support of the people so that he could win the election. For this, meeting were organized. Since the party did not have at that time any base in the rural areas of the State, Choudhury lost the election. He secured only 5.34 per cent of votes.

Ravi Janaki Rao, a Kamma Brahmin, a reputed retired teacher, the 'priest' of the Komtis, an extremely popular figure, commanded maximum respect in the village. He was profoundly admired by one and all. Out of love and affection the villagers invited him to all their festivals like marriage etc. But unfortunately such a known personality was completely ignored by the political bosses of the area like the M.L.A. or former M.L.A., as he was not choosen as a candidate either for the office of Sarpanch or the Samiti Member. The reason for this was not far to seek. He was not in the good books of the leaders. However, it was his personality that attracted the people, cutting across the castes, political colour and boundaries, to his side. His victory was certainly a major set back to both of the state leaders. Of course, in course to time, forgetting the past differences, he started supporting Usha Devi. It may be noted here that both Sarpanch and the Samiti Member became very close as their enemies were the same and did their best to promote the developmental activities of the village.

Assembly Elections and Factions

As stated earlier, Nuapada was a part of parlakhemundi and thereafter Digapahandi (Badakhemundi) Assembly constituency and Bhanjanagar (Scheduled Caste) Parliamentary constituencies. After the delimitation of Parliamentary and Assembly constituencies order, 1961 and the Gazette of 1965, the village came under the Ramgiri (Scheduled Tribe) Assembly and Koraput (S.T.) parliamentary constituencies. However, since 1974, it has been a part of the Chikiti Assembly and Berhampur Lok Sabha Constituencies. The Table 7.7 reflects the candidates who won on different party tickets at the different times from the Assembly constituency of which Nuapada was a part.

Table 7.7

Sl. No.	*Elected Representatives to the Assembly*	*Political Party*	*Years of Elections*	*Constituencies*
1.	Jagannath Mishra	Communist	1952	Parlakhemundi double member Constituencies
2.	Anaga manjari Devi (W)	Congress	1957	Digapahandi
3.	Raghunath Mahapatra	,,	1961	,,
4.	Arjun Singh	,,	1967	Ramagiri (ST)
5.	Gorsanga Sabar	,,	1971	,,
6.	Satchitananda Deo	,,	1974	Chikiti
7.	Jagannath Pati	Janata	1977	,,
8.	C.D. Samantara	Independent	1980	,,
9.	,,	Cong. (I)	1985	,,
10.	Usha Devi (W)	Janata	1990	,,
11.	C.D. Samantara	Ind.	1995	,,

Earlier, the people of Nuapada, as was the case elsewhere in India, were not that politically conscious. All their political activities including casting of votes were mostly influenced by their leaders. In other words, most of the villagers were "dictated" by their "masters" and played to their tunes. Acting as a link between the leaders and the people, the faction leaders of the village played a key role in the electoral process. The political scenario, however, changed in 1974 when Nuapada became a part of the Chikit Assembly Constituency. The people started playing a different role in politics, which was unknown to them two decades back. They came in contact with the state—level leaders, interacted with them, discussed with them their problems. No more they were "feeling shy" exchanging their ideas with the latter.

It is a fact that different factions have supported different candidates contesting the Assembly elections at different time. For example, in 1952 Assembly election while Sunkuru Jagannath and Gala Chineya supported the communist candidates Jagannath Mishra, Silla Shankar Narayan rallied round and backed the Congress candidate.

It is significant to note that not all the factions necessarily extend their support to one candidate or a political party during the election. But strangely in 1957 Assembly election all of them got united and supported Ananga Manjari Devi, wife of the Zamindar of Badakhemundi, who contested on a Congress ticket. The socio-economic and political background of the candidate combined with their love and admiration for the Congress party brought all the factions under the umbrella of the Congress candidate. History repeated again in 1961 and 1967 Assembly elections. The last election presented a new political picture and assumed a new dimension when Arjun Singh, a Scheduled Tribe school teacher contested from the Ramagir (reserved for Schedule Tribes) constituency. He hailed from Siripur a nearby village of Nuapada, constituting a part of the then Nuapada Gram Panchayat.

The people of Nuapada evinced a keen interest in his election by extending him all sorts of cooperation including financial help. Arjun Singh won the election. Voters were, however, disappointed with his inefficiency and incapacity to deliver the goods. All their hopes were belied. Although communication and water problem were solved to some extent, the credit went to Sunkuru Jagannath, the then Sarpanch of the village and Dibakar Patnaik, the then District Board President.

It is interesting to note that when Arjun Singh filed his nomination as an independent candidate in 1971 Assembly elections, most of the faction leaders, dissatisfied with his performance, supported the Congress candidate, Gorsanga Sabar. Singh was, however, supported by factional leaders like Sunkuru Jagannath and Gala Chineya. Sabar won the game. The 1974 Mid-term Assembly election witnessed a multi-cornered contest involving three candidates, namely,

Satchidananda Deo	(Congress),
Jagannath Pati	(Swatantra) and
Damburudhar Panigrahi	(independent)

It may be noted that the people of Nuapada came to know about these candidates for the first time. But the faction leaders knew Satchidananda Deo (Congress) much earlier because Chikiti is very near to Nuapada. Their visit to Chikiti in connection with party programmes helped them to come in close contact with him. Therefore, almost all the faction leaders supported him, who was not only a very good person but also contested on the Congress ticket, the party which had a hypnotic effect on them as well as the voters. Deo won election. But he became very unpopular in the area, particularly among the Komtis. In 1975, when S. Jagannath, a Komti landlord and faction leader, approached him to rescue the landlords from the clutches of the Orissa Land Reforms Act (which put a ceiling on the possession of land by a family. Excess land is to be surrendered to the government), he turned down his request. This enraged the Komti factions who became very hostile to him.

In 1977 Assembly election, Jagannath pati, who contested unsuccessfully the 1974 election to the Assembly, contested from the Chikiti Constituency on a Janata Party ticket. It was expected that either Deo, former M.L.A., or Chintamani Dyan Samantara would be the candidate from the Congress. But surprisingly neither of them got the Congress ticket. The person chosen for it was no other than Binayak Acharya himself, the then Chief Minister of Orissa. Damburudhar Panigrahy, an unknown face, contested as an Independent candidate.

Acharya was a candidate both from Chikiti and Berhampur Assembly Constituencies. The faction leaders of Nuapada thought that if he won the election from both the constituencies, naturally he would leave the chikiti constituency because Berhampur is his own place as well as a prestigious constituency in Ganjam District. Therefore, the young leaders of the village were instructed by the factional leaders to ask Acharya which constituency he would retain in case he won both the constituencies.

Jagannath Pati, was a known face in the area. Not withstanding his failure in 1974 election, he maintained a good rapport with some factional leaders of the village. In 1977 election, there was a wave in favour of the Janata Party. Hence, the young leaders as well as the people of the village favoured Pati. But some old Congress leaders naturally supported Acharya. Since Panigrahi had no reputation in the village, people did not support him. In this election, irrespective of their party affiliation, the people supported Pati, who was considered as the local candidate. He also got the support of different factions who in the past had voted for the Congress. The result was obvious. He won the election. The Janata "wave", dominance of "localism", support from various faction leaders, Acharya's contest from both the constituencies—all these went in favour of Pati.

In 1980, Assembly elections were held after the Lok Sabha general elections, in an atmosphere surcharged with the Congress wave. As there was Indira-wave, the Congress (I) came to power with an overwhelming majority in the Lak Sabha. It won a land-slide victory. Therefore, there was a pro-Congress atmosphere before the Assembly elections were held in the state. It was widely expected that the Congress (I) would come to power in various states when Assembly elections were held. Therefore, there was a scramble for Congress (I) tickets. For the Chikiti Assembly Constituency there were two applicants: C.D. Samantara and Satchidananda Deo. The former was the ex-chairman of the Patrapur panchayat samiti while the latter was the ex-M.L.A. of Chikiti. There was a tussle between them to get the party ticket. Samantara, considered as a 'protege' of R. Jagannath Rao, the M.P. form Berhampur parliamentary constituency and a former union minister. He, therefore, went to New Delhi to influence Indira Gandhi through him in securing a ticket for him. However, all his efforts went in vain as Deo got the ticket. Disappointed, he (Samantara) returned to his area. However, this could not dampen his spirit as he consulted with his friends and followers, whether he should contest the election. Most of them urged him to contest as an independent candidate. But it was a great risk for him as one of his opponents would be Jagannath Pati, the out-going M.L.A. and another would be Deo, an ex-M.L.A. and the Congress (I) candidate.

Notwithstanding his weak position vis-a-vis other candidates, he decided to file his nomination as an independent candidate. The Chikiti Assembly Constituency witness a multi-cornered contest with five candidates in the fray. They were: Satchidananda Deo (Congress), Jagannath Pati (Congress-Urs.), C.D. Samantara (Independent), Kunja Bihari Nayak (Independent) and Ram Prasad Maharan from the CPI (M).

Though, there were five contestants in the fray it was actually a triangular fight among Deo, Pati and Samantara. Other candidates were insignificant because they did not have any political base in the area. Moreover, in this triangular fight most of the faction leaders preferred Samantara to others. This support was issue-based rather than interest-oriented. Because in 1975, as said earlier, the then M.L.A. Deo, did not come to the rescue of the land-owners of the village, who were apprehensive of losing their lands following the implementation of Orissa Land Reforms Act. Secondly, people opposed Deo, the sitting M.L.A., when the latter opposed the construction of a temporary barrage by the people on the river "Bahuda" at the upper level as this would help the irrigation of lands. Deo not only opposed it but also gave direction to the local authorities to demolish the barrage. As a result, most of the farmers in the village were not only adversely affected but also nurtured a grudge against him.

Pati was opposed by most of the factions because he proved to be a political opportunist by changing his party affiliation from the Janata Party to Congress (Urs). So, ultimately Samantara was their only choice.

Following Samantara's victory in 1980 election, factional leaders like the "Mahanta" and Rama Rao become powerful. It is a known fact rather a reality in politics that leaders close to the

M.L.As. and M.Ps. become more active as they have a support base. The 'Mahanta' and Rao took advantage of Samantara's position and urged him to see that a bridge was constructed over the river Bahuda. The work was done. But it was in the year 1984. The belated action, however, gave a tremendous satisfaction to the people of the area.

In 1985 Assembly election there was a neck-to-neck contest in the Chikiti Assembly Constituency, involving Usha Devi from the Janata Dal and Samantara from the Congress. The latter was declared elected.

It is significant to note that in the 1984 Gram Panchayat election when Samantara supported Rama Rao for the post of Sarpanch, most of the faction leaders including the "Mahanta" became hostile to him (Samantara). But when he came to village and approached all these faction leaders individually requesting them to forgive him and forget the past, the political scenario took a different turn as leaders like Mahanta, Raghunath Tripathy, Gala Chineya and others supported him (Samantara). S. Jagannath, who, in fact, supported the Congress (Urs) candidate in 1980 Assembly election, changed his side when he supported Samantara on the ground that the latter took all the measures for the construction of a bridge over the river Bahuda.

It is significant to note that faction leaders of Nuapada are "opportunists" as is evident from their unholy alliance with different party leaders. They change their sides, their political colour and political behaviour. It is quite pertinent to note that while the faction leaders support one party or a candidate their children support the oppositions. It is because whoever comes to power, he would be ultimately helpful to them by serving their purpose. Factional leaders like Epari Simanchal, T. Nageswar, Hrusikesh Nayak and some sub-factions supported Usha Devi. Samantara won the election. Although these leaders projected themselves to be the supporters of Samantara, in fact, they motivated the voters in favour of Usha Devi. When Samantara came to know about this from his supporters like Sarathi Dakua and the "Mahanta", he became extremely furious and to avenge this insult and double-dealing. On his suggestion and order, the shops and mills of the Komtis and others were raided. By doing so, he wanted to teach them a lesson. His action also sent them a signal, what would be in store for those who betrayed him, deceived him and disobeyed him. Those who were affected by raid started appeasing Samantara. At the same time, significantly, they also wanted to take revenge on him.

The 1990 Assembly elections gave them an opportunity. They strongly opposed him. The election atmosphere was then surcharged with the Janata wave in Orissa. Factions and their leaders were also not happy with him as instead of taking any interest in the developmental activities of the area of shielded his younger brother, Krishna Chandra Dyan Samantara, who was power-drunk and a perpetrator of crimes in the society. The unsocial and criminal activities of the latter certainly tarnished the image of his elder brother. The latter himself incurred the displeasure of the people by interfering too much in the activities of the institutions.

It may be noted that conflict between him and Ananta Pradhan a leader of Kampa Community, resulted in its division into two factions: 'Kampa' and 'Pradhan'. A separate society known as 'Pradhan Samaj' was registered and its supporters supported the Janata candidate. Their number in Chikiti constituency was about 6,000. The people of Kampa (original caste), with a strength of 4,000 favoured Samantara. By observing the political scenario of the Chikiti constituency, the factional leaders of Nuapada like Epari Simanchal, Silla Sudarshan, Epari Tripati, Tumulu Nageswar, Sunkuru Sabreya (son of Sunkuru Jagannath), Gala Chineya, T. Ramnath, Ananda Jani and others supported Usha Devi, who contested on a Janata Dal ticket. She approached the voters, met them personally, went from door to door, requested the women voters in particular to support her in the election. The leaders like B. Rama Rao, T. Harishchandra, one faction of Dera community, Raghunath Tripathy supported Samantara. Whenever the latter conducted the meeting for election, the factional leaders used to attend the meeting, assured him of their help. But inwardly they opposed him for the reasons mentioned above. Samantara lost the election and Usha Devi won it.

After the election was over, the faction leaders, who supported Usha Devi, secured certain benefits by exploiting her office. T. Nageswar, Barat Bhadranchal, Epari Tripati, S. Sudarshan, S Badri Narayan, Ananda Jani and other elites of Nuapada became powerful. Some of them influenced her to transfer officials and employees working in different offices of the village. Contracts for the construction of roads and bridges were awarded to them. But unfortunately they were not sincere as their works were found to be unsatisfactory by the Block Development Officer. As a result payment was held up. T. Nageswar then approached her to help him. But as she had already taken the officer into confidence, she remained silent. Nageswar's interest was affected and soon developed a misunderstanding between the two. His discontentment and dissatisfaction gave rise to hostility, adversely affecting the relationship between the two. In due course of time, the relation between the leaders like T. Nageswar, Ananda Jani (Sarpanch), Silla Sudarshan Rao and Usha Devi became very much strained.

The election of 1995 was altogether a different election in the electoral history of India. It had its impact on the factional politics in the village. Because of electoral reforms the earlier electoral practices were replaced by new ones. Like the previous elections, the 1995 election also witnessed a multi-cornered contest in the Chikiti Assembly constituency. The contenders were: Durga Prasad Reddy (Congress-I), Usha Devi (Janata Dal), Jagannath Pati (B.J.P.), C.D. Samantara (Independent), D. Padmavati (Independent). As mentioned earlier, the opportunistic support of different factions to different candidates did not work this time. Because faction leaders could not assess the electoral prospects of different candidates. Unlike the previous elections, this time there was no campaigning through posters, bill boards, leaf-lets or the use of microphones. Even public meetings were not organized by the leaders. Door to Door campaigning became the order of the day.

It is because of change in the political scenario following Elections Commission's strict order to all the political parties, to follow in letter and spirit its "diktats" relating to the conduct of elections, major faction leaders were confused as to whom to support. Since they had some bitter experience and hostile relations with Samantara who contested as an Independent candidate they supported Usha Devi. Barat Rama Rao, B. Ganeshu, M. Bighnesu, B. Abbayi, M. Bairi and others, however, supported Samantara. Leaders like T. Nageswar, Ananda Jani helped Durga Pratap Reddy (Congress-I). Each faction wanted that its candidate should win the election. However, with the support of the faction led by

B. Rama Rao, M. Bairi, B. Ganeshu, B. Abbayi could mobilize the village labourers, small farmers, artisans and others in favour of Samantara, who won the election. Surprisingly after the election was over, every faction claimed that it supported him. Since he was an experienced politician, he ignored all those factions opposed to him.

It may, therefore, be observed here that factional politics in Nuapada centres round political opportunism rather than genuine issues.

Lok Sabha Elections and Factions

Faction leaders of Nuapada normally interact more with the M.L.As. than with the M.Ps. as the former happens to be more close to them geographically. In other words, at normal times the linkage between the M.P. and the faction leaders is not that strong. However, the latter plays a major role at the time of parliamentary elections. The candidates seeking election to the Lok Sabha heavily depend upon their vote banks for their electoral success. But this becomes easier and possible only when they act through the village leaders who know the people's minds, are aware of their problems, can influence them easily. Hence, their role assumes much significance at the time of elections. Extension of support to the M.P. (candidate) by the people and the village leaders is mainly influenced by factors like caste and his relationship with the M.L.A. It is not that difficult for the candidate to influence the voters if the M.L.A. also belongs to his political party. Undoubtedly, the M.L.A. will support him with all his resources. But it is not the case if they belong to opposite parties or groups or camps. M.L.A.'s relationship with the faction leaders, often, makes or mars the future of a candidate willing to have an entry into the Lok Sabha.

It may be noted that since Independence, the people of Nuapada have been extending their support to candidates seeking office on a Congress ticket, except, of course, in 1984, 1989 and 1991 general elections to the Lok Sabha. The reasons for this have been explained earlier. They feel that Congress, which brought freedom to the country, only can provide a stable government at the centre. To them, there is none who can replace the Congress or can be considered as an alternative to it. It is, therefore, not a matter of surprise if the Congress continued to sweep the polls until 1991. Factions had little role to play in these elections. But Komti factions became active during the elections held in 1984, 1989 and 1991 as Surya Narayan Patro, a Komti by caste, joined the fray. Hailing from Berhampur he contested in these elections on a Janata Dal ticket. He was supported by S. Sudarshan Rao, T.N. Murty, E. Abbayi, T. Raghunath, E. Simanchal, B. Bhadranchal as they were not happy with the role, performance and activities of C.D. Samantara as an M.L.A. His role particularly during the 1984 Gram Panchayat Election in supporting B. Rama Rao created bitterness in the minds of faction leaders and it had its impact in 1984 general election to the Lok Sabha. R. Jagannath Rao who was representing the constituency for more than 20 years won the election and Patra was defeated.

In 1989 Parliamentary elections, Patra who again joined the fray, was supported by S. Sudarshan, T.N. Murty, E. Abbayi, E. Simanchal, E. Tripati, Gala Chineya, Ch. Simanchal, mainly because he belonged to their caste and they were hostile to Samantara for his activities. Since he (Samantara) was their enemy, the Congress candidate for the Lok Sabha elections, Gopinath Gajapati Narayan Deo, also became their natural enemy. Inspite of the opposition to Deo from most of the factions he came out with flying colours.

During the 1991 Lok Sabha elections the Berhampur Parliamentary constituency of which Nuapada is a part, witnessed a multi-cornered contest. It is significant to note that all the factions were divided into two groups: one led by Samantara and the other by Usha Devi. Both the leaders accepted the election as a challenge to their career. Hence, their efforts to bring success to their party candidates. It was a fight between the M.L.A. and ex-M.L.A. Both tried to mobilize the support of faction leaders of Nuapada. The victory of Deo in the election was a severe setback to the Janata Dal and its leaders.

In 1996 general election to the Lok Sabha, while B. Rama Rao, S. Shankar Narayan, T. Harischada, N. Bairi, R.N. Tripathy, K. Krishna Rao, Bodedi Ganeshu, Godavari Nayak, T. Premanjali (w) supported P.V. Narasimha Rao, a congress candidate, S. Sudarshan, E. Simanchal, G. Chineya, Ananda Jani, H.K. Nayak, Babu Pradhan, Hari Sethi, raillied round the Janata candidate

Sugyani Kumari Devi, the 'Queen' of Khallikote. Samantara and his supporters supported Narasimha Rao and the opposite factions extended their support to the Janata candidate. Rao won the election.

Sex and Factions

Sometimes sex also plays an important role in creating factions in the village. Scholars like Lewis have observed that "Quarrels over sexual offences may also lead to the development of factions in the village". There is a popular saying that 'dharas' (factions) revolve around wealth, women and land. As said earlier, during 1938–40 factionalism in Nuapada centered around sex. It is, however, significant to note that the sex-based factions in Nuapada were purely temporary in nature.

Educational Institutions and Factions

Education plays a key role in political socialization of individuals in a society.[19] It promotes virtues; dispels ignorance; fosters harmony; develops citizenship qualities; makes an individual conscious of himself—of his rights and duties; helps him to understand a problem in right perspective; increases his awareness of social, economic and political issues; encourages him to raise his voice against exploitation, fight against injustice and discrimination; goads him to discharge his duties faithfully and creates an atmosphere for him to fulfil himself and realise his best self.[20] It helps in bringing an allround development in the society and changes the outlook of the individuals. Keeping in mind the importance and significance of education, important leaders like T. Krishna Murty, Narasingha Panigrahy, Raghunath Tripathy, S. Ram Das Ratna Subudhi, T. Egnesham, Dr. Sudarshan Rao and others gave importance to the promotion of education in Nuapada. Their dream was partly realized when a primary schools was started in the year 1923–24. This year hearalded a new era in the history of spreading education in the village. Thereafter, another M.E. School, a high school (1941), a Girl's high school (1981), a College (1980) were established at different times. But, unfortunately, all these educational institutions are riddled with factionalism.

It is very unfortunate to note that some members of the Komti community were strongly opposed to the establishment of a high school. They did not want to make any contribution—financial or otherwise—towards the spread of education. Hence the rift started between the supporters and the opponents of the school. The latter could not succeed in their attempt to stall the project. Notwithstanding all their protests and oppositions, a school was established in 1941. T. Patita, a widow belonging to the Komti community, died without naming any one as her legal heir. She had left behind some property—both in cash and kind—with T. Krishna Murty who donated the same to the high school. A Trust was made, of which the 'Mahanta', S. Jagannath, and some members of the Komti community were its members. T. Patita's donation was utilized for the development of the school which was under the control of the District Board, Chikiti since 1945 for a period of ten to twelve years.

After the dissolution of the District Board, a special officer was appointed to look after the school. At that time it was converted to a 'C' type High school. During the tenure of Lingaraj Panigrahi as the Education Minister of Orissa, all the 'C' type schools were declared as government high schools. So when it became a government institution, its committee diverted the 'Patita fund' towards the development of the 'Satya Narayan Temple' managed by the Komti community. Cunningly the committee of the High School did not hand over the documents pertaining to the landed property to the government. It was also alleged that the fund was misutilized and misappropriated. Although the other castes knew about it, they did not protest against the Komtis as all the members of the Patita Trust except the 'Mahanta' belonged to the Komti community. Mahanta spent most of his time in Berhampur which is away from Nuapada. Whenever he used to come to village, he did not take any interest in its affairs.

In 1978, Braja Sundar Panda, the then sub-Post Master of Nuapada, took initiative for the establishment of a college at Nuapada. He observed that in the village most of the Komtis belong to the upper strata of the society. Hence, if they are convinced of the utility or usefulness of a college, it would not be difficult to set up a college. So, he began to motivate the leading personalities of the village and organised various meetings to discuss the matter. But the leaders were diffident as they felt that to run a college was not an easy task. Besides, it would be difficult to meet the recurring expenses of the college in future till it got the grants-in-aid from the government. Some faction leaders like B. Rama Rao, T. Mohan Rao, B. Ardaraju and T. Ramanath motivated others to drop the proposal as it would be very expensive for them. However, when Panda gave them the statistics about their business prospects following the establishment of a college they were convinced of its importance. Yet, they did not prefer to become the president or secretary of the College Governing Body. They wanted to remain as its members only. In 1980, the college was established. The 'Mahanta' became the president of the Governing Body. Some Komti factions, who were opposed to the presidentship of the 'Mahanta' as well as the establishment of the college, did not associate with the college matters. When the college was inaugurated with pomp and fun on 22nd August, 1980, the faction leaders opposed to it felt extremely unhappy and boycotted the same. They felt that if the college passed through any financial crisis in future, the responsibility of looking after it would be thrust on them. In other words, they would be asked to bear the financial burden. Certainly it would be taxing them.

It is interesting to note that 'Barapataka' was convened by 'Desi Behera' on the suggestion of the Governing Body of the college. Important persons of the village were requested to make liberal contributions to the growth and development of the college. And in this connection a development committee was constituted to collect donations from each and every family of the village. It is very pertinent to observe that in the meeting it was decided what amount should be paid by which family. In other words, the donation amount to be collected was fixed and thrust upon. The families were rather forced to pay. The principle who should pay what was to be rigorously implemented. It is very significant to note that those who were reluctant to pay the amount were threatened of dire consequences, particularly the lands would not be allowed to be cultivated. Those who did not have the 'fixed amount' to contribute to the college development fund, were asked to borrow the amount from the bank and discharge their obligations. Those who opposed this decision, described it arbitrary and whimsical.

But inspite of their opposition, the committee went ahead with its mission of collecting donations. And surprisingly, one lakh rupees was collected within twenty four hours. It is interesting to note that the medical officer, revenue inspector and other officers of the village also contributed to the college development fund. The bank remained opened throughout the night. The opposite factions, though contributed donations under threat, started many litigations against the college authorities. It is very unfortunate to observe that a few students resorted to violent means to collect donations. They did not spare even the bus drivers. Once they detailed a bus owned by the Zamindar of Chikiti and demanded that the driver should pay something to the college fund. On refusal, the bus was detained in Nuapada. Following this incident, members of the Zamindar family registered cases in the police station and students involved in this became the victims. As a result, some false cases were filed against them. When they were involved, their parents requested the Governing body to interfere in the matter and as a result the conflict between the students and the opponents of the college, in fact, became the conflict between the College Governing Body and their opponents. Some police cases were also registered. The "Barapataka" on an occasion and in one of the issues also imposed a find of five hundred rupees on Raghunath Tripathy, a retired teacher. He was to pay for the mischievous activities of his son Bhaskar Tripathy, a teacher in a local Government High School. He appealed the M.L.A., Samantara, who also happened to be his relative, to help him. The latter was in dilemma because the 'Mahanta', a member of Barapataka who also very close to him. So, he suggested Tripathy to inform the police. However, within a span of three months, all the cases were compromised in the presence of the Deputy Superintendent of Police and others.

Thereafter, the 'Mahanta' proposed in the Governing Body meeting that the 'Patita Fund' be utilized for the development of the college. Being a member of the trust he explained how the funds was to be utilized. Other members belonging to the Komti Community placed this matter in their caste council. So those who opposed to the college and Governing Body thought to establish a girl's high school with the help of the said fund. Braja Sundar Panda, the initiator and promoter of the college who maintained a balance between both the groups, encouraged them to start a school for girls. He also succeeded in pacifying the aggrieved

Governing Body members of the College by arguing that let them start a high school which would feed the college. Finally the girl's high school was set up in September, 1981.

The result of the Panchayat election of 1984 had a great repercussion on the functioning of these educational institutions. Because S. Badri Narayan, son of a member of the college Governing Body, was defeated in the election to the Panchayat because of the interference of the local M.L.A., Samantara in favour of Rama Rao. Therefore, for some time the entire Governing Body became hostile to Samantara, as the Sarpanch B. Rama Rao was opposed to the Governing Body. Anyhow, after the no confidence motion was passed against the Sarpanch, the 'Mahanta' became the Sarpanch in the bye-election to the Gram Panchayat in 1985.

It may be mentioned here that when the college received the grant-in-aid from the government in 1985, Samantara succeeded in becoming the president of the Governing Body. By that time, he had already assumed the office of Deputy Speaker of the Orissa Legislative Assembly. Even though he became the president, he usually did not attend its meetings and assigned the duty to the 'Mahanta' to preside over them. In the parliament elections the Komtis and other followers supported Surjya Narayan Patro (Janta Dal) because of caste feelings. Therefore, Samantara became terribly angry with the Komtis. He supported the 'Mahanta' and completely ignored the Komtis and their supporters without giving any importance or weightage to their views even though they were also the members of the Governing Body. Therefore, cleavages started gradually in the Governing Body. Meanwhile, Braja Sundar Panda was transferred to Bhata Kumarada sub-post office and thereafter he resigned from his service and entered into the political field. When he visited Nuapada he criticized Samantara in strong words. This enraged the latter and his supporters, including a few members of the Governing Body. Samantara asked them not to entertain Panda and take his views seriously. At the same time, some members of the Governing Body were the blind supporters of Panda who always stood for the development and prosperity of the College. Personal rivalry between Panda and Samantara had its impact on the functioning of the college as its Governing Body who divided into two groups; one supporting Panda another favouring Samantara. It may be observed here that in one of the General Body meetings of the Governing Body held on 25 October, 1987, Samantara scolded a few committee members like Gala Chineya, Sankar Narayan and others. Chineya, an active worker of the College, not only strongly resented against Samantara but also tendered his resignations from the Governing Body. Shankar Narayan also followed his foot-step. Their resignations from the Governing Body adversely affected the developmental activities of the college.

Factional Politics in Nuapada had its impact even on the student politics because different factions were actively and directly involved in the students union election. In 1987 following the admission of Rabi Narayan Dyansamantara, son of the M.L.A., into the college, a demand was made for the election to the student's union. The college authority agreed to this demand. But, unfortunately, the M.L.A.'s son was defeated. This was treated as a great humiliation and insult to the M.L.A. Blinded by his love for his son, the latter pressurized the 'Mahanta', President of the Governing Body, to reconsider the election result and declare his son elected. But latter was helpless to do any favour to R.N. Dyansamantara. Again in the year 1988 because of the factional politics within the Governing Body of the college, the principal denied to hold the college union election and decided to nominate the representatives to the students union. While the factions aligned to the M.L.A. supported it, it was at the same time strongly opposed by the opposite group led by Braja Sundar Panda who strongly argued in favour of the election. The latter apprehended that the M.L.A's son might be nominated as President of the Students Union, in case there was no election. The academic atmosphere was vitiated and polluted by arguments and counter arguments over the conduct of the election. More and more number of students joined the campaign demanding for immediate election. Student leaders outside Nuapada took up he issue and organized a students strike supported by different factions opposed to C.D. Samantara. But due to the pressure from the government, strike was suppressed. Neither the election was held nor the principal nominated any one to the union. But it exposed the extent of factional politics in the village and its impact upon the students.

Factional Politics in the village witnessed what is called the worst kind of diplomacy causing much loss to the college. After the shifting of the college building, the Komtis wanted to purchase the old building which was donated by the 'Mahanta'. But the amount fixed by the Governing Body under his control was not acceptable to them. Besides, there were also some legal problems in the disposal of the old building. But the Komtis crooked up a diplomacy by paying one thousand rupees as advance to the 'Mahanta', though they knew it pretty well that it would be difficult to get the clearance from the Endowment Board. When the case was pending with the Board, they took away the assets of the old building and used the same in the Girl's High School building and used the same in the Girls's High School building established by them. However, Samantara, the M.L.A., with a view to get the support of the Komtis, interfered and allowed them to purchase the old building. But the latter did not purchase for two reasons. First, the sale was to be cleared by the Endowment Board. Secondly, their aim was to see that the Governing Body, consisting of the 'Mahanta' and members mostly belonging to him, was put to loss.

The college Governing Body suffered a lot due to political interference and the infighting among the members of different factions. Though, people were protesting against the interference of Samantara, things did not change even after Mrs. Usha Devi of Janata Dal became the M.L.A. in 1990. She also started appointing her own party members in the Governing Body. Developmental works were neglected by her. It is very unfortunate to observe that those teachers and leaders opposed to such activities of the M.L.A., had to face her wrath as she wanted to teach them a lesson. Things turned worse when she herself became the president of Governing Body, in spite of the fact that the Orissa Education Rule categorically states that the Collector should be its President.

Co-operatives and Factions

The Co-operative system, which stands for self-help and mutual help, has been established in rural India as the crisis-manager of rural people and with a view to bring an end to the exploitation of the poor by the middle men and the money-lenders of the village. So different types of Co-operatives like Credit Co-operatives, Marketing Co-operatives, Producers Co-operatives have been established in rural India to bring an alround development of the people, particularly in the fields of business and agriculture.

Accordingly, in Nuapada village a number of Co-operative Societies have been established. However, since 1970s, some of them have become defunct due to mismanagement and loss. At present, there are three societies; namely, Service Co-operative, Weavers' Co-operative and Arnapurna Weavers' Co-operative Societies. The first one, set up in 1939, seeks to provide agricultural loans, fertilizers, etc., to the peasants. Besides, it also distributes essential commodities like sugar, wheat, kerosine, etc., to the villagers at a subsidiary rate. It has about four hundred members and two hundred of them are at present active. It is managed by its own members who elect one among them as its president. At the time of election to this office different political parties interfere thereby giving rise to factionalism.

The Weavers' Co-operative Society, set up in 1951 under the leadership of G. Chineya, B. Abbayi and others, includes—the members of the Dera Community not only of Nuapada but also of other villagers like Kolipentho and Kumarada. The main objective of this society is to provide the raw-materials to the weavers at a cheaper rate and purchase the clothes from it at a higher price.

It may be noted that Co-operative Societies have been set up with a hope that they would work in an atmosphere that would ensure an all-round development to its members. But all these hopes have been belied as factionalism has become a way of life for them. The Weavers Co-operative Society is not an exception to this rule. The Weavers' of Nuapada are divided into two groups belonging to two different areas: Bada Dera Sahi and Sana Dera Sahi. While the leader of the latter group is Gala Fakir, the farmer is led by Khadi Chandra and others. Socio-Economic factors are mainly responsible for the growth of factionalism. Gala Fakir's decisions to ostracize a member of his community, who had married a Christian girl was resented by one section of community. This was the beginning of the end of social harmony and cohesion. The community split into two groups. The Komtis, who used to lend money at higher interest to the Deras, could no more exploit the latter because of their protection by the Co-operative Society. Injured and wounded mentally, they awaited with patience to take vengeance against the Deras and factionalism with in the community gave the Komtis a great opportunity to exploit the situation. Following factionalism, the Weavers' Co-operative Society was bifurcated. Another Society known as the Arnapurna Weavers' Co-operative Society was set up amidst stiff opposition at sana Dera sahi, under the leadership of Gala Chineya.

It is very interesting to note that soon after the establishment of the new society, G. Chineya did his best to create a rift among the members of the old Weavers' Co-operative Society. He instigated some of its members against the corrupt functioning of its secretary, Manimi Bighnesu. As a result, they openly demanded the letters resignation. But, on the other hand, he was strongly supported by some other members of the society and the factional rivalry within the Dera community led by B. Ganeshu and others took a violent turn. The Secretary was locked up. And the matter was referred to police and Assistant Director to Textiles, Berhampur. The latter asked all the Executive Members to resign and following their resignation he appointed one of the supporters of M. Bighnesu as the Secretary. This aggravated the situation. The two intra-factions got involved in a violent fight against one other. Police had to rush to the village to take a stock of the situation. When the Director of Textiles came to know about all these intra-factional activities he suggested the Government to take-over the management of he Co-operative. Before doing so, the government locked it for some days. And the result was the poor weavers were the worst sufferers.

Thus, factional politics in the village has not only disturbed the political institutions but also has made the socio-economic institutions the centre of factional politics. As a result, institutions like Co-operatives, whose main motto is to give justice to the poor people through the united effort have become the targets. Factional politics has not only affected the efficacy and efficiency of such institutes but also protected the vested interests of the middle men and the business people have been benefited highly. To put it in other words, factional politics in institutions like Co-operatives have gone against the interests of the rural poor.

This factional politics has also impeded the development and prosperity of the members of the Co-operatives. That is why a sum of thirty four lakh rupees, which was sanctioned to both the co-operatives jointly for the construction of hospitals, schools, sanitation, electricity etc. under the scheme of Integrated Rural

Development for Weavers, has not so far been implemented. This highly speaks of dysfunctional role played by factionalism is rural government and politics.

Cultural Association and Factions

Cultural associations are formed to promote the intellectual and cultural activities of the people; advance their knowledge and culture and enrich their social life. But unfortunately, these cultural activities are mostly responsible in promoting factionalism in Nuapada. The formation of cultural associations has given rise to conflict between the Deras supported by the 'Mahanta', and the Komtis. The conflict between the two can be attributed to the fact that, the Deras under the guidance and supervision of the 'Mahanta' staged a number of plays during the late 1920s. A 'fund' was created and the profits from these dramas was deposited in it. The Komtis tried to control it without contributing anything towards the staging of the dramas. This interesting phenomenon has been explained earlier. But, however, the Komtis also organized another association named as "Bagha Akhada". The members were K. Rama Murty, T. Narseya, Epari Lingarju, Tumuly Bighnesu, Barat Appana, Sunkuru Jagannath, Raghunath Tripathy and Sevaka Ratna. Since those eight persons organized it, it was locally also termed as "Astha Malla".

Thus, the village society, its environment and its life have been polluted because of the development of these cultural associations.

It is, however, significant to note that notwithstanding the deeply rooted factionalism that has retarded the process of development in the village, at times particularly at the time of celebration of village festivals like 'Thakurani Yatra' or 'Sitalasasthi Yatra', the Deras get themselves united and take keen interest in making them successful. Their efforts, their unity, their co-operation—all these are highly praiseworthy even though these are purely temporary in nature.

References

1. Lewis, Op. cit., p. 114.
2. Chaudhury, Op. cit., p. 179.

3. Fukunaga, Op. cit., p. 30.

4. R. Nicholas "*Factions : A comparative Analysis*", M. Banton (ed.), in Political Systems and the Distribution of Power, ASA Monograph, No. 2, (New York: Fredrick A. Praeger, 1965) p. 46.

5. Epstein, Op. cit.

6. Beals and Siegel, Op. cit.

7. Pocock, Op. cit.

8. Epstein, Op. cit., p. 139.

9. See, Srinivas, Op. cit., p. 18 and also his *Social Change in Modern India*, op. cit.

10. Srinivas, Op. cit.

11. Rastogi, Op. cit.

12. Somjee, Op. cit., p. 2.

13. See, Rajat Suhra Mukopadhay, "*Party Politics in Panchayat*", Social Change, Vol. 14, No. 2, June 1984, p. 53.

14. Ibid.

15. Alok Kumar Bandyopadhyay, "*Village Panchayat—A Bird's Eye View*", Economic Affairs, 26(3) July–September, 1981, p. 170.

16. Nagesh Jha, *Leadership and Local Politics, A Study of Meerut, District in U.P.*, (New Delhi: Popular Prakashan, 1979), p. 7.

17. Mukhopadhyay, Op.cit., p. 55.

18. Bhargava and Torgal, Op. cit.

19. K. S. Padhy and P.K. Panigrahi, *Socialist Movement in India*, (New Delhi: Kanishka Publishing House, 1992) p. 205.

20. Ibid.

8
Summary, Conclusion and Findings

Factionalism in rural government and politics constitutes an important area of enquiry in the social sciences. Hence, scholarly interest in the shape and mode of operation of rural government in India has grown immensely at present as is evident from the review of literature. But the existence of rural government in India is a very ancient phenomenon. About 80 per cent of the total population in India belonging to different castes, religions and culture live in villages covering 70 per cent of its territory. Barring the occasional emergence of urban civilization, as in the case of Mahenjodar and Harappa,[1] the rural character of Indian society has remained intact and even today this is true in most parts of the country. When Gandhi, Father of the Nation, said that "India lives in villages," he was accurately analysing the nature of Indian society. In this respect, India widely differs from the western countries which turned predominantly urban at the advent of the industrial revolution. It remained untouched by the industrial revolution. It remained untouched by the industrial revolution primarily due to the conservative nature of the rural population and fear of accepting anything new. No doubt, foreign rulers[2] also devised the system of government for the rural areas which left the initiative in the hands of the village people themselves in the form of Panchayati Raj system. But the system was not based on a truly democratic set-up. As a result, once prosperous village societies continued to be the cess-pools of ignorance, illiteracy, poverty and prejudices.

No doubt, after independence, efforts have been made to give power to the rural people and undertake projects for their upliftment. Indian democracy is still striving hard for its success in the rural areas where majority suffer in the midst of grinding poverty. No doubt, steps have been undertaken by the authorities in the past and present by adopting many socio-economic measures for improvement of the villages and giving political rights to the villagers to form rural government in the shape of Panchayati Raj system. But a number of social, economic, religious and political forces have contributed to the success and failure of such efforts. Hence, an attempt has been made here to highlight the impact of such forces on the rural government and politics in India with special reference to a particular village named Nuapada in the State of Orissa.

Democratic political organization of India in the post-independent era has set the villages in the main stream of the nation. The villagers are to exercise their franchise in the elections of the Panchayati Raj at the grass-root level, the Assembly at the State level and the Lok Sabha at the National level. In fact, electoral politics presumably politicize the people in the national perspective. Thus, factional leaders have nexus at the supra-village level. These, in fact, provide strength to them in the village politics. Thus, the factional politics of a village is studied in a wider context rather then in isolation from it.

Factionalism, basic to most communities and an intrinsic part of political life[3] is a growing phenomenon in Indian Government and Politics, infecting local, state and national politics. Political parties, trade unions, village communities and even voluntary associations have become crisis-ridden, with the increasing factional activities.

The rural India, which appears outwardly to be calm and quite and seems to be characterized by peace and harmony, has, in fact, been experiencing and experimenting with conflict and hostility.[4] Now every village has become more or less a centre that can be treated with contempt and suspicion. Factionalism, jealousy, deceit and inter-personal rancour have become common characteristics of the present day rural life.

The earliest interest in factions come from political scientists (Lasswell, 1931), while social anthropologists only became aware of their significance during the past few decades. Firth (1957) was the first to make an attempt to set out systematically some of their functions and structural characteristics. He treated them as informal counterparts of more formal political groupings and noted that members were recruited according to structurally diverse principles. Nicholas (1965) also viewed factions as essentially systematically organized conflict groups in balanced opposition to each other.

It is to be noted that factionalism as a phenomenon has, however, been studied for the first time by Oscar Lewis.[5] He enjoys the credit of being a pioneer in the study of factionalism and for having drawn the attention to such an important aspect of the socio-political life in the Indian village.

Among the research works on rural political behaviour, concentration has been upon the trends of intra-caste and inter-caste factions which received attention it he 1950s–1960s. Typically, one of the studies considered that rural India is a "Faction Society".[6] Bottomore reviewed village studies and noted the existence of factionalism, which has become rampant in the rural politics, to be the characteristic of traditional village structure itself.[7] However, factionalism in the village owes its origin and growth to caste conflict, personal considerations, lust or greed for power and higher status and the desire of feudal leaders to perpetuate their dominance in the village life. On the other hand, poverty, illiteracy, lack of political consciousness have added fuel to the fire. Thus, in course of time, factionalism has assumed different dimensions and roles in different rural areas depending upon caste, wealth, landed property and electoral politics. In some villages, religion and culture are also responsible for its growth. As a result, every village community has lost its significance as a 'community'. Appropriately, Baviskar has emphasized the need to study the organization and functioning of factions at various levels of politics.[8] To him, factional politics refers to the power groups.[9] Quarrels, rivalries and legal wranglings in the Indian village are transfigured by factional politics. Beals and Siegel[10] argue that factional conflict involves both 'stress' and 'strain'. In their view it reflects a lack of unity and cohesion and inability of people to co-operate in community action. They attribute the divisiveness to rapid social change occurring in the village community.

In India, faction is an important and universal feature of local politics.[11] There are village level research studies on socio-political life, referring to faction and factionalism as a wide-spread phenomenon, and describing the numerous ways in which individuals and groups from alliances with each other and are involved in some conflicts. Each emphasizes the different ways or manners in which factions perform their functions in different situations.

Factionalism is linked with power politics. It is an expression of political struggle for power and prestige. Masaaki Fukunaga has rightly observed that whether or not a given conflict is resolved, is not important to understand factionalism. What is important is that it is a dynamic process resulting from continuously shifting alliances and coalitions which people make with each other to achieve what they might think as their political goals at a given time.[12] In fact, factions centre around some kind of political and economic power. On some occasions like elections to the gram panchayat, co-operative societies, state assembly, factional activities become more prominent. Normally, a kind of cold war exists between two potential warring groups. When it erupts, caste, party and interest appear to be the most important factors of factionalism in the villages.[13]

S.C. Dube[14] on he basis of an empirical study of four villages in Madhya Pradesh disproved the usefulness of the concept of dominant caste and suggested alternatively the dominance of a faction consisting of the several castes in the villages which is more useful for understanding power.[15] Because power is the process of exercising control over others in the society and that is acquired through controlling, influencing and manipulating the will of others in favour of either an individual as in the case of factions or a group as in the case of a political party. D. K. Samanta in his study on "Determinants of political factions in a Deccan Village" observes that "Factional politics emerges out of conflict and competition for acquiring access to power. Man to man relationship guided by various socio-economic reasons is also of great relevance to factional politics."[16]

A study of factionalism provides some clues to the social scientists, administrators and people involved in rural government and politics to know about the causes of factionalism and their role at panchayat samiti, district and state level. One can also know about the link of the rural factional leaders with the district and state level leaders. Without studying factionalism, it would be impractical to give ideas on rural problems and assess the success or failure of programmes meant for solving the problems of rural areas. In other words, the study will give a realistic orientation to the people who are working in different developmental programmes in rural areas and can work in a better way for the success of such programmes.

Factions are essential elements of political process and also seem to activate the process of modernization.[17] And therefore, today, it is important to re-examine and verify as to how political process and activities of factions are performed within a given community. The term "factions" has come to be used in the analysis of the Indian rural political structure and this is recognized as being "deeply significant in analytic research and expansional concept."[18]

Factionalism is a characteristic form of conflict. As a special field of investigation it leads to an understanding of the functioning of social systems under co-operation and competition. It helps us in studying the formation and operation of factions within a political system. Factionalism, which can be studied as an ideology, refers to the role of leaders in dividing the people as their respective followers. The former take up the role of patrons and try to channelise the developmental resources in favour of their respective followers, regions and communities. The present power politics, developmental schemes, and allocation of resources have been examined from this perspective regarding factionalism as an ideology.[19]

No doubt, day by day, social scientist have engaged themselves in the study of factionalism in rural government and politics. But hardly any study has been made on this aspect in Orissa, a backward state of India having 80 per cent of rural population. Especially, an exclusive study on an Orissan village in southern part of Orissa characterised by social prejudices, poverty and backwardness has become imminent. Hence, importance of the present study that has made an attempt to highlight the causes, role, linkages, patterns and other factors of factionalism in an Orissan village located in the southern part of Orissa.

The term 'Faction' generally refers to any group of a larger unit, which works for the development of a particular group of persons or of an area. It arises in the struggle for power and represents a division on details of application and not on principles. It is a coalition of individuals personally recruited by or an behalf of, an individual in competition with another individual or coalition with whom he was formerly united. Factions compete for honour and/or the control of resources.[20] The central focus of a faction is the leader who has recruited it. Ties between leader and followers are usually personal, although followers sometimes recruit other on behalf of their leader. Factionalism—the competition between factions for scarce resources of power—can take many forms and has been recorded in all parts of the world, although the most numerous and detailed descriptions come from India.[21] Factions are fundamental political units and factionalism the most elementary political process.[22]

The term faction has been employed as an opprobrious epithet in the political field since Roman days: the word arose from the name given to the divisions into which Roman charioteers were separated.[23] A ruling group finds it convenient to stigmatize its rivals within the organization, and the epithets which are most effective convey the innuendos of willful self-seeking. Those who are in power have the benefit of the assumption that they represent the collective interests in substance as well as in form. A faction seems to subordinate the public good to private gain and thus the term takes its place in the dialectic of the political struggle, especially as a means of defence and counter-attack by those in power. The epithet is quickly taken up by those who concur in the established policies or who are loyal to the ruling personnel and hurled against the dissenters. The intensive study of individuals has repeatedly demonstrated the ambivalent attitudes which characterise so many human relationships. Those who acquiesce in any authoritarian regime repress more or less successfully their own hostility against that regime. If authority is challenged from without it tends to reactivate a struggle within the personalities of the loyal, who seek to protect themselves from this struggle by attacking the dissenter. Casting opprobrium on the challenger is a protective reaction which externalizes the individual conflict and hastens the removal of the disturber from the environment.[24]

Factionalism occurs in situations of rapid social change and is one of the processes, adjustment leading to a situation of dynamic equilibrium.[25] Sometimes it manifests a definite class bias. No doubt, it brings about social change. But it is not exclusively a product of changes in the wider society. Rival factions far from being in balanced opposition, differ in respect to access to resources and strategy, internal organization, ideology, social composition and symbolism. Although the number of competing factions can vary, there are usually two. Often one is associated with the dominant power configuration in the community, focussing on the headman, chief or dominant landlord. This coalition takes the form of establishment. It is usually conservative; it has access to a range of resources, including the most important cultural symbols and it tends to be defensive and concerned with protecting its superior position. Aligned against this power bloc is a category of persons who are dissatisfied with the way in which those with superior power wield it. Although initially they may be merely disgruntled, they may later organize a rival coalition and compete for resources. They form the opposition faction. Opposition factions, if they persist over time, tend to develop a more tightly-knit organizational structure in order to compete effectively against their more powerful rival.

Because factionalism takes place in a social framework in which unity and consensus is generally regarded as an ideal, it is seen as divisive, a temporary unpleasantness, the details of which should not be discussed with outsiders.

Thus, one can recognise various general ideas of factions in the studies on Indian local level politics; which were considered by different scholars in their own way.

The present study reveals that like other Indian villages, Nuapada is also a faction-ridden society. The origin of factionalism dates back to 1920s and it is the product of several factors, social, economic, cultural and political. Factionalism is not only a growing phenomenon in village politics of Nuapada but also is so deeply rooted that it is found to be a curse to its simple and easy-going life, a hindrance to its developmental process, a detriment to its unity, integration and cohesiveness, a threat to its stability and strength, a check on its growth and prosperity, a blow to its calm and serene atmosphere. In other words, it is quite harmful, dangerous and dysfunctional to the society in every aspect of human life. Factionalism, a deadly evil, has torn apart the village community and spread its tentacles in every sphere of life, thereby eating away its vitals and sapping its strength. It has vitiated the atmosphere, corrupted the people and degraded the community.

It is found that the Komtis, because of their superior economic power, exert a tremendous influence in village politics. Their exploitation through money-lending has also given rise to factionalism in Nuapada. At present there are nine factional groups in the village, all working against one another. As a result, the interests of the village have not only been neglected and ignored but also sacrificed at the altar of narrow and selfish interest of the faction leaders and groups.

Factionalism centres around castes, issues, culture, regions, languages etc. It is very disheartening to note that a particular caste is fragmented into several sub-groups or factional groups which stand at loggerheads on several issues.

It is pertinent to note that since factional groups in Nuapada are primarily kinship grouping and mainly centre around caste they are permanent in nature. At times they are the product of other factors like marriage etc. Initially, they tend to be non-political but in due course of time they become political as it is very different to remain aloof or keep oneself free from the arena of politics. Political and non-political spheres are so inter-linked and interdependent, and interact with one another so closely that one does not know when it has become political. Political colour or political affiliation of a faction changes from time to time if the situation changes.

Leaders play an important role in factional politics of Nuapada. Hailing from a varied socio-economic and political background, they are politically affiliated, have linkages with political leaders at the state and national levels, extend their support to political parties and leaders contesting the elections to various offices. Factionalism assumes a new dimension and plays a different role at the time of assembly and parliamentary elections. It is, thus, evident that factional leaders are not only highly politicized but also have made politics self-centered and individual-oriented.

Village government has been created with a view that it would promote the development of the village and political parties would not participate either directly or indirectly in its affairs. They should keep a distance from the village government and politics. The structure of the village government rests on this foundation. But it is very unfortunate to note that political parties are now playing an active role in the government of Nuapada, thereby belying all the hopes and expectations of the founding-fathers of the village government in modern India. Too much interference by the political parties poses a serious threat to the spirit of the village government.

It is very unfortunate to note that notwithstanding their strong support to the theory of non-party system in the rural government, they have moved far away from what they profess. A wide gulf exists between what they profess and what they practise. Steps should be taken to change the panchayat statute to bring an end to the interference and involvement of political parties in the village government and politics. This will go a long way in curbing factionalism in Nuapada politics.

It is very sad to note that the village government of Nuapada has failed to deliver its goods. Narrow and selfish interests of the leaders has kept them bound to their own personal development. The conflict among the factional leaders has threatened the effective functioning of the village government in Nuapada.

Women constitute half of the population. But unfortunately, they are deprived of their dues and have been victimized in the male-dominated society. Steps have been taken to restore their status by providing them necessary facilities including education and employment in various services. Of late, the government of India and different state governments including the Government of Orissa have adopted certain measures to uplift them politically. The first step they have taken in this regard is to reserve 30 per cent of seats for them in the panchayat bodies by amending the Constitution (73rd and 74th Amendments of 1992). Significantly, the Government of Orissa took steps in this regard earlier (1991).

In Nuapada panchayat, out of eleven seats four are reserved for women. Earlier, they were passive in their action. But now they are playing an active role in the village politics. Their active participation can be directly linked to their education, supports from their family members, etc.

Factionalism often breeds contempt and gives rise to violence, thereby causing a loss to life and property and posing a threat to law and order situation.

Factional politics in Nuapada has not only affected the village politics but also infected the co-operatives and educational institutions. It will continue to be an integral part of village politics as long as the people and their leaders have not changed their outlook, attitudes and perceptions. The founding fathers' dream about the village government can be realized if they leaders do not run after power. Instead of being power-seekers, they should be men of character, integrity and honesty. Upon them rests the functioning of the panchayat government. Its efficacy and efficiency and the future of the village largely depend on how the factional leaders behave in the village politics.

References

1. E.J.H. Mackay, "*Further Excavations at Mahenjo-daro*", Vol. 1–2, (Delhi: 1938), also see, R.C. Manjumdar (ed.), *History and Culture of Indian People*, Vol. I (Bombay: Bharati and Vidya Bhavan Series, 1951), pp. 172–76.

2. During the Muslim period (1192–1707 A.D.) a centralized form of local-self government was maintained. Kotwal was the most important of the local officers. The local government in India as is found in its present form is primarily a British innovation. It was, in fact, the creation of Lord Ripon in 1882.

3. Jeremy Boissevain, "Factions", in Adam Kuper and Jessica Kuper (eds.), The Social Science Encyclopedia (London: Routledge and Kegan Paul, 1985), p. 289.

4. S.S. Sharma, "*Factions: Antecedents and Consequences, A Comparative Study in two Villages in a Block in Western Uttar Pradesh*—A Report (unpublished), 1985, p. 1.

5. Masaki Fukunaga, "Society, Caste and Factional Politics: Conflict and Continuity in Rural India", (New Delhi: Manohar Publisher, 1993), p.1.

6. Baljit Singh, "*Next Step in Village India*", (Bombay : Asia Publishing House, 1961), p. 4.

7. Sharma, Op. cit.

8. B.S. Baviskar, "*Factions and Party Politics*", General Elections in

an Assembly Constituency in Maharashtra, Sociological Bulletin, 1971, 20(I), pp. 54–77.

9. A. R. Beals & B.J. Siegel, "*Divisiveness and Social Conflict : An Anthropological Approach*", California: Stanford University Press, 1966.

10. Fukunaga, Op. cit., p. 2.

11. Ibid., p. 15.

12. B.K. Nagla, "*Factionalism, Politics and Social Sturcture*", Jaipur: Rawat Publications, 1984, p. 202.

13. Nagla, op. cit., p. 2.

14. S.C. Dube, "*Caste Dominance and Factionalism*", *Contributions to Indian Sociology*, No. 2, 1968, pp. 58–81.

15. Sharma, op. cit., p. 2.

16. D.K. Samanta, "Determinnants of Political Factions in a Deccan Village", Journal of Indian Anthropological Society, Vol. 17, 1982, p. 215.

17. The term "modernization" is derived from the Latin word "modo" which means "just now". Modernization is not the same as Europeanization or Westernization. Though, Europe and other Western nations constitute one of the major sources of modernization, the latter itself is a synthesis of modernization, the latter itself is a synthesis of old and new ways, and differs according to the prevailing situation. Modernization denotes a process of long-range cultural and social change accepted by members of the changing society as beneficial, inevitable, or on balance desirable. (Robert E. Ward and Dankwart A. Rustow (eds.), Political Modernization in Japan and Turkey (Princeton, New Jersey: Princeton University Press, 1968), p. 3.

    Modernization is comprehensive concept aimed at capturing, describing and evaluating the profound qualitative and quantitative changes that have taken place in human society from sixteenth century onewards. "The process of modernization which began in Italy in the fifteenth century and spread in most of the West over the following five hundred years is now worldwide...." (Joseph La Palombara, "*Distribution and Development in Modernization*" in Myron Weiner (ed.), *Modernization: The Dynamics of Growth*, (Voice of America Forum Lectures, 1966, p. 252). Modernization is the current term for an old process—the proces of social change.

To Cyril Black, modernization is "the process by which historically evolved instituions are adapted to the rapidly changing conditions that reflect the unprecedented increase in man's knowledge, permitting control over his environment, that accompanied the scientific revolution". (Cyril E. Black, "*The Dynamics of Modernization*", (New York: Harper and Row, 1966, p. 7).

D.A. Rustow defined modernization as the process of "rapidly widening control over nature through closer co-operation of man". (D.A. Rustow, A. *World of Nations: Problems of Political Modernization*, (The Brokings Institution, 1967) pp. 275–76.

18. D.F. Miller, "*Faction in Indian Village Politics*", (Pacific Affairs, Vol. 38, No. 1, 1965), p. 17.

19. Boissevain, op. cit.

20. Ibid.

21 Ibid.

22. Oscar Lewis, "Village life in Northern India," Urbana: University of Illinois Press. 1958.

23. Harold D., Lasswell, "Factions", in Encyclopaedia of the Social Sciences, Vol. 6, pp. 49–51.

24. Ibid.

25. Beals and Siegel, Op. cit.

Bibliography

Almond, A. Gabriel and G. Powell, Comparative Politics: A Developmental Approach (Boston: Little, Brown 1966).

____________ and S. Verba, The Civic Culture (Boston: Little, Brown, 1965).

Bachenniemer, R. "Elements of Leadership in an Andhra Village" in Richard L. Park and I. Tinker (eds.) Leadership and Political Institutions in India (Princeton, N.J. : Princeton University Press, 1959).

Bada, C.R., "Emerging Pattern of Rural Leadership", Indian Journal of Public Administration, 23(3), July–September, 1977.

Bailey, F.G., Caste and Economic Frontier (Manchester: Manchester University Press, 1957).

____________, "Politics and Society in Orissa", Advancement of Science, May, 1962.

____________, "Politics and Society in Contemporary Orissa" in C.H. Philips (ed.) Politics and Society in India (London: 1963).

____________, "The Study of Politics in Village India", Paper presented at the Annual Meeting (16th) of the Association for Asian Studies, (Washington D.C., March, 1964, Memeo).

Baloff, Max (ed.) The Federalist (Oxford: 1948).

Bandyopadhaya, Alok Kumar, "Village Panchayat—A Bird's Eye-View", Economic Affairs, 26(3) July–Sept., 1981.

Baviskar B.S., "Factions and Party Politics", Economic and Political Weekly, Vol. 3(12), 1971.

Beals, Alan R., "Leadership in Mysore Village", in Richard L. Park and I. Tinker (eds.) Leadership and Political Institutions in India, (Princeton: Princeton University Press, 1959).

____________ and B.J. Siegal Divisiveness and Social Conflict (Stanford: Stanford University Press. 1966).

Behura, N.K., "Conflict, Politics and Harmony", Man and Life, 1978.

Bendix, Reinhard and Seymour Martian Lipset (eds.) Class, Status and Power: Social Stratification in Comparative Perspective (London: 1974).

Bhatia, B.M., "Price Policy, Agriculture and Economic Growth, IASSI Qly., Vol. 11, No. 1, 1992.

Bhargava B.S. and V.N. Torgal, "Factionalism : A Study of a Panchayat in Karnataka, Qly. Journal of Local—self Government Institute, Bombay, Vol. 51–52, (1980–82).

____________, "Politico-Administrative Dynamics in Panchayati Raj System" (Delhi: Ashish Publishing House).

Bhambhri, C.P., "Political Parties and Panchayati Raj: Some Theoritical Consideratioins", in M.V. Mathur and Iqbal Narain (eds.), Panchayati Raj, Planning and Democracy (New Delhi: Asia Publshing House, 1969).

Biossevain, Jeremy, "Factions, Parties and Politics in Malta", American Anthropologist, 66, 1964.

Brass, Paul R., "Factionalism and the Congress Party in U.P.", Asian Survey, Vol. 4 (1964).

____________, "Factional Politics in an Indian State, the Congress Party in Uttar Pradesh", (Berkeley : University of California Press, 1965).

____________, "Caste, Faction and Party in Indian Politics", 2 Vols. (Delhi: Chanakya Publishers, 1984).

Brown L.B. "Ideology" (London: Cox and Leymen Ltd., 1973).

Burja, Jannet, "The Dynamics of Political Action: A New Look at Factionalism", Anthropologist, 1975.

Black, Cyril E., The Dynamics of Modernization (New York: Harper and Row, 1966).

Chance, Normana, "Factionalism as a Process of Social and Cultural Change", In M. Sheriff (ed.) Inter-group Relations and Leadership (New York: John Wiley and Sons, 1962).

Chauhan B.R., A Rajasthan Village (New Delhi: Vir Publishing House, 1967).

Choudhury, B.C., Social Change, Social Structure and Modernization: A Linkage Process of Political Devleopment in an Orissan District," Unpublished Ph.D. Dissertation, Berhampur University, 1991.

____________, R.K., Caste and Power Structure: A Study of a Harayana Village, Unpublished Thesis, 1984.

Cohn, Bernard S, "The Changing Status of a Depressed Caste", In Mckim Marriott (ed.), Village India, (Chicago: Chicago University Press, 1957).

Daniel Thorner, The Shaping of Modern India (New Delhi : Allied Publisher, 1980).

David Pocock—"The Bases of Faction in Gujarat", British Journal of Sociology, 8, 1957.

Dube S.C., Indian Village (Bombay: Allied Publisher Pvt. Ltd., 1965).

Das Gupta, Biplab and W.H. Morris Jones, Patterns and Trends in Indian Politics; An Ecological Analysis of Aggregate Data on Society and Elections (New Delhi: Allied, 1975).

Das, B.C., "The Dynamics of Factional Conflict: A Study of the Dimensions of Electoral Conflict in an Assembly Constituency in Orissa", The Indian Political Science Review, Vol. XI, January, 1977.

____________, "Government and Politics in Orissa since Independence—A Bird's Eye-view", The Indian Political Science Review, Vol. XII, 1977.

Das, Biswarup, The Bhaumakaras: Budhist Kinds of Orissa and their Times (New Delhi: Oriental Publishers and Distributors, 1978).

Dash, S.C., "Government and Politics of Orissa", Indian Journal of Political Science, Vol. 26, 1965.

Edward, J. Jay, "Authority Structure, Factions and Social Change in a Chatisgari Village" in Giri Raj Gupta (ed.) Cohesion and Conflict in Modern India (Delhi: Vikas Publishing House, 1978).

Elliot, Corolymn, "Caste and Faction Among the Dominant Castes" in Rajni Kothari (ed.), Caste in Indian Politics (New Delhi: Orient Longmans, 1970).

Emmerich Herbert and Richard Garnett, "Electoral Process" in Enclyclopaedia Britanica (Macro), Vol. 6. (U.S.A.: The University of Chicago Press, 1977).

Firth, Raymond, "Introduction to Factions in Indian and Overseas Indian Societies", The British Journal of Sociology, Vol. 8, No. 4, 1957.

Fukunaga, Massaki, "*Society, Caste and Factional Politics: Conflict and Continuity in Rural India*" (New Delhi : Manohar, 1993).

Fred I. Greenstein and Nelson W. Polsby (eds.), Hand Book of Political Science, Vol. III, (Amssa Chusetts: 1973).

____________, Hand Book of Political Science, Vol. IV (London : Addison-Welsey Publishing Company, 1975).

Gangrade, K.D., "Leadership in Rural India: An Analysis of Some Trends" in Alfred Desouja (ed.), Leadership and Development (Delhi: Manohar, 1978).

George, Murdock, "Social Structure of a Tanjore Village" in K. Ishwaran (ed.) Changes and Continuity in India's Village (New York: Columbia University Press, 1970).

Hanchett, S.L., "Changing Economic, Social and Ritual Relationship in a Modern South Indian Village", University Films International, 1970.

Hunter W.W., The Imperial Gazetter of India, Vol. V (London: 1885).

Iqbal Narain et. al., Election Studies in India (New Delhi: 1978).

Ishwaran, K.; Tradition and Economy in Village India (Bombay Publishers Pvt. Ltd., 1966).

Jena, B.B., People, Culture and Polity (Delhi: Kalyani, 1980).

____________ and J.K. Baral, "A Fresh Look at Vote Banks: Some Case Studies from Orissa", Indian Journal of Political Science, Vol. 40, No. 3, Sept., 1979.

Jeorges, B., "Leadership and Social Changes", in J.W. Airan (ed.), The Nature of Leadership (Bombay: Lalvani Publishing House, 1969).

Jha, Shree Nagesh, Leadership and Local Politics: A Study of Meerut District in Uttar Pradesh (Bombay : Popular Prakashan Pvt. Ltd., 1979).

Jones, Rodeny W., Urban Politics in India: Area Power and Policy in a Penetrated System (Berkeley: University of California Press, 1974).

Jones, W.H. Morris, The Government and Politics of India (London: Hutchinson, 1971).

Joseph, P. Harris, "Electins, Encyclopaedia of Social Science, Vol. V–VI, (New York: MacMillion, 1962).

Kaur, Satinderjit et. al., "Role of Village Leaders in Rural Upliftment", Krurukshetra, September, 1993.

Khare, R.S., "Group Dynamics in a North Indian Village", Human Organisation, Vol. 21, No. 3 (1962).

Kothari, Rajni (ed.) Caste in Indian Politics (New Delhi: Orient Longmans).

Lewis, Oscar, Group Dynamics in a North Indian Village (Delhi: Planning Commission, 1954).

____________, Village life in Northern India, (Urbana : University of Illinois Press, 1958).

Lipset, S.M., "Political Sociology" in N.J. Smelser (ed.) Sociology: An Introduction (New Delhi: Wiley Eastern, 1970).

Mackay, E.J.H., Further Excavations at Mahenjo-daro, 2 Vols. (Delhi: 1938).

Mackenzine, "Elections", International Encyclopaedia of Social Science (New York: Collier Macmillan, 1968).

Mahapatra, J.K., Factional Politics in India, (Allahabad: Chugh Publications, 1985).

__________ and U.M. Das, "Agranrian Transition and Social Development in Orissa", Indian Journal of Political Science, Vol. 54, No. 2, April–June, 1993.

Mahatab, Harekrishna, History of Orissa, Vol. I (Cuttack: Prajatantra Prachar Samiti, 1959).

Majumdar, D.N., "Fluidity of Status Structures in India, in A.R. Desai (ed.), Rural Sociology in India (Bombay: Popular Prakashan, 1969).

__________, R.C. (ed.), History and Culture of Indian People, Vol. I (Bombay: Bharati and Vidya Bhavan Series, 1951).

Mann, R.S., Social Structure, Social Change and Future trends (Jaipur: Rawat Publications, 1979).

Mathur, P.C., "Political Corolaries of Panchayati Raj" in M.V. Mathur and Iqbal Narain (eds.), Panchayati Raj, Planning and Democracy (New Delhi: Asia Publishing House, 1969).

Mayor, Adrian C., Peasant in the Pacific: A Study of Fiji Indian Rural Society. (London: Raefledge and Kegan Paul, 1961).

Mc Cormack, William C., Changing Leadership of a Mysore Village, Unpublished Ph.D. Thesis, University of Chicago, 1956.

__________, "Factionalism in a Mysore Village", in Park and Tinker (eds.), Leadership and Political Institutions in India (Princeton : Princeton University Press, 1959).

Mashreque M. Shairul and M. Rahul Amin, "Politics of Factionalism in Rural Bangladesh", IASSI Quly. Vol. 11, No. 2, 1992.

Mehta, Sushila, Social Conflicts in a Village Community (Delhi: S. Chand and Co. Pvt. Ltd., 1971).

__________, S.R., Emerging Pattern of Rural Leadership. (New Delhi: Wiley Eastern Pvt. Ltd., 1972).

Michael, Hechter, "Group Farmation and the Cultural Division of Labour", American Journal of Sociology, Vol. 84, No. 2, September, 1978.

Mishra, Bishnu, "Caste, Class and Power: A Study of an Orissan Gram Panchayat", Unpublished M.Phil dissertation, Berhampur University.

Mishra, S.N., "Identifying the Rural Elite. A case study of Amarpur Gram Panchayat", Indian Journal of Political Science, 40(30) September, 1979.

____________, "Election and Political Development in Orissa" in A.P. Padhi (ed.) Indian State Politics : A Case Study of Orissa (Delhi: B.R. Publishing Corporation, 1985).

Mohanty, Surendra, Kulabrudha (Cuttack: Lark Books, 1978).

____________, "Satavdira Surya" (Cuttack: Lark Books, 1970).

Mukherjee, Prabhat, History of Orissa, Vol. VI (Bhubaneswar : Utkal University).

Mukhopadhya, Rajatsubhra, "Party Politics in Panchayat", Social Change, Vol. 14, No. 2, June, 1984.

Murdock, G., Review of Caste in India (New Delhi: Rawat Publications, 1977).

Nagla, B.K., Factionalism, Politics and Social Structure in Jaipur: Rawat Publication, 1984).

Nanda, Sukadev, Coalitional Politics in Orissa (New Delhi : Sterling Publishers, Pvt. Ltd., 1979).

Nicholas, Ralph W., "Factions: A Comparative Analysis" in Michael Banton (ed.), Political Systems and the Distributiion of Power, A.S.A. Monograph, No.2 (New York : Frederik A Praeger).

____________, "Village Factions and Political Parties" Journal of Commonwealth Studies, Vol. 2, 1963.

Opler, M.E. and R.D. Singh, "Economic, Political and Social Change in a Village of North Central india", Human Organisation, Vol. II, No. 2, 1952.

Padhy, K.S., Corruption in Politics (Delhi: B.R. Publishing Corporation, 1986).

____________, "Politics of Corruption in Orissa", in A.P. Padhi (ed.) Indian State Politics : A Case Study of Orissa (Delhi: B.R. Publishing Corporation, 1985).

____________ and P.K. Muni, Corruption in Indian Politics : A Case Study of an Indian State (Delhi: Discovery Publishing House, 1987).

____________ and P.P. Tripathy, Voting Behaviour of Tribals in India (Delhi: Kanishka Publishers and Distributors, 1994).

____________ and P.K. panigrahi, Socialist Movement in India (Delhi: Kanishka Publishing House, 1992).

Panda, B.S., Gandhi Krishna Murty (Berhampur: Gopinath Press, 1979).

Panda, K.C., Factional Politics in Rural Orissa, Unpublished Ph.D. Thesis, Sambalpur University, 1981.

Panigrahi, K.C., History of Orissa (Hindu Period) (Cuttack: Kitab Mahal, 1981).

Patnaik, B.K., The Politics of Floor-Crossing (Cuttack : Santosh Publications, 1985).

____________, N. and Lakshmi Narayan H.D., Factional Politics in Village India", Man in India, Vol. 49, 1969.

Petrullo, L. and B.N. Bose, (eds.), Leadership and Inter-personal Behaviour (New York : Holt Rinehart and Winston, 1961).

Palombara, Joseph La, "Distributiion and Development in Modernization" in Myron Weiner (ed.), Modernization: The Dynamics of Growth, (Voice of America Forum Lectures, 1966).

Pocock, David F., "The Bases of Factions in Gujarat", The British Jouirnal of Sociology, Vol. 8, 1957.

Prasad, Narmadeshwar, "Panchayatraj Problems of Reorganization" in M.V. Mathur and Iqbal Narain (eds.), Panchayati Raj, Planning and Democracy (New Delhi: Asia Publishing House, 1969).

Ranganath, "The Changing Pattern of Rural Leadership in U.P., Indian Academy of Social Sciences, New Delhi, 1971.

Rao, Ranga K., Village Politics: A Longitudinal Study (Bombay: Popular Prakashan).

____________, K.V., "Politics in Orissa, Social Ecology and Constitutional Compulsions", Indian Journal of Political Science, Vol. 26, 1965.

____________, "The Pattern of Orissa Politics", in Iqbal Narain (ed.), State Politics in India, (Meerut: Meenakshi, 1967).

____________, M.S.A., "Urbanization and Social Change", in Urban Sociology in India (Delhi : Orient Longman, 1974).

Rastogi, P.N., The Nature of Dynamics of Factional Conflict (Delhi: Macmillon Company of India Ltd., 1975).

Ray, B.C., Foundations of British Orissa (Cuttack : New Studnets Store, 1969).

____________, N.S., "A Short History of Creation of Orissa as a Separate State", Utkal Prasanga, Special Issue, 1975.

Richard, D. Lambert, "Some Impact of Urban Society Upon Village Life" in Roy Runner (ed.) India's Urban Future (Berkeley: University of California Press, 1962).

Richard, L. Park and I. Tinker, Leadership and Political Institutions in India (Princeton, N.J. : Princeton University Press, 1959).

____________, R. Fagen, The Components of Communication Net Works—Politics and Communication (Boston: Little, Brown, 1966).

____________, T. Morris and malvin Seeman, "The Problem of Leaderhsip : An Interdisciplinary Approach", American Journal of Sociology, Vol. 56, No. 2.

____________, The Congress party in Rajasthan (Delhi: Oxford University Press, 1972).

Robert, Red Field & Alfonso Rajas, Chan Kan & Maya Village (Chicago: Chicago University Press, 1964).

Rustow, D.A., A World of Nations: Problems of Political Modernization (The Brokings Institution, 1967).

Sahu, N.K., *et. al*, History of Orissa (Cuttack: Nalanda Publishers, 1985).

Samanta, D.K., "Determinants of Political Faction in a Deccan Village", Journal Indian Anthropological Society, 17, 1982.

Saran, Parmatma, *Rural Leadership in the Context of India's Modernization* (New Delhi: Vikas Publishing House Pvt. Ltd., 1978).

Sesadri, K., *Political Linkage and Rural Development* (Delhi: 1976).

______________, *Rural Unrest in India* (New Delhi: Intellectual Publishing House, 1983).

Sharma, S.S., "Faction: Antecedents and Consequences: A Comparative Study in two Villages in a Block in Western Uttar Pradesh—A Report (Unpublished).

Shekerappa, V., "Does Priority Sector Lending Help the Poor?" Kurukshetra, July, 1994.

Singh, Harjinder, Village Leadership, A Case Study of Village Mohali in Punjab (New Delhi : Sterling Publishers Pvt. Ltd., 1968).

Singh, Baljit, *Next Step in Village India* (Bombay: Asia Publishing House, 1961).

______________, Surendra, "Leadership and Factionalism", Eastern Anthropologist, 31(3), July–September, 1978.

Sisson, Richard, *The Congress Party in Rajasthan: Political Integration and Institution–Building in an Indian State*" (Berkeley: University of California Press, 1972).

Somjee, A.H., *Democracy and Political Change in Village India: A Case Study* (New Delhi: Orient Longman, 1971).

Srinivas, M.N., "The Dominant Caste in Rampura", American Anthroplogist, Vol. 61, No.1, 1959.

_____________, "The Social System of a Mysore Village" in Medium Marriot (ed.), *Village India*, (Chicago: University of Chicago Press, 1955), and also his "Social Change in Modern India", (Berkeley, University of California Press, 1966).

_____________, "Future of Indian Caste", Economic & Political Weekly, Annual Number, Bombay : February, 1979.

Subramanyam, Y.S., *Social Change in Village India: An Andhra Case Study* (New Delhi : Prithviraj Publishers, 1975).

Sukla, N.K., *The Social Structure of an Indian Village* (Delhi: Cosmo Publications).

Tannenabaum, Weschler and Massarik, *Leadership and Organisation* (New York: McGraw-Hill Book Co., 1961).

Taylor, C.C. et. al., India's Roots of Democracy (Delhi: Orient Longman).

Tead, O., *The Art of Leadership* (New York: McGraw Hill Book Co., 1936).

Thirumalai, S., "Trends in Rural Change" in A.R. Desai (ed.) *Rural Sociology in India* (Bombay: Popular Prakashan, 1969).

Turnover, V.W., *Schism and Continuity in an African Society* (Manchester: Manchester University Press, 1957).

Varma, S.P. & Iqbal Narain, *Voting Behaviour in Changing Society* (Delhi: 1973).

_____________, *Modern Political Theory: A Critical Survey* (New Delhi: Vikas Publishing House Pvt. Ltd., 1975).

Weiner, Myron, *Party Politics in India : The Development of a Multi-party System* (Princeton: Princeton University Press: 1957).

Wood, Evelyn, *Patterns of Influence within Rural India in Park and Tinker* (eds.).

Yadav, J.S., "Factionalism in a Haryana Village", American Anthropologist, Vol. 70, 1968.

[Report]

— Agricultural Census of Orissa Board of Revenue, Orissa, 1970–71.

— Census of India, 1961, 1981 and 1991.

— Administrative Inquiry Committee Report, Government of Orissa, 1958.

— District Statistical Hand Book, Ganjam, 1965.

— The Ganjam District Manual, Government of Madras, 1918.

— District Statistical Hand Book 1990–91, Ganjam.

— Delimitation of Parliamentary and Assembly Constituencies Order, 1961, Orissa.

— The Orissa Gazette, Extraordinary No. 1503, Cuttack, June 27, 1965.

— Third Supplement to Hand Book of Important Notifications, circulars and orders, 1978, Home Election Department.

— Economic Survey 1991–92, Government of Orissa.

— Indian Statutery Commission Report, Vol. 1, Calcutta, 1930.